Secrets of
New England Cooking

Secrets of New England Cooking

Ella Shannon Bowles
and
Dorothy S. Towle

Illustrated by
Wenderoth Saunders

DOVER PUBLICATIONS, INC
Mineola, New York

This book is dedicated
to
Lillian Siemering,
mother of one author, friend of the other,
in deep appreciation of
the assistance she has given in its preparation

CONTENTS

FOREWORD

Aunt Fanny Aldrich was considered the best cook in the neighborhood—high praise in a town where most women prided themselves on serving three tasty square meals a day. But Aunt Fanny went a step further and gave a lot of extra touches to her food. She put rose petals, dried in cinnamon and sugar, and chopped butternuts in her mincemeat. She baked black bass in spiced apple juice, and added nutmeg and a dash of lemon to corn fritters.

Her Canada plum pies were culinary masterpieces. Her delicate crabapple jelly in fluted tart shells quivered when you looked at it. Her creamshortened freckled doughnuts never soaked fat. The filling of her pumpkin pies was like golden custard. Her fruitcakes grew richer and plummier with age. Her light soda biscuits would melt in your mouth.

In their old age, Aunt Fanny's two grandsons, gossiping under the maples, emphatically told their grandsons and their grandsons' wives that no one in the world ever cooked like their Grandmother Aldrich. And their eyes grew dreamy with memories of wild strawberry short-cakes, blackcap custard pies, and blueberry johnnycakes.

Aunt Fanny's headstone in the roadside graveyard is moss-stained, and her grandsons too are dead. City folks now spend their summers in the old white house by Gale River. But her reputation as queen of the kitchen still lingers in the village of Franconia, for she was one of those natural cooks who are "born with a mixing spoon in one hand and a rolling pin in the other." New England has produced many. They in-vented baked Indian pudding and apple pandowdy. They established the boiled dinner as a Thursday institution, and Boston baked beans and brown bread as the typical Saturday night supper.

Year after year, they exchanged cooking secrets. They discussed their favorite dishes at tea drinkings and quiltings, at church socials and sewing clubs. They made town meeting dinners and grange suppers famous. Their clam chowders, stuffed baked lobster, chicken and dum-plings, and blueberry pies brought tourists by the dozen to their door-steps. Their "receipts" traveled along inland waterways and in oxcarts to the back country; they went west in covered wagons; they rounded the Horn in sailing vessels.

But all the good dishes did not come from country kitchens. Europe was practically a next-door neighbor, and daily life in New England cities showed its influence. Cooks in the mansions of Portsmouth and Boston added subtle Continental touches to the food served formally in the best London manner. Many of their recipes are now part of our regional cooking tradition.

But whenever and wherever they have lived, most people of New England have demanded rich savory food. Colonial men and women were rigid in doctrinal matters, but they certainly were not rigid in affairs of the table. Nor were they unduly frugal when they could get supplies. The Pilgrims ate groundnuts during the first hard winter, but they preferred better food when it became available. The citizens of old Boston liked hasty pudding but did not call for it every time they sat down to a meal. They enjoyed highly seasoned food and plenty of it—eels stuffed with spices and baked in wine, for instance. The patriots gladly ate simple dishes during the war with England, but they were delighted when restrictions were removed and dining again became something to talk about. Country cooks might be somewhat "near" with "boughten" things—but they were amazingly lavish with home-grown foods, and butter, cream, and eggs.

Styles in cooking changed, of course, as time went on, especially after the *Grand Turk* made its famous trip, bringing new beverages and foods from the China seas. And more and more delicacies came to the kitchen as Yankee sailing vessels went to and from the West Indies, Hong Kong, Calcutta, and "up the Straits." Lucy Larcom says that, in her childhood, jars of tropical fruits, tamarinds, ginger root, and other spicy appetizers were as common as barberries and cranberries in the cupboards of Beverly housekeepers.

But New England cooks continued to use the native fruits and berries and the vegetables from their kitchen gardens. They still did much baking with corn meal, and they seasoned dishes with salt pork. They stuffed roast chicken with dressings flavored with home-grown herbs. They put roadside tansy in their crumbly cheeses. They dug greens and roasted corn on the cob. They made spicy gingerbread and warm apple-sauce for supper. But they did not serve pie for breakfast. Oh, a piece now and then, perhaps, but not as a usual thing. That idea came from the fact that in brick-oven days the pandowdy from the Saturday after-noon oven appeared on the Sunday morning breakfast table. And break-fast was a good hot meal, certainly greatly needed, for the only food afterward until sunset was a cold snack at the noon house between the long morning and afternoon sermons.

To tell an interesting story about the history of New England cook-ing, we have not conventionally arranged the recipes. You will find rules for baking cakes, making pies, and cooking meat in the chapters, "Indian Inheritance," "Brick-Oven Cookery," and "Maple Trees and Beehives," as well as under the usual headings.

If at first glance there seems to be an overabundance of recipes for baked Indian pudding, our excuse is that we want you to see that, when properly made, this old New England dessert is not the insipid pasty concoction often served under that name. There is a knack to getting the rich color and blend of flavors that make a perfect pudding. Every New England cook is likely to have a pet recipe which she thinks is better than that of her neighbor, and we have tried to give you a variety to choose from.

We adapted some of the recipes for Yankee dishes from old regional cookbooks, modifying the more ancient rules to meet present-day conditions. We have substituted measurements by spoon and cup for gills and pounds, but have kept the homely phrases "butter the size of an egg," "butter the size of a walnut," and a "pinch" of this or that. Yankee cooks always say "try out" when they draw the fat from pork by frying. So we have used the term too. If original directions called for cream of tartar and soda, we listed these ingredients, but have not designated any particular grade of white flour. It should be sifted before measuring.

The old names are given to the dishes. We have also used local names, especially in the chapter, "Doughnut Crock and Cooky Jar." And we have spelled the popular Indian meal breakfast cake four different ways—jonne cake, journey cake, jonny cake, and johnnycake—depending on the time the recipe originated. We also have used the words frying pan, skillet, and spider interchangeably.

ACKNOWLEDGMENT

Many of the recipes in this book were given by the descendants of the cooks who made them famous. These especially have the genuine New England flavor. Friends and neighbors have been generous in telling how they make their favorite dishes, and we also have drawn freely on personal experience in cooking for our families.

To all who have assisted in the preparation of this book we wish to express our thanks. We are particularly grateful to: Harriet Bowles, Harriet Charles, Esther Barraclough, Peggy Wyman, Elizabeth Pierce, Wilfred Harwood, Albion Hodgdon, Bessie York, Mrs. W. C. Pulsifer, Catherine McGregor, Janet Towle, Harriet McCroary, Ashton Rollins, Evelyn Knight, Ada Lundholm, Martha Carpenter, Mary Hurd, Elizabeth Ellis, Helen McLaughlin, Berdille Eldredge, Marian Blewett, Adele Ells, Cornelia Wadleigh, Marguerite Adams, Francis Robinson, and to the State of Maine Development Commission.

We think fondly too of Aunt Fanny Aldrich who really gave us the idea for this cookbook. We hope that you will find evidences of her deft hand and her imagination in every recipe and that the dishes you make will be as delicious as those she whipped up more than eighty year ago.

ELLA SHANNON BOWLES
DOROTHY S. TOWLE

Durham, New Hampshire

SECRETS OF
NEW ENGLAND COOKING

1. INDIAN INHERITANCE

Not all the secrets of New England cookery can be traced back to the Indians. Many receipes that have given the Maine to Connecticut region its culinary reputation are adapted from "rules" or "receipts" that originally came from old England. Just the same, the Indians had quite a hand in our present-day bill of fare. Some of their foods our "great-greats" did not like, but others they took over enthusiastically, permanently putting them in the larders of their descendants. Crops from primitive garden patches, wild plants the Indian women gathered in spring, native nuts and berries, and maple sweets, not to mention a large variety of fish and game, inspired New England dishes that are famous all over the United States today.

Topping this list is maize or corn, which is planted, cultivated, and prepared for the table practically as it was when Samoset met the Pilgrims. The Indian method of roasting ears of corn in ashes is a simple process but still there are rules to follow. The corn should be "in the milk" and freshly gathered. The clean hardwood ashes should be hot, but not so full of coals that the ears of corn will burn.

Popcorn is also a gift from the Indians and so is sagamite, a dish we know as hulled corn. Indian women, pounding out meals of varied texture in their stone corn mills, also made nasaump, a word the Rhode Island colonists shortened into samp. Samp makes a delicious though hearty breakfast porridge.

It did not take our ancestors long to find ways of improving on the Indian corn mills. They liked corn meal so well that they soon invented contrivances to grind it. One of their favorite corn meal dishes was hasty pudding, or stirabout pudding. Hundreds of New Englanders were raised on mush and milk, and liked it too, if you can believe Joel Barlow, the Hartford wit, who eulogized hasty pudding in verse.

Crisp hot ashcakes, baked Indian fashion among the hearth ashes of the kitchen fireplace, were a popular breakfast bread in New England for many years and everyone who has heard anything about New England cooking knows of the famous Rhode Island jonny cakes, sometimes called scalded corncake, or breakfast bannocks. These cakes are not easy to make, but there is no corncake to be compared with them when they come sizzling hot and just right from the griddle.

Indian beans were similar to some of the varieties we raise today. The Indians used them in ashcakes, in stews, and cooked with other vegetables, especially corn. The corn and bean combination is the dish most of us call succotash, which really is not the Indian name. "Corn boiled whole" was the meaning of the Narragansett word *m' sickquatash*. It was applied by an early traveler who thought it was an Indian dish of corn, beans, and bear flesh.

Some of the early explorers found that the Indians on Cape Ann cultivated artichokes and used them in stews and soups. Usually the women cared for the gardens, but for some unknown reason the men raised the artichokes. The explorers liked the tubers and took some back to Europe where they became popular, especially in Spain. There they were called girasoles, a word the rougher English tongue turned into "Jerusalem."

As soon as the first green shoots appeared above the ground after the long cold winter, the Indian women hunted for the rootstocks of ostrich fern and bracken and for fiddleheads, the new coiled fronds, which they prized. In Maine today, ostrich fern fiddleheads, still considered a great delicacy, are gathered just as the new leaves unfold and before leaflets begin to show, a period lasting hardly more than a week around the first of May. Ferns other than the ostrich and bracken are worthless as food, so if you cannot identify these two varieties, let ferns alone.

The Indians also prized milkweed as a potherb. They ate both the young shoots and the pods.

CORN ROASTED IN ASHES

Pull back the husks from ears of freshly gathered corn, remove the silk, and replace the husks. Tie the tips of the husks together. Bury the ears in hot ashes and let them stay for twelve to fifteen minutes. Brush away the ashes and turn back the husks. Rub butter over the corn and eat the ears from the husks.

Another method is to pull back the corn husks and wrap a piece of bacon around each ear. Replace the husks and roast the ears in the usual way.

TOASTED GREEN CORN

Boil the ears of corn as directed for Boiled Corn on the Cob. Spread with melted butter and broil over coals for about five minutes, turning the ears so they will brown evenly. Serve with more butter and salt.

BOILED CORN ON THE COB

Always cook corn on the cob as soon as possible after it has been picked. Husk the ears and remove the silk. Put them in a deep kettle and cover with boiling water to which one tablespoon of sugar has been added. Boil from six to ten minutes, depending on the age and tenderness of the corn. Drain and wrap the ears in a napkin. Serve with plenty of butter.

FRIED CORN

The following two recipes are tried-and-true corn dishes that are popular in New Hampshire.

Cut the corn from the cob, using a sharp knife, and cutting only about half the depth of the kernels. Then with the back of the knife scrape off the rest of the pulp. Put bacon fat and a little butter in an iron skillet. Use one-third cup of fat to five cups of corn. When the fat is hot, add corn and enough water to make a gravy-like mixture. Season to taste with salt and pepper. Cook five minutes, stirring constantly. Reduce the heat and cover the skillet. Let the corn simmer for about twenty minutes longer, stirring occasionally. It should be quite thick when ready to serve. Serves eight to ten.

CORN POPPED IN A KETTLE

Put a mixing spoon of lard and one teaspoon of salt in the bottom of a heavy kettle. When hot, turn in a cup of shelled popcorn. Stir briskly, using a long-handled mixing spoon. When the kernels begin to pop, cover the kettle. Shake rapidly until the kettle is filled with fluffy white kernels. Discard any old maids left in the bottom of the kettle. Turn the corn into a large bowl, yellow crockery preferred. Turn a liberal amount of melted butter over the corn. Sprinkle with salt, if needed.

HULLED CORN

Put two teaspoons of soda with one quart of yellow corn. Cover with cold water, adding more as needed until the hulls are loosened. Drain and wash off the hulls. Boil the corn again in clear water. Change the water again and cook the corn until the kernels are very soft. The time depends on the kind of corn, but it will take one and a half hours or more. Serve hot with butter or with milk, or cold with milk. In the country, hulled corn is often eaten for Sunday night supper. Serves ten.

INDIAN SAMP

Use hard kernels of corn of the current year and have them cracked very coarse. Put two cups of this corn in a kettle and pour cold water in it, well over the top of the corn. After the hulls rise, pour off the water through a sieve into a pail. Throw away the chaff, turn the water back on the corn, and stir it. Repeat this process until the samp is free of chaff. Then using the water that has been poured on and off, boil the samp. Add more water if necessary. Cook at least one hour, or until soft. Serve in bowls with plenty of rich milk. If you like your breakfast cereals sweetened, pour a little maple syrup, honey, or molasses over your serving. Serves six.

HASTY PUDDING

2 1/2 cups boiling water   3/4 teaspoon salt
1 cup corn meal

Put salted water in a deep kettle. When it boils vigorously, sprinkle in the corn meal, stirring it all the time. Cook thirty minutes over direct heat. If you use a double boiler, cook the pudding one hour. Serve in deep bowls with plenty of milk. Sweeten to taste with maple syrup, honey, molasses, or sugar. Serves six to eight.

FRIED MUSH

Prepare Hasty Pudding. Rinse a bread pan with cold water and turn hot mush into it. When cold, remove the mush from the pan and cut into three-quarter-inch slices. They may be pan-fried in hot fat in a skillet, or dipped in beaten egg, rolled in crumbs, and fried in deep fat. Serve for breakfast, accompanied by curls of crisp bacon or thin slices of perfectly browned salt pork. Serves six. Your great-grandmother would have advised you not to serve fried mush in summer.

ASHCAKES

2 cups corn meal   1 tablespoon maple sugar
1 teaspoon salt   Boiling water

Mix the corn meal, salt, and maple sugar with enough boiling water to make a dough you can handle. Let it stand for an hour. Then mold the dough into cakes about one inch thick. Wipe a clean place on the warm hearth and place the cakes on it. Cover with hot ashes and bake about forty-five minutes. Shake off the ashes and very quickly dip the cakes in a dish of hot water. Wipe with a cloth and serve immediately with butter. Makes about twenty-four cakes.

RHODE ISLAND JONNY CAKES

These jonny cakes should be made from white bolted meal; yellow corn meal will not do at all. This recipe came from South County, Rhode Island.

You will need two saucepans to start Rhode Island jonny cakes. In one saucepan, put one cup of white bolted meal and half a teaspoon of salt. Place the saucepan on the range where the contents will be kept hot without burning. The other saucepan should contain actively boiling water. Wet the meal carefully with the boiling water, stirring in a little at a time until it makes a crumbly mass, but not a dough. Stir briskly, being careful not to let the mixture stick on the saucepan.

When the corn meal is wet and swollen, add milk until the mass will hold its shape when dropped from a spoon. This will require considerable judgment on your part. If the mixture is too soft, it will spread on the griddle; if too stiff, the jonny cakes will be hard and tough. Grease the griddle, and with a spoon drop the mixture on it in small oval shapes. Pat them into cakes about three-quarters inch thick. Makes one to one and a half dozen cakes.

Move the cakes about on the griddle after they set and begin to brown. If they seem too stiff, moisten the top with milk. When brown on the underside, put a little cooking fat on the top, and turn the cakes over. Add fat as needed to make good brown crusts.

When the cakes are done, let them stand in a warm oven with the door open. This not only keeps the cakes hot but also makes them puff slightly. Rhode Island jonny cakes are especially delicious when served with beach-plum jelly.

SCALDED CORN BREAD

Here is an old-fashioned johnnycake, baked in the oven, not on the griddle.

1 quart water-milled corn meal	3 eggs, well beaten
Boiling water	1 pint buttermilk
1 teaspoon salt	1 teaspoon soda
1 tablespoon butter	1 tablespoon warm water

Scald the corn meal with enough boiling water to moisten. Beat in the salt and butter. Mix eggs well with the corn meal. Add the buttermilk and then the soda thoroughly dissolved in the warm water. Beat hard for three minutes. Put in a large baking pan and bake in a rather quick oven, 425 degrees F., for forty minutes. This corn bread is moist and a little heavy. It may be eaten with butter or with cream and maple syrup.

CENTURY-OLD PLYMOUTH SUCCOTASH

"One quart of large white beans, not the pea beans; six quarts of hulled corn; six to eight pounds of corned beef from the second cut of the rattle rand, which should be corned for only three or four days; one pound of salt pork, fat and lean; chicken weighing four to six pounds; one large white turnip; eight or ten medium-sized potatoes.

Wash the beans and soak them overnight in cold water. When boiling, change the water and simmer until soft enough to mash the beans to a pulp and the water is nearly absorbed.

Wash the salt pork and the corned beef. About eight o'clock, put them in cold water in a very large kettle, and skim the water as they begin to boil.

Clean and truss the chicken as for boiling, and put it with the meat about an hour and a quarter before dinnertime. Allow a longer time if a fowl is used, and keep plenty of water in the kettle.

Two hours before dinnertime, put the beans, mashed to a pulp, and the hulled corn into another kettle with some of the fat from the meat in the bottom to keep them from sticking. Take out enough liquor from the meat to cover the corn and beans, and let them simmer where they will not burn. Stir often, and add more liquor if needed. The mixture should be like a thick soup, and the beans should absorb all the liquor, yet they must not be too dry.

Pare and cut the turnip into one-inch slices; add it about eleven o'clock, and the pared potatoes half an hour later.

Take up the chicken as soon as tender, so that it may be served whole. Serve the beef and pork together; the chicken, turnip, and potatoes each on separate dishes; and the beans and corn in a tureen. The meat usually salts the mixture sufficiently, and no other seasoning is necessary. Save the water left from the meat to warm the corn and beans the next day, and serve the meat cold. This will keep several days in cold weather, and like many other dishes, it is better when warmed over, so there is no objection to making a large quantity. Serves ten to twelve."

BAKED CORN AND BEANS

Here is another old-time corn and bean dish which is a great favorite in New England, but it is in no sense succotash. In one family this recipe has been in constant use since the 1830s.

In sweet-corn time, prepare a pot of Boston baked beans. Half an hour before the beans are ready to serve, take them from the oven and remove the pork. Have ready boiled corn cut from the ears. Use plenty of corn and stir it thoroughly into the beans. Put the bean pot in a moderate over, 350 degrees F., and bake the beans and corn about twenty-five minutes.

DEEP-DISH BAKED SQUASH

Cut a Hubbard squash in pieces and steam for thirty to forty minutes, or until tender. Drain and remove the pulp from the shell. Mash the pulp and put it through a strainer. For every two cups of pulp, add the following ingredients:

2 tablespoons butter	1 egg yolk, beaten
1 tablespoon cream	Salt and pepper to taste
1 teaspoon maple sugar	1/2 cup buttered cracker crumbs

Mix the first five ingredients with the pulp, and turn it into a buttered baking dish. Cover with the cracker crumbs. Bake thirty minutes in a hot oven, 400 degrees F. Serves four to six.

PAN-FRIED SUMMER SQUASH

Thoroughly wash summer squash, but do not remove the skin. Cut crosswise in slices about half an inch thick. Dip the slices in beaten egg diluted with one-quarter cup milk and seasoned with salt and pepper; then dip them in fine cracker crumbs and fry in bacon fat until brown on both sides. A two-pound squash serves four to six.

NEW ENGLAND STANDING DISH
(Stewed Pumpkin)

We give this recipe as Josselyn recorded it nearly three hundred years ago.

"The Housewives' manner is to slice them [pumpkins] when ripe and cut them into Dice, and so fill a pot with them of two or three Gallons and stew them upon a gentle fire the whole day. And as they sink then fill again with fresh Pompions not putting any liquor to them, and when it is stir'd enough it will look like bak'd Apples, this Dish putting Butter to it and a little Vinegar with some Spice as Ginger which makes it taste like an Apple, and so serve it up to be eaten with fish or flesh."

PUMPKIN MARMALADE

You might not care for the pumpkin sauce which our ancestors liked so well. But if you have "a sweet tooth" you probably will find a marmalade made of pumpkins and oranges very delicious. The following recipe is at least fifty years old and is still used in a New Hampshire family.

7 pounds pumpkin   5 oranges
5 pounds white sugar   1 lemon

Pare pumpkin and cut it into cubes. Add sugar. Let set overnight. In the morning, cook slowly for about five hours, stirring often to prevent scorching. Add the juice of the oranges and the lemon, and the rinds cut into small pieces. Cook until the rinds are soft. Turn the mixture into hot glass jars. When cool, cover with melted wax. Makes three to four pints.

BOILED JERUSALEM ARTICHOKES

Wash and pare Jerusalem artichokes. Cover with cold water, adding about one-quarter cup of vinegar to keep them from darkening. Let them stand about half an hour, then drain and cook in boiling salted water until tender, about twenty-five minutes. Watch closely and remove the tubers from the water just as soon as they become soft. If cooked too long, they will harden again. Season with salt and pepper. Dip each tuber in melted butter and put them in a serving dish. Sprinkle with finely chopped parsley. They may also be served in cream sauce or scalloped.

ARTICHOKE FRITTERS

Another recipe for preparing Jerusalem artichokes comes from a Boston cook.

Boil one pound of Jerusalem artichokes until tender, about twenty-five minutes. Cut them in quarters. Cover with a mixture of olive oil, vinegar, salt and pepper, and finely chopped parsley. Let them stand for half an hour, then drain the pieces and dip in the following batter:

1 cup flour	1/2 cup ice water
1/2 teaspoon salt	1 tablespoon olive oil
1 teaspoon baking powder	1 lemon, juice
Pinch of cayenne	1 egg white
2 eggs	

Sift the first four ingredients. Add the two eggs alternately with the ice water. Add the olive oil and lemon juice. Beat the extra egg white and add it to the mixture. Immediately place the mixture in the refrigerator to chill. Fry the fritters in deep hot fat, dropping them from a large spoon. Drain on soft paper and sprinkle with a very little salt mixed with a pinch of dry mustard. Serves four.

FIDDLEHEADS ON TOAST

Gather the tender young unrolled fronds of the ostrich fern. Allow four or five to a serving. Be careful to keep them from wilting. Rub off the hairy portions. Wash thoroughly and remove the dry papery scales, including those in the tightly coiled leaf tips and hard bases of the stalks. Sprinkle freely with salt. Boil in a little water or steam about half an hour. Serve in lengths on toast, dressed with melted butter, hot cream, or thin cream sauce.

SOUFFLE OF FIDDLEHEADS

1 cup chopped cooked fiddleheads	1/2 lemon, juice
1/2 cup thick white sauce	Salt and pepper to taste
1/2 onion, minced	3 egg whites, stiffly beaten
3 egg yolks, well beaten	

Combine all the ingredients except the egg whites. Blend thoroughly. Quickly fold in the egg whites and pour the mixture into a greased baking dish. Set in a pan of hot water and bake in a moderate oven, 350 degrees F., for fifty minutes, or until firm to the touch. Serve immediately. Serves four.

CREAMED MILKWEED SHOOTS

The time to gather milkweed shoots is in the late spring or early summer when they are only a few inches high. Allow four to six shoots for each serving. Rub them between your hands to remove the wool and wash them thoroughly. Put the shoots in a large saucepan and cover with boiling water. Add a little salt and boil until tender, at least half an hour. Change the water twice during the cooking period to remove the milky juice. Drain the shoots and cover with hot seasoned cream, or serve on toast with cream sauce.

2. FROM SEA AND POND

Fish has been a staple food in New England since the earliest days. "Fresh cod in summer is but coarse food to us," the Pilgrims told their friends in England. From then on, right up to the present, with New England the center of the country's fresh fish industry, cod, mackerel, haddock, halibut have been important foods—especially cod, the cornerstone of the fortunes of the original codfish aristocracy, and the symbol of the state sovereignty of Massachusetts.

Most non-New Englanders have cod in mind when they ask for a good fish recipe. You cannot go wrong with the baked cod recipe given here, though you need not be restricted to getting the sacred cod to the dinner table in the best Bostonian manner. You can cook almost any kind of fish by this recipe, that is, if it is large enough to bake. And do not forget that boiled potatoes and small whole beets cooked with melted butter should always accompany "Cape Cod turkey" to the table.

In New England, baked mackerel gives baked cod a run for its money.

This highly flavored fish is fat, which makes it excellent for the oven and alien to the frying pan.

It is the consensus in New Hampshire's Great Bay region that no other fish can touch sea or striped bass as a prime dinner dish. Cod, halibut, and sea bass are all fine fish for boiling or, to be absolutely correct, for simmering. Some cooks are content to boil fish in plain salted water. But others—and these are the wise ones—lace the water with vinegar or sour wine and add vegetables and piquant seasonings.

The opening of the creamy white blossoms of the shadbushes on river banks is a perennial sign that it is shadding time in New England. The delicately flavored white-fleshed shad were an important source of food in early New England. The silver harvest was garnered in great quantities to be eaten fresh or salted down by the barrel for winter use. The way of cooking shad given here is an old favorite.

Most sportsmen prefer brook trout popped into a frying pan right from the stream or hung from the small end of a birch sapling before an open fire. North country fishermen will have nothing to do with trout the day after they are taken. The fish lose flavor, they say. They claim too that trout taken in different waters have varying flavors.

Ask any New Englander of the seacoast region what tongues and sounds are, and he will show the greatest surprise. "Why, cod's tongues and cheeks, of course!" he will say. Then he is quite likely to add, "And they're mighty good eating, too!"

Salt cod was a staple of all New England larders, a stand-by for making hearty breakfast and dinner dishes. It was served Saturday noon in the best families, and the Saturday dinners of John Hancock and his wife, Dorothy Quincy, were especially famous. They served codfish every week, keeping open house for everybody who cared to attend. The codfish were arranged on crested pewter platters that were ordered from England expressly for the purpose.

Kedgeree is not strictly a New England dish, but it was very popular on Beacon Hill tables in the 1850s. We would like to say that this breakfast dish of fish, rice, and eggs was brought to Boston from India, but this would not be true. It came to New England, as have so many other good standard dishes, from England. The recipe given here is from

Godey's Lady's Book, which had as its editor, a New Hampshire attorney's widow, Sarah Josepha Hale.

BAKED MACKEREL

First, as the Nantucket fishermen say, "sleever" your mackerel. In off-island speech this means to cut each side of the fish away in one piece from head to tail. Clean the fish and rub salt on the inner side. Place in the baking pan, skin side down. Over the fish pour one cup of milk, seasoned with salt and pepper. Bake in a moderate oven, 350 degrees F., for fifteen minutes. Add two cups of hot thin cream and cook fifteen minutes longer, or until the fish is tender and amber-colored. A medium-sized mackerel will serve four to six.

BAKED SHORE COD

Remove the fins, then scale and clean a four- to five-pound cod. Rub the inside portion with salt. Let the fish stand for ten minutes. Stuff loosely and sew up. Put waxed paper in the bottom of the baking pan and lay the cod on it. The paper will help when removing the fish to the platter. Lay thin slices of salt pork on the fish, and dredge with flour. Pour one cup of cold water around the fish. Bake in a moderate oven, 350 degrees F., for one hour, basting frequently. Remove the fish and thicken the sauce with one tablespoon of flour made into a paste with a little cold water. Season with salt and pepper. Serves six.

Old-Time Crumbly Fish Stuffing

1 cup cracker crumbs	1 teaspoon capers
1/4 teaspoon pepper	1 teaspoon chopped pickles
1 teaspoon salt	1/4 cup finely chopped salt pork
1 teaspoon minced onion	1/2 cup rich cream
1 teaspoon chopped parsley	

Mix in the order given. This makes a very crunchy stuffing. If you prefer a stuffing that is more moist, use stale bread crumbs moistened with a beaten egg and a little water. Add the same seasonings.

If you want a company dinner dish, stuff the cod with two cups of oysters rolled in seasoned cracker crumbs and moistened with one-half cup of melted butter.

KITTERY BAKED HALIBUT

4 thin slices salt pork	1 cup milk
1 onion, sliced	1 bay leaf
2 1/2 pounds halibut	Salt and pepper
3 tablespoons butter, melted	1 lemon, juice
3 tablespoons flour	

Lay the slices of salt pork on the bottom of a baking dish and cover with half of the onion slices. Place the halibut on them. Turn half the butter and the remainder of the onion slices over the halibut. Then add the rest of the butter. Sprinkle with the flour. Pour the milk around the fish; add the bay leaf and salt and pepper. Squeeze the juice of the lemon over all. Cover and bake twenty-five minutes in a moderate oven, 350 degrees F. Remove the cover and cook twenty minutes longer. Serves six. Serve with the following sauce.

Lobster Sauce

2 egg yolks	1/2 lemon, juice
1/2 cup cream	1/2 cup lobster, cut in very small
1/3 teaspoon salt	pieces
Dash of cayenne	Coral
1/2 cup boiling water	

Add the egg yolks to the cream, one at a time, then beat for five minutes. Add the salt, cayenne, and boiling water. Put the mixture in a double boiler and stir until thick, two or three minutes. Add the lemon juice, lobster, and coral. Serve at once.

OGUNQUIT BAKED HADDOCK

A good many New Englanders would vote for haddock as their favorite fish. This is the way it is prepared in a popular seacoast resort on the Maine coast. By this method the fish is cooked very slowly; in some cases the process goes on for hours.

Clean and prepare a six-pound haddock for baking. Cut notches in each side of the fish, about half an inch apart. Fill each notch with a wedge of salt pork. Cover the fish with flour and put in a large baking pan. Turn half a cup of water around the fish. Bake very slowly at 325 degrees F. until the fish is tender, basting frequently. When ready to serve, cover with a sauce made by boiling one cup of water with one tablespoon of flour mixed with a little water. Add butter the size of an egg. Boil about five minutes. Add two cups of hot cream seasoned to taste. Turn the sauce over the fish and serve immediately. Serves six to eight.

BAKED SEA BASS

Clean and skin a sea bass. Rub the inside with salt and fill with any preferred fish stuffing. Sew up the fish and place it on the rack of the baking pan. Cover with white wine or milk. For a six-pound bass, bake about one and one-half hours in a moderate oven, 350 degrees F. Serves six to eight.

NEW ENGLAND COURT BOUILLON

Mince an onion, a stalk of celery, and a few sprigs of parsley. Fry them in a little butter; add two tablespoons salt, a bay leaf, three whole cloves, two quarts of boiling water, and one pint of cider vinegar or sour wine. Boil about fifteen minutes. Strain the liquid before using.

BOILED SALMON WITH NEW PEAS

For each person to be served, allow half a pound of fresh salmon steak. If you use hot water for boiling the fish, add salt and one tablespoon of lemon juice or cider vinegar. If possible, use court bouillon. Put the liquid in a kettle deep enough so it will cover the fish. Wrap the salmon steaks in a thin cloth to keep them from losing their shape, and place them in the kettle. Simmer, but do not boil, for twenty minutes. Remove the fish to a platter and cover the fish with egg sauce. Serve with buttered garden peas.

Drawn-Butter Egg Sauce

1/2 cup butter or other table fat	1/2 teaspoon salt
2 tablespoons flour	1/4 teaspoon pepper
1 cup hot water	2 hard-cooked eggs, sliced
1 cup hot fish stock	

Melt half of the fat in a saucepan. Sir in the flour until smooth. Pour in the hot water and fish stock, stirring vigorously. Cook for five minutes. Add the remaining fat, seasonings, and hard-cooked eggs.

BOSTON BROILED SCROD

Small or medium-sized fish that have been split down the back, fish steaks, and fish fillets are at their best when properly broiled. This is particularly true of scrod, the name the fish trade gives to young codfish and small haddock.

In certain Boston hotels, broiled scrod, served with a bowl of melted butter, laced with lemon juice, is a dish that gourmets ask for again and again. The following recipe is basically one that has been used by a New England family for three generations at least.

While the broiler is heating, scrape and remove the scales from the fish, taking care not to break the skin. If the fish is small, broil it whole; if rather large, cut it into strips. Rub the broiler with a piece of salt pork and place the fish on it, skin side down. Sprinkle with melted butter and broil thoroughly on one side. Turn the fish to the other side, being careful not to break the skin. Sprinkle again with melted butter and continue broiling. It takes about thirty minutes to broil a medium-sized fish. Season with salt and pepper, and send to the table piping hot. Serve with slices of lemon and melted butter. Allow one-half to three-fourths pound of fish for each serving.

All kinds of fish may be broiled, but if rather large pieces are used, it is a good idea to put them in a moderate oven for about fifteen minutes before they are placed on the broiler.

TONGUES AND SOUNDS

Soak the tongues and sounds in cold water overnight. In the morning, drain them and cover again with cold water. Bring to just below the boiling point and simmer for thirty minutes. Serve with Drawn-Butter Egg Sauce.

BAKED SALMON TROUT

According to Mrs. Harland, "Handle the beauty with gentle respect while cleaning, washing, and wiping him, and lay him full length, still respectfully, in a baking-pan, with just enough water to keep him from scorching. If large, score the backbone with a sharp knife, taking care not to mar the comeliness of his red-spotted sides. Bake slowly, basting often with butter and water. By the time he is done—and he should be so well looked after that his royal robe hardly shows a seam or rent, and the red spots are still distinctly visible—have ready in a saucepan a cup of cream—diluted with a *few* spoonfuls of hot water, lest it should clot in heating—in which has been stirred cautiously two tablespoons of melted butter and a little chopped parsley. Heat this in a vessel set within another of boiling water, add the gravy from the dripping pan, boil up once to thicken, and when the trout is laid—always respectfully—in a hot dish, pour the sauce around him as he lies in state. He will take kindly to the creamy bath, and your guests will take kindly to him. Garnish with a wreath of crimson nasturtium-blooms and dainty sprigs of parsley, arranged by your own hands on the edge of the dish, and let no sharply spiced sauces come near him. They would but mar his native richness—the flavor he brought with him from the lake and the wild-wood. Salt him lightly, should he need it, eat and be happy."

PAN-FRIED TROUT, WHITE MOUNTAIN STYLE

Cook trout just as soon as you can after taking. Use a pair of kitchen scissors to slit one side of the fish. Clean and wash it quickly under very cold water. Try out pieces of salt pork to make enough fat so there will be about one-quarter inch in the bottom of the pan. Roll the trout in seasoned corn meal. Fry it in the hot pork fat, first on one side, then on the other. Turn carefully. Do not burn or overcook. Arrange on a platter surrounded by crisp salt pork slices. Serve with country fried or Lyonnaise potatoes. Perch may be cooked the same way. They should be served with wedges of lemon.

FRIED PICKEREL, COUNTRY STYLE

Clean the fish and cut it into uniform pieces about an inch thick. Roll the slices in flour or corn meal. Try out slices of salt pork until you have about half an inch of fat in the bottom of the frying pan. If necessary, add table fat to make the desired quantity. Fry the pickerel in the fat, turning each piece when it is browned. Drain on paper.

Serve the pickerel with the following gravy made in the frying pan. Remove any scraps of fish or meal that remain in the pan. Turn in one-quarter cup of boiling water and add one cup of rich hot cream. Let boil two minutes. Thicken with one tablespoon flour, stirring vigorously. Season with salt, pepper, and chopped parsley. Turn the sauce into a deep platter and lay the fish in it. Garnish with slices of crisp fried pork. Allow a half-pound fish for each serving.

BAKED SHAD

1 good-sized shad	2 tablespoons table fat
2 cups stuffing	1/2 cup hot water
Slices of salt pork	1 tablespoon ketchup
1 cup hot water	Slices of lemon

Clean the fish and stuff and lay it in a baking pan. Put the slices of salt pork on top of the fish. Surround with cup of hot water. Baste with fat and one-half cup of hot water. Bake in a hot oven for about ten minutes, then lower to moderate heat, and bake for half an hour. Remove the fish to a hot serving platter. Add the ketchup to the juices in the bottom of the pan. If too thick, add a little water. Pour over the fish. Garnish with the slices of lemon. A three-pound shad serves six.

CONNECTICUT RIVER PLANKED SHAD

Clean a three-pound shad and remove the head. Split the fish entirely open and nail it to a board of hardwood. Set the board in front of the open fire. Broil until the fish is brown and cooked through, about twenty minutes. Remove it from the plank; spread the fish with butter, salt, and cayenne pepper, and serve it from the plank.

Walnut or butternut pickles are delicious accompaniments to planked shad. Serves six.

BAKED BLACK BASS

Prepare a good-sized bass for baking in the usual way, and use the following stuffing:

2 cups stale bread crumbs	1 cup hot water
1/2 cup table fat	Salt and pepper
Few sprigs of sweet herbs	1 egg, beaten

Stuff and sew up the fish. Score both sides, cutting down to the bone. Put a thin slice of salt pork in each incision. Baste often, first with melted butter and water, then with drippings from the fish and pork. Bake in a moderate oven, 350 degrees F., one hour. Serves six.

FRIED EELS

Skin the fish and let it stand in boiling water for a few minutes. Cut into three-inch pieces. Roll in a mixture of flour and corn meal. Pan-fry in hot fat until brown. Allow one-half pound for each serving.

LAKE COUNTRY FRIED SMELTS

Clean and wash the smelts. Drain, salt them, and let stand for half an hour. Roll in a mixture of corn meal and flour. Drop into two inches of boiling fat and fry until crisp and brown. The secret of cooking smelts is to have them crisp. Allow five to eight smelts, according to size, for each serving.

NEW ENGLAND CODFISH DINNER

1 1/2 to 2 pounds salt cod	12 small beets
1/4 pound salt pork	6 onions
6 potatoes	1 1/2 cups medium white sauce

Cut the codfish in portions suitable for serving. Cover with cold water and let it stand for about one and one-half hours, changing the water several times. Drain, cover with fresh cold water, and bring slowly to the boiling point. Drain the codfish again and keep it hot. Dice the salt pork and cook in a frying pan until crisp and brown. Cook the vegetables separately. Arrange the codfish on a hot platter and cover with the white sauce. Garnish with pork and arrange the vegetables around the edge of the platter. Serves six.

WHITE MOUNTAIN PICKED FISH

2 cups salt codfish, picked into small pieces	1 tablespoon flour
	2 cups rich milk
1/2 cup melted butter	2 eggs, slightly beaten

Freshen the codfish and let simmer for ten minutes, then drain. Melt the butter in a saucepan and thicken with the flour, stirring vigorously. Add the milk gradually. Cook five minutes. Add the codfish. In about ten minutes, stir in the eggs. Serve at once with baked potatoes and pickled beets. Serves six.

SALT CODFISH WITH PORK SCRAPS

Here is an old-time supper dish that is still served frequently in northern New Hampshire.

Freshen enough strips of salt codfish to make a meal for your family. One pound of salt fish will serve six. Put strips in cold water and bring to the simmering point, but do not boil. Try out a number of thin slices of salt pork. When they are nicely browned, remove them to a hot platter. Drain the codfish strips and turn them into the hot pork fat.

Take them out as soon as they are heated. They should be removed when they are white and tender, not browned. Serve the codfish with the pork scraps around it, and pour a little hot fat over all.

YANKEE FISH PIE

Fish combines so well with other ingredients that it is always excellent in made and casserole dishes. The following recipe is an old one that makes use of both cod and oysters.

Flour, seasoned with salt and pepper	1/2 lemon, juice
	Water
1-pound cod, boned and cut in pieces	1 tablespoon butter
	2 cups mashed potatoes
7 large oysters	1 tablespoon milk

Roll the pieces of cod in the seasoned flour and place them in a greased baking dish. Pour the oysters and their liquor over the cod. Sprinkle with the lemon juice and dredge lightly with the flour. Add enough water to cover the mixture. Dot with bits of the butter. Bake slowly for half an hour in a slow oven, 325 degrees F. Cover with the mashed potatoes and brush the crust with the milk. Return to the oven until the potato crust is browned. Serve at once. Serves six.

SMOKED FISH CASSEROLE

1 1/2 pounds finnan haddie or other smoked fish	3 cups hot milk
	2 hard-cooked eggs, diced
Milk	2 tablespoons chopped green pepper
Water	
4 medium boiled potatoes, diced	Salt and pepper
5 tablespoons table fat	4 slices bread, cubed
4 tablespoons flour	1 tablespoon butter

Wash the fish, cut in half crosswise, and put it in a baking pan. Add enough milk and water to cover. Soak for half an hour, then bring to a boil, and let simmer fifteen minutes. Drain the fish and remove the skin and bones. Flake the fish and add it to the diced potatoes. Make a sauce of the fat, flour, and milk. Add the fish and potato mixture, the eggs, and the seasonings to the sauce, then turn it into a casserole. Brown the bread cubes in one tablespoon of butter, and place on top of the mixture. Bake one-half hour in a moderate oven, 350 degrees F. Serves six.

SUNDAY MORNING FISH BALLS

There are a number of tricks to making fish balls. The water should be drained from the potatoes and codfish the instant they are cooked. Then they should be placed in a saucepan, covered with a clean cloth, and allowed to dry out. Unless this is done, the fish balls will not hold together properly when dropped in the hot fat. The fish and potatoes should be combined while still hot, and after the other ingredients are added, the mixture must be kept hot until all the fish balls are fried. Do not fry more than five fish balls at a time, and reheat the fat after each frying.

1 cup raw salt codfish, picked into very small pieces
2 cups sliced potatoes
1 teaspoon butter
1/8 teaspoon pepper
1/4 teaspoon salt
1 egg, well beaten

Freshen the codfish slightly. Put it on top of the potatoes in a kettle, cover with boiling water, and cook until the potatoes are soft. Drain off all the water. Mash the fish and potatoes, and beat together, using a fork, until the mixture is very light. Add the butter and seasonings, and then the beaten egg. Drop by spoonfuls into two inches of smoking hot fat. Fry about one minute. Dip the spoon in the fat before taking up the mixture for each fish ball. Serves six.

1840 FISH HASH

Prepare fish as for fish balls. Chop cold potatoes fine and mix with the fish. Fry six slices of salt pork. Remove the slices, but leave the fat in the skillet. Turn the hash mixture into the fat. Add half a cup of boiling water. Brown the hash, being careful not to burn it. Fold the mixture as you would an omelet. Garnish with salt pork slices.

MRS. HALE'S RECIPE FOR KEDGEREE

"Take some fish that has been dressed, bone it carefully, and pull it into small bits. Add hard-boiled eggs, chopped, and as much rice, well-boiled, as you require to fill your dish. Mix all these well together, with sufficient butter or cream to moisten them, adding a little cayenne, mustard, and salt. Put all into a saucepan and stir with a fork (not a spoon) until quite hot. The fire must not be too fierce, and the dish must be served up very hot."

3. OUT OF THE LOBSTER POT

THE Pilgrims found Cape Cod a bleak place in November, 1620. Fortunately they soon made friends with the Indians who taught them to supplement the meager supply of food left from their long sea voyage with shellfish from the bays and shallow inlets. In December, 1621, Edward Winslow, the chronicler of those early days, wrote: "Our bay is full of lobster all summer. . . . We have mussels . . . at our door. Oysters we have none near, but can have them brought by the Indians when we will."

Steamed clams and mussels made the first meal the Pilgrims had on land. Today, no summer is really perfect for the New Englander until, napkin under chin, he has eaten his fill of fresh steamed clams, dipped in broth and then in melted butter. Two varieties of clams are abundant in New England, the hard and the soft. Of the hard clams, known as quahogs, the large ones are used for soups, chowders, and fritters, and the littlenecks and cherrystones are steamed or served raw.

When an industry assumes an important place in a community, a whole new vocabulary springs up. The expression, "chowderheaded old clam," arose because the old and tough quahogs were used for chowder and the tender ones for other purposes. In the same way we got the expression, "Don't be a clam," meaning closemouthed.

The center of the New England oyster business for many years was around Wellfleet on Cape Cod. There in 1802, twenty-five vessels were engaged in cod, mackerel, and oyster fishing. People of that day believed the world had no better oysters than those found near Wellfleet.

In the 1850s, Rhode Island began developing beds in Narragansett Bay with oysters brought from the Chesapeake region, but the industry was interrupted by the Civil War. The Rhode Island oysters never gained favor with the old-timers, however, who continued to believe that imported oysters could not hold a candle to the native ones.

So popular were oysters that taverns and eating places, well into the nineteenth century, made a specialty of oyster suppers in winter months. In late autumn, oysters and clams were buried in beds of damp sea sand mixed with Indian meal. Watered twice a week, plump fresh oysters were always available for rich pies on cold winter evenings. At fashionable parties in the middle 1800s, these and oyster patties were midnight supper favorites. Both creamed and curried oysters were served in patty shells. Those who did not have oysters stored in their cellars pickled a few to enjoy with eggnog on New Year's Eve. It has always been the rule to serve oysters only in months that have the letter R in their names.

Even in colonial times, oysters were shipped far inland. Piled in saddlebags to be carried by horseback, and later packed in kegs and flour barrels or loaded on spring wagons, oyster caravans journeyed into northern New York and Vermont. There many a housewife would swap butter, cheese, homespun cloth, or yarn for one or two dozen oysters.

English visitors did not take any more kindly to American oysters than Americans in England took to Brussels sprouts. Thackeray, eating his first raw oyster at the Parker House, remarked that he felt as though he had just swallowed a baby. Many persons share this dislike, but for those who have cultivated the taste, raw oysters cannot be matched by other seafoods of which New England has such a luscious abundance.

STEAMED CLAMS

Allow between ten and fifteen clams per person. Scrub with a brush and wash in cold running water. Pick out all the broken shells and be sure the clams are fresh and alive. Fresh clams have thin, tightly closed shells; do not use any that are even slightly opened. Put the clams in a kettle, adding half a cup of boiling water to each four quarts of clams. Cover tightly and steam until the shells are partly opened. Be careful not to overcook. Serve with a cup of broth and a dish of melted butter.

CLAM BROTH

After steaming, remove the clams. Strain the liquid through a double thickness of cheesecloth, being sure not to disturb the sand that may be in the bottom of the kettle. If you want to serve clam broth alone as a first course, simmer the clams until the shells are well open, using a little more water than you allow for steamed clams, or use a court bouillon as for mussels. Then strain the broth. Serve very hot either plain or with a spoonful of salted whipped cream.

FRIED CLAMS

Allow one quart of shucked clams for six persons. Clean the clams well and dry them. Dip in egg beaten lightly with a tablespoon of cold water, then in fine bread crumbs or corn meal. Fry in deep fat until brown. Drain well on absorbent paper.

STATE OF MAINE CLAM FRITTERS

24 clams	1 tablespoon melted butter
1 egg, yolk and white beaten separately	1/4 teaspoon salt
	1/2 cup flour
1/2 cup milk	

Beat the egg yolk, add the milk, butter, salt, and flour. Fold in the stiffly beaten egg white. Drain the clams, dip them in the batter, and fry brown. Serves four.

CONNECTICUT SCALLOPED CLAMS

1 cup bread crumbs	1 tablespoon minced onion
2 cups chopped clams	1/4 cup top milk
Salt and paprika	1/2 cup clam juice
1 tablespoon minced parsley	1 tablespoon butter

Place a layer of bread crumbs and a layer of chopped clams in a buttered baking dish. Sprinkle with the seasonings. Add another layer of crumbs, clams, and seasonings. Cover with the milk and clam juice, finishing with a layer of crumbs. Dot with the butter and bake twenty minutes in a hot oven, 400 degrees F. Three tablespoons of sherry added to the dish improves the flavor. Serves six.

MAINE DEVILED CLAMS

2 cups clams	1/2 cup minced celery
1/2 cup liquor	4 tablespoons butter
1 teaspoon lemon juice	1/8 teaspoon pepper
2 tablespoons minced onion	1/4 teaspoon prepared mustard
2 tablespoons minced green pepper	3/4 cup cracker crumbs

Chop the clams fine, add the lemon juice, and let the clams simmer in their own liquor five minutes. Cook the minced onion, green pepper, and celery in the melted butter until tender. Mix with the remaining ingredients, add to the clams, and bake in quahog shells or ramekins twenty minutes in a moderate oven, 350 degrees F. Serves six.

KENNEBUNKPORT CLAM PIE

2 slices salt pork	Salt and pepper
1 onion, minced	1 cup chopped clams
3 potatoes, cubed	Pie crust

Try out the salt pork, add the minced onion, and fry until light brown. Add the potato cubes and salt and pepper. Cover and cook slowly until the potatoes are done, adding just enough water to keep them from burning. Add the clams and put the mixture in a buttered baking dish. Cover with a rich pie crust, and bake in a moderate oven, 350 degrees F., until brown. Do not use a lower crust as it is apt to get soggy. Serves four.

CREAMED CLAMS

25 soft clams
3 tablespoons butter
3 tablespoons flour
1 cup clam liquor

Salt and pepper
1 cup scalded milk
Toast or patty shells

Chop the clams coarsely. Melt the butter, add the flour, and blend. Add the clam liquor, and cook until smooth. Add the clams and seasonings, reheat to boiling, stir in the hot milk, and cook one minute. Serve at once on toast or in patty shells. Serves six.

SCALLOPED OYSTERS

1 quart oysters and liquor
1 cup bread crumbs
2 cups cracker crumbs
1/2 cup melted butter

1/2 teaspoon salt
1/2 teaspoon pepper
1 cup cream or top milk

Clean the oysters. Mix the bread and cracker crumbs and the butter, salt, and pepper. Cover the bottom of a buttered baking dish with a thin layer of crumbs, add half the oysters and liquor, cover with crumbs, and add another layer of oysters, liquor, and crumbs. Pour the cream over the top. Bake in a moderate oven, 375 degrees F., for thirty to forty minutes. Serves six to eight.

OYSTER COCKTAIL

16 small raw oysters
2 tablespoons ketchup
1 tablespoon lemon juice
3 drops Tabasco sauce

1/2 teaspoon horseradish
2 drops onion juice
2 tablespoons minced celery
Salt to taste

Mix, chill thoroughly, and serve in cocktail glasses. Allow eight oysters to a person.

FRIED OYSTERS

Drain and clean the oysters. Season with salt and pepper. Dip in flour, beaten egg, and then in fine bread crumbs, cracker meal, flour, or corn meal. Fry in deep fat until brown. Drain on absorbent paper and serve hot, garnished with lemon and parsley. Allow six oysters to a serving.

PIGS IN BLANKET

Drain and clean the oysters. Wrap each oyster in a small piece of bacon and skewer it with a toothpick. Either fry or broil until the bacon is brown. It will take about one-quarter pound of bacon for each dozen oysters. Allow four to six oysters to a serving.

OYSTER PATTIES

1 quart oysters	1 wineglass white wine
2 tablespoons butter	1 lemon, juice
1 tablespoon flour	Salt and pepper
1/2 teaspoon mace	Patty shells

Melt the butter, add the flour and other seasonings. Add the oysters and cook them until the edges curl, stirring constantly. Fill the patty shells and serve at once. Serves eight.

CURRIED OYSTERS

1 pint oysters	1/4 teaspoon salt
1/4 cup butter	1/8 teaspoon pepper
Oyster liquor and cream	1/2 teaspoon curry powder
1 1/2 tablespoons flour	Steamed rice or patty shells

Clean the oysters and cook them in half the butter until the edges curl. Drain the oysters and add enough cream to the liquor to make one cup.

Blend the remaining butter and flour, add the liquid, and stir until smooth. Add the seasonings and oysters. Cook in a double boiler ten minutes and serve hot on steamed rice or in patty shells. Serves four.

CREAMED OYSTERS

1 pint oysters	1/8 teaspoon pepper
2 tablespoons butter	1/2 teaspoon celery salt
2 tablespoons flour	1/4 teaspoon paprika
1 cup oyster liquor and cream	1 teaspoon sherry
1/2 teaspoon salt	Patty shells or toast

Drain the oysters. Melt the butter, add the flour, then the oyster liquor plus enough cream to make one cup. When cooked smooth, add the spices and oysters. Cook in a double boiler until the oysters are thoroughly heated and the edges begin to curl. Add the sherry and serve in patty shells or on toast. Serves four. The recipe may be varied by using equal amounts of oysters and mushrooms or oysters and minced ham.

OYSTER PIE

1 quart oysters and liquor	1/2 cup cracker crumbs
Salt and pepper	2 tablespoons butter
Dash of mace	Pastry
1/4 cup white wine	

Drain the oysters, season with salt, pepper, and a dash of mace. Add the wine, crumbs, and melted butter. Line a pie tin with rich pastry, add the oysters, and cover with the oyster liquor. Cover with a top crust and bake in a moderate oven, 375 degrees F., for thirty to forty minutes, or until the crust is brown. Chicken stock may be used in place of white wine, and mushrooms added if desired. Serves six.

Oyster and celery pie: Follow the above recipe and add one cup of celery in place of the wine and cracker crumbs.

Yankee oyster pie: Use cream in place of the wine and oyster liquor.

BAKED OYSTERS

12 large oysters	2 cups thick white sauce
1/4 cup melted butter	Salt, pepper, paprika
1 small onion	Grated cheese
6 mushrooms	Minced parsley

Wash the oysters, place in the deep half of the shells, cover with half of the melted butter, and broil until the edges curl. Sauté the onion and mushrooms in the remaining butter, add the white sauce, and season with salt, pepper, and paprika to taste. Put as much of the sauce on each oyster as the shell will hold, sprinkle with grated cheese and parsley, and place under the broiler flame until the cheese melts. Allow three to six oysters to a serving.

PICKLED OYSTERS

1 quart oysters	1 cup dry white wine
1 cup oyster liquor and water	1 cup hot vinegar
1 1/4 teaspoons salt	2 tablespoons pickling spice

Wash and clean the oysters. Add enough water to the oyster liquor to make one cup. Add the oysters and cook until the edges curl. Remove the oysters, add the vinegar and pickling spice. Boil ten minutes, skim, add the wine, pour over oysters, and put in jars. If there is not enough liquid, add half vinegar and half water mixed with two parts wine. Bring to a boil before adding.

STEAMED MUSSELS

Wash the mussels thoroughly, scrub the shells with a brush, and pull out the black hairy beards. Mussels are best steamed in a court bouillon, but may be steamed similar to Steamed Clams.

Put the mussels in a pot with only the water that clings to them. For two dozen mussels, add a pinch of thyme or several sprigs of fresh thyme, half a bay leaf, one small chopped onion, one-quarter clove of garlic, salt, pepper, and half a cup of white wine. Cook over a low flame, shaking a few times until the shells open. Serve either with butter as steamed clams or with a sauce. Allow six mussels to a serving.

Sauce for Mussels

Melt one teaspoon of butter for each dozen mussels and pour into the strained mussel liquor. Add salt and pepper to taste. Pour over beaten egg yolk, and blend. Add chopped parsley.

FRIED MUSSELS

Wash the mussels, drain and dry them well. Sprinkle with lemon juice. Roll in flour seasoned with salt and pepper, dip in slightly beaten egg, roll in cracker crumbs, and fry in deep fat. Allow six to a serving.

The recipe for clam cakes also may be used for mussels. For creamed mussels, use the recipe for creamed clams. Be sure to sprinkle mussels with lemon juice before adding them to the batter or cream sauce.

MUSSELS AU GRATIN

1 chopped onion	1 tablespoon lemon juice
2 tablespoons butter	1 cup bread crumbs
2 tablespoons flour	2 cups mussels
1 1/2 cups mussel liquor	Grated cheese
Salt and pepper	

Sauté the onion in butter, add the flour, and blend. Add the mussel liquor and stir until smooth. Add salt and pepper. Sprinkle the lemon juice on the mussels. Put a layer of the bread crumbs in a buttered casserole, then a layer of mussels, and a layer of sauce. Top with the bread crumbs, sprinkle with grated cheese, and bake twenty minutes in a moderate oven, 375 degrees F. Serves six.

BOILED LOBSTER

For those who have never cooked a lobster, just a word of advice about buying.

Lobsters in New England are sold alive or green, cold boiled, or as picked lobster meat. Live lobsters have their claws plugged with a small piece of wood or held securely with a strong rubber band. If you value your fingers, do not remove the plugs until the lobsters are boiled or prepared for cooking. Chicken lobsters weigh just under a pound; medium lobsters, a pound or two pounds; and oversize, from two pounds up. Lobsters over three pounds are inclined to be tough, so buy the smaller sizes.

Be sure the lobsters are alive when you buy them and cook them as soon as possible. Live lobsters are a mottled greenish blue with red flecks. When cooked they turn a bright scarlet. If it is necessary to keep live lobsters for any length of time, place them in the coldest part of the refrigerator, but do not put them directly on ice.

Allow at least a pound of live lobster per person, and when using fresh or canned picked lobster, count on one and a half pounds of meat for six people.

The inexperienced cook is sometimes concerned about what parts of the lobster to eat. All but the stomach, or lady, can be eaten; this is the hard sack in back of the head. The spongy grayish white substance that covers the body and the inside of the large shell is the lung, and is thrown away, although it is not harmful.

Both the coral or roe—the bright scarlet substance found in the body—and the greenish liver or tomalley are edible. Many persons consider the tomalley the best part of the lobster.

In boiling allow enough water to cover the lobster, the amount depending on the size of the kettle. Two or three quarts for each lobster and two to three tablespoons of salt is about right. Bring the water to a good boil and then plunge the lobster in head first. Cover and count the boiling time after the water begins to boil again. If you are near the shore and get your lobsters from a fisherman, he will usually bring seaweed with him. In this case, plunge the lobster into boiling unsalted water, and cover with a layer of seaweed. Boil for fifteen to twenty minutes. Remove from the water and drain several minutes before serving.

If lobsters are to be served cold, allow them to cool at room temperature. Do not place them in the refrigerator until they are completely cooled, and do not put them under cold running water.

To serve boiled lobsters, twist the large claws from the body and crack gently with a nutcracker or hammer. Be sure not to pound or bruise the tender meat. Lay the lobster on its back, and with the point of a sharp knife or scissors, cut down the middle, beginning at the head and continuing to the end of the tail. Remove the lady and the black vein that runs the length of the tail. The small claws may be left on, or removed and used as a garnish.

Place the lobster on a small platter, arrange the claws around it, and garnish with sliced lemon and sprigs of parsley. Serve with a side dish of melted butter and French fried potatoes or potato chips.

BROILED LOBSTER

Insert a sharp knife into the back of the lobster between the body and the tail to sever the spinal cord and kill the lobster. Then run a sharp knife on the underside from head to tail, cutting entirely through the shell. Break open as you do for a boiled lobster. Remove the stomach and the intestinal cord. Brush the inside with melted butter and sprinkle with salt and pepper. Arrange on a broiler pan. Broil eight minutes on the shell side and six minutes on the meat side. Crack the claws, and serve with melted butter.

Lobster prepared as above and baked for twenty to thirty minutes in a moderate oven, 375 degrees F., is not as dry as broiled lobster.

BAKED STUFFED LOBSTER

Mix the tomalley and coral to a smooth paste with one-fourth cup cracker crumbs for each two-pound lobster. Season with salt, cayenne, and Worcestershire sauce. Spread the lobster cavity with this mixture, sprinkle with one tablespoon minced parsley and one tablespoon minced onion, mixed with one-fourth cup cracker crumbs. Dot with butter. Place in a broiler pan, bake fifteen minutes in a moderate oven, 350 degrees F., and broil fifteen minutes longer. Serve with melted butter and lemon slices.

DEVILED LOBSTER

Deviled lobster may be made by following the recipe for scalloped lobster below, adding one-fourth teaspoon dry mustard, one-half teaspoon onion juice, and one-fourth teaspoon cayenne. Deviled lobster must be highly seasoned to be tasty.

SCALLOPED LOBSTER

1 1/2 cups lobster meat	1 egg, well beaten
1 cup milk	Salt and pepper
2 tablespoons butter	2 teaspoons lemon juice
1 tablespoon flour	Buttered crumbs

Cut the lobster meat into pieces. Make a white sauce of the milk, butter, and flour. Blend in the well-beaten egg, add the lobster meat, salt and pepper to taste, and the lemon juice. Put in a buttered baking dish and cover with the crumbs. Bake twenty minutes in a moderate oven, 350 degrees F., or until the crumbs are brown. Serves four to six.

LOBSTER THERMIDOR

3 medium boiled lobsters	1/4 teaspoon paprika
1 cup sliced mushrooms	2 egg yolks, beaten
1 teaspoon minced onion	1 cup grated cheese
3 tablespoons butter	2 tablespoons sherry
2 tablespoons flour	1 tablespoon lemon juice
1 1/2 cups top milk	1/8 teaspoon cayenne
1/2 teaspoon dry mustard	Salt to taste

Split the lobsters. Remove the meat and cut it in large pieces. Add the liver and coral. Reserve the lobster shells. Sauté the onion and mushrooms in the butter for three minutes, blend in the flour, add the milk, and stir until thick. Add the mustard, paprika, beaten egg yolks, and three-fourths of the cup of cheese. Stir until the cheese is melted. Add the lobster meat, the remaining ingredients, and salt to taste. Put the mixture in the lobster shells or in a buttered casserole, sprinkle with the remaining cheese, and brown in a hot oven, 450 degrees F. Serves six.

LOBSTER CUTLETS

2 1/2 tablespoons butter	1/2 teaspoon salt
1/3 cup flour	1/4 teaspoon pepper
1 cup milk	2 cups cut lobster meat
1 egg yolk, beaten	1 1/2 tablespoons lemon juice

Melt the butter, add the flour, milk, and beaten egg yolk. Cook until slightly thickened. Season with the salt and pepper, add the lobster meat and lemon juice, and cool. Shape into cutlets, roll in bread crumbs, beaten egg, in crumbs again, and fry in deep fat. Serves six.

LOBSTER NEWBURG

4 tablespoons butter	1 cup cream
2 cups diced lobster meat	3 egg yolks, beaten
1/4 cup sherry	Salt, pepper, cayenne
1 tablespoon brandy	

Melt the butter in a double boiler, add the lobster meat, and cook three minutes, stirring constantly. Add the sherry and brandy. Heat the cream and mix with the beaten egg yolks. Add this to the lobster. Stir until thickened, but do not allow to boil. Season to taste with salt, pepper, and cayenne. Serves four to six.

CURRIED LOBSTER

1 medium boiled lobster	1 teaspoon curry powder
1 cup milk	Salt and pepper
2 tablespoons flour	1 cup cream
2 tablespoons butter	

Remove the meat from the lobster and cut into pieces. Add the tomalley and coral to it. Heat the milk, add the flour blended with the butter, curry powder, salt, and pepper. Add the cream and lobster meat, and cook in a double boiler until thickened. Serves four.

BOILED SHRIMPS

Shrimps are not so plentiful as lobsters, clams, and oysters in New England, but are popular with most lovers of sea foods. The shrimp is a small crustacean resembling a lobster. When bought in the market, the head is often removed, but the thin paperlike shell is left on the rest of the body. The black vein running down the back should always be removed after cooking.

Wash the shrimps and drop them in boiling salted water to cover, allowing one tablespoon salt to each two quarts of water. Cover, and simmer fifteen to twenty minutes, or until the shells turn pink and the shrimps are tender. Drain and remove the shells and the black vein.

FRIED SHRIMPS

For fried shrimps, follow the recipe for Fried Oysters.

EAST INDIA SHRIMP CURRY

1/2 cup minced onion	1/4 teaspoon ginger
6 tablespoons butter	1 cup chicken broth
6 tablespoons flour	2 cups top milk
2 1/2 teaspoons curry powder	2 1/2 pounds boiled shrimps
1 1/2 teaspoons salt	1 teaspoon lemon juice
1 1/2 teaspoons sugar	6 cups boiled rice

Sauté the onion in the butter, add the flour and seasonings. Blend, add the chicken broth and milk. Cook in a double boiler, stirring constantly until thickened. Add the shrimps and the lemon juice. Heat well and serve with the boiled rice. One cup of boiled celery may be added, if desired.

As accompaniments serve bowls of shredded raw coconut, chopped salted almonds, chopped diced bacon, and chutney. Serves eight to ten.

OYSTER AND SHRIMP PIE

1 quart oysters	1 teaspoon salt
1 cup shrimps	1/8 teaspoon pepper
1/3 cup butter	1/2 cup chopped celery, or
1/2 cup flour	1 tablespoon chopped parsley
Milk	Pie crust

Wash and drain the oysters. Scald and strain the liquor. Remove the shells and veins from the shrimps. Melt the butter, add the flour, and the strained liquor plus enough milk to make three cups. Blend well. Add the oysters and shrimps and the seasonings. Pour into a buttered baking dish, cover with pie crust, and bake in a hot oven, 400 degrees F., for forty minutes, or until brown. Serves six to eight.

BOILED CRABS

Wash the crabs thoroughly and plunge them head first into boiling salted water, using one tablespoon salt to each quart of water. Cover and boil twenty minutes. Drain and cover with cold water. Break off the claws and the tail or apron on the underside of the shell. Separate the shells and remove the intestine, sand bag, and gills found between the top shell and the two halves of the body. Crack the claws, and with a nut-pick remove the meat in as large flakes as possible.

CRAB MEAT AU GRATIN

2 tablespoons butter	1/8 teaspoon pepper
2 tablespoons flour	2 cups cooked crab meat
1 cup rich milk	1/2 pound grated cheese
1/4 teaspoon salt	

Melt the butter in the top of a double boiler, add the flour and milk, stirring until smooth. Add the seasonings and crab meat. Put in a buttered casserole, sprinkle with the greated cheese, and brown under the broiler flame. Serves six.

CRAB MEAT À LA KING

Melt two tablespoons butter, add three tablespoons flour, and stir in one and one-half cups rich milk. Cook until thick and smooth, add three-fourths teaspoon salt, one beaten egg, one and one-half cups crab meat, one-fourth pimiento cut in strips, one tablespoon lemon juice, and one-half cup mushrooms. Reheat to the boiling point, but do not stir too hard. Add two tablespoons butter, and serve on toast points garnished with strips of pimiento and parsley, or serve in patty shells. Serves six.

DEVILED CRABS

2 cups crab meat	1/2 teaspoon salt
1/4 cup sherry	1 teaspoon dry mustard
1 teaspoon Worcestershire sauce	White pepper
3 egg yolks, beaten	2 cups milk
3 tablespoons butter	1/2 cup buttered bread crumbs
2 tablespoons flour	

Mix the crab meat with the sherry, Worcestershire sauce, and egg yolks. Melt the butter, stir in the flour mixed with the seasonings. Add the milk, and stir over the heat until thick. Add the crab meat, and blend well. Fill the crab shells with the mixture, sprinkle with the buttered crumbs, and bake in a moderate oven, 375 degrees F., for ten minutes until brown. Serves six.

Some recipes call for minced hard-cooked eggs, minced parsley, lemon juice, and horseradish. Their use depends on whether you like highly seasoned dishes. For the above recipe, one-half teaspoon horseradish and two tablespoons lemon juice would be sufficient, and two hard-cooked eggs minced fine.

FRIED SOFT-SHELLED CRABS

Soft-shelled crabs are another New England delicacy. They are usually served fried, but may be broiled. The back of the soft-shelled crab tapers to a point at each side. Lay the crab on its face, and pull back each point, pulling off all the spongy material that is exposed. Then turn the crab on

its back, and with a knife remove the apron or tail which laps under-
neath and all the spongy substance under it. Drop the crabs in boiling
water to cover, adding one tablespoon salt to each quart, then cover and
boil twenty minutes.

Prepare six crabs as described above. Beat two eggs, roll the crabs in
cracker crumbs, dip in egg, roll in fine cracker crumbs again, and fry in
deep fat for about eight minutes, or until golden brown. Drain on absorbent paper. Sprinkle with salt and pepper and serve with tartare sauce.
Serves six.

FRIED SCALLOPS

Cut a pint of scallops into three-fourth-inch cubes. Roll in flour seasoned with salt and pepper, then in beaten egg and in fine cracker
crumbs. Fry in deep fat and serve with tartare sauce. Serves four.

HUNTINGTON SCALLOPS

3 tablespoons lemon juice	1 egg, beaten
1 tablespoon olive oil	1/4 cup bread crumbs
1 teaspoon salt	2 tablespoons grated cheese
1/2 teaspoon pepper	3 tablespoons minced ham
1/2 teaspoon minced parsley	1 teaspoon minced chives
1 quart scallops	

Make a marinade of the first five ingredients. Put the scallops in the
marinade and let stand thirty minutes. Drain. Dip the scallops in the
beaten egg, and roll them in the remaining ingredients. Fry in hot fat.
Serves six.

SCALLOP CASSEROLE

1 1/2 pints scallops	1/2 teaspoon pepper
4 tablespoons butter	1/2 teaspoon dry mustard
1/2 onion, sliced	1 tablespoon lemon juice
4 tablespoons flour	2 teaspoons parsley
2 cups milk	Buttered crumbs
1 teaspoon salt	

Clean the scallops. Sauté the onion in butter until brown, add the flour, milk, and other seasonings. Cook until smooth. Add the scallops, turn into a buttered baking dish, cover with the buttered crumbs, and bake thirty minutes in a moderate oven, 350 degrees F. Serves six.

SCALLOPED SCALLOPS

For scalloped scallops, follow the recipe for Scalloped Oysters.

CREAMED SCALLOPS

For creamed scallops, follow the recipe for Creamed Oysters.

4. CHOWDER KETTLE AND
SOUP TUREEN

Every New England girl who lived within sound of the sea, four or five generations ago, counted a chowder kettle as an essential part of her "setting out." When a bride left the family homestead, she carried with her a huge iron pot in which to make the hearty dish of fish, swimming in rich broth flavored with salt pork and onions.

Long before her banns were cried, a seacoast bride had learned all the tricks of successful chowder making: how to select a freshly caught cod or haddock of just the right size; how to boil the head to add goodness to the dish; how to try out salt pork without scorching the fat or blackening the onions fried in it. She knew that fish slices must not lose their shape and turn into a pulpy unappetizing mass, and that milk must be heated to keep it from curdling when added to the simmering contents of the kettle. But above all, the chowder must be dished up at exactly the

46

crucial moment and turned into the great tureen steaming hot and giving off a delectable odor that was a hurry-up dinner call to everyone who smelled it.

Clam chowder has always run fish chowder a close second in New England; in fact, today there are many people who are so convinced that it heads the list, they will drive for miles to find the type that exactly suits their fancy. Round-shelled quahogs, or cherrystones, make delicious chowder, and are much used in Rhode Island. The controversy of tomatoes versus no tomatoes in clam chowder started in this little state. Some Rhode Island people maintain as stoutly as the citizens of Maine that this vegetable never should go into the chowder kettle. Their opponents contend that it greatly improves the color and flavor of the dish. Be that as it may, the name of the state has become identified with the tomato variety of clam chowder.

As far back as the thirteenth century, English gentry ate soup at least once a day. "Dried peas and bacon water," watercress soup, cabbage soup, cheese soup, and "poor man's soup" made of odds and ends gathered together on short warning were old favorites. Better soups were spiced with marjoram, sage, sweet basil, or with mace, nutmeg, and cinnamon. Served in wooden trenchers or in pewter porringers, these soups were soaked up with bread, and for many families were the whole meal, but a substantial and tasty one.

Meat soups were of two kinds: brown, similar to the French *pot au feu,* made of beef or mutton and of marrow bones; and white, made of veal, chicken, or turkey. Nearly every New England family had long-handled slender marrow spoons to scoop the marrow from the center of the bones, for it was regarded as a great delicacy. Cooked marrow also was sprinkled with salt and pepper and eaten on fresh bread or made into small balls to be served with soup. Many cooks cracked the soup-bone and browned part of the meat in the melted marrow to make a rich-bodied soup.

Cooks on Nantucket whalers and other seagoing vessels frequently served lobscouse, a dish made of salt beef—familiarly known as "salt horse"—potatoes, onion, and pepper stewed together. Inland a similar dish was often called spoon meat because it provided most of the dinner and could be eaten with a spoon. First, the dinner kettle was partly filled with water and hung on the crane. When the water boiled, fresh meat, or salt meat when fresh was not available, cut in small pieces, was dropped in. Then vegetables and whole spices were added. At first the dish was thickened with corn meal, or at sea with powdered hardtack; later, potatoes were used.

In the days when every sea captain was expected to bring home a turtle and a keg of pickled limes, turtle soup was served frequently in seaport towns. Cuffy Cockroach, a slave belonging to Jahleel Brenton of Rhode Island, acquired such a reputation as a turtle cook that he was loaned to his master's friends on special occasions.

In the back country of Maine and New Hampshire and on Cope Cod, snapping turtles were abundant in all the fresh-water ponds. Old-timers thought there was nothing quite as tasty as snapper soup. One of Maine's tall tales is of a snapping turtle that was kept in a swill barrel until it grew to weigh eighty-six pounds.

NANTUCKET FISH CHOWDER

1 medium-sized fresh codfish, sliced	2 tablespoons flour
1/2 pound salt pork, sliced	1 1/2 cups hot milk
3 medium-sized onions, sliced	2 teaspoons salt
Water	1/4 teaspoon pepper
	Soda crackers

First, put the fish head in a saucepan, cover with cold water, and start it cooking. Then try out the salt pork in a skillet until the slices are crisp and brown. Remove the pork and fry the sliced onions in the fat until very light brown. Cut the pork slices into bits, add them to the fat and onion, and put the combination in the chowder kettle. Add the codfish slices and the strained water in which the fish head was boiled. Then add enough water so the liquid stands about two inches above the fish. Cook slowly for about twenty minutes. Make a paste of the flour and a little cold water. Mix with the hot milk and stir into the chowder. Add the seasonings, and let the chowder boil up once. Place halved soda crackers in the bottom of a tureen and turn the hot chowder over them. Serve at once. Serves four to six.

RHODE ISLAND SEA BASS CHOWDER

5 slices salt pork	Pinch of summer savory
4 pounds sea bass	Boston crackers
3 thin slices bacon	Water
4 medium-sized onions, sliced	2 tablespoons butter
Handful of chopped parsley	2 tablespoons flour

Dice the pork and fry it in the chowder kettle until crisp. Cut the sea bass in two-inch cubes and put in the kettle. Place the strips of bacon on top. Cover with the slices of onion. Add the parsley and summer savory and a layer of split crackers. Continue with the layers until all the fish is used. The top layer of crackers should be buttered. Add cold water to cover. Cook gently one hour. Using a skimmer, remove the solid parts of the chowder to a serving dish. Cream the butter and flour, and thicken the liquid. Let it boil up once. Serve with sour pickles and stewed tomatoes. This is a very rich chowder. Serves six.

DOWN-EAST CLAM CHOWDER

The home cook usually makes her chowder with shucked clams, she may even use canned clams; but the genuine shore cook will have nothing to do with either. She demands freshly dug clams still in their shells, using about half a peck for a medium-sized chowder. First, she scrubs the clams thoroughly with a small brush and then puts them in a large kettle with just enough water to keep the bottom layer from burning. When the clams at the top have opened, she takes them from the shells. Then she removes the skins, and cuts off all the black ends.

The following rule for clam chowder calls for shucked clams; but you can use clams in the shell, if you prefer. If fresh clams are not available, a good chowder may be made with canned clams, preferably the whole ones.

1 quart shucked clams

2 cups cold water

1/4 pound salt pork, sliced

1 onion, sliced

4 cups cubed potatoes

1 teaspoon salt

1/8 teaspoon pepper

4 cups boiling water

4 cups hot milk

4 tablespoons butter

3 tablespoons flour

8 large crackers

Pick over the clams and pour cold water over them. Strain the water and clam juice, and put it aside. Chop the leather straps or hard portions of the clams. Cut the pork in small pieces and try it out. Cook the onion in the fat until soft. Put a layer of potatoes in the chowder kettle, and add the chopped clams. Sprinkle with the salt and pepper. Add the boiling water and cook fifteen minutes. Add the hot milk, the soft portions of the clams, and the butter. Cook three minutes. Reheat the clam juice, thicken with flour, and add the mixture to the chowder. Let the chowder come to a boil, and turn immediately over split crackers in a soup tureen. Serves ten.

RHODE ISLAND CLAM CHOWDER

1 slice salt pork, diced

2 large onions, sliced

4 cups sliced potatoes

2 cups boiling water

1 quart quahogs, hard parts
    chopped

1 cup stewed tomatoes, strained

1/4 teaspoon soda

2 cups hot milk

Salt and pepper

2 tablespoons butter

6 large crackers

Try out the pork in a skillet. Cook the onions in the fat until light brown and soft. Put in a chowder kettle and add the potatoes. Cover with the boiling water, cook about ten minutes, then add the chopped parts of the clams. Cook until the potatoes are partly done. Stir the soda into the tomatoes, and add them with the soft parts of the clams to the chowder. Simmer until the potatoes are done. Add the hot milk, seasonings, and butter. Split the crackers, dip them quickly into the chowder, then place in the bottom of a tureen, and turn the steaming hot chowder over them. Serve at once. Serves eight.

PAWTUCKET CHICKEN CHOWDER

2 tablespoons chicken fat	1 cup cooked cubed chicken
1 onion, sliced	1 cup hot milk
2 stalks celery, minced	1 tablespoon flour
2 cups sliced potatoes	1 teaspoon salt
2 cups hot water	1/8 teaspoon pepper

Melt the chicken fat, add the vegetables, and cook until the potatoes are soft. Add the hot water and chicken. Bring to a boil. Add the hot milk, thicken with the flour, and add the seasonings. Serve very hot. Serves four.

SALT PORK CHOWDER
(Salt Pork Stew)

It is often hard to tell where a chowder leaves off and a stew begins. The two recipes given here are known in the White Mountains as stews; in the coastal part of New England they are referred to as chowders. But under whichever name they appear, they are substantial tasty dishes and are inexpensive to make.

Do not depend on salt pork chowder as an unexpected-company dish. It needs planning and slow cooking to bring it to the peak of perfection. Nor should you prepare the ingredients with a niggardly hand; every experienced mountain cook will tell you that the dish is much better warmed over than on the day it first comes from the kettle.

3 large carrots	8 medium-sized potatoes, cut in
3 medium-sized onions	cubes
1/8 pound salt pork	8 cups boiling water
	Salt and pepper

Slice the carrots and onions, and put them in a chowder kettle. Cover with water and cook about half an hour. Slice the pork and fry it in a skillet until brown. Add the fat to the vegetables; there should be about five tablespoons. Add the potatoes, boiling water, and seasonings. Cook until the potatoes are soft. The pork slices may be diced and added, if desired. Serves eight. About twenty minutes before serving, add dumplings made as follows:

Dumplings

1 teaspoon baking powder	1/2 teaspoon salt
2 cups flour	Sweet milk
1 teaspoon table fat	

Sift the baking powder with the flour. Work in the table fat. Add the salt and mix with milk until the mixture will drop from a spoon. Drop the dumplings on top of the boiling chowder. Cover the kettle closely, and do not open for twenty minutes.

PARSNIP CHOWDER
(Parsnip Stew)

"Parsnips are poison unless they are first frozen" is an old New England superstition, but it was exploded years ago. But the fact remains that parsnips are sweeter and better if they remain in the ground under a snow blanket until spring. Parsnip chowder, or stew if you prefer, should be made from freshly dug parsnips touched by Jack Frost or kept at 40 degrees or below by modern storage methods. It is a waste of time and food to make this dish from shriveled parsnips, for they do not have good texture or the right flavor.

1/3 cup diced salt pork	4 cups hot milk
4 medium-sized onions, sliced	2 tablespoons table fat
2 cups pared and sliced parsnips	Salt and pepper
1 cup cubed potato	1/2 cup rolled cracker crumbs
2 cups boiling water	

Try out the salt pork. Add the onions and cook until light brown. Remove the pork scraps, if desired. Turn into a kettle and add the parsnips and potatoes. Add the boiling water and cook until the vegetables are soft. Add the milk, table fat, and seasonings. Just before the chowder comes to a boil, add the cracker crumbs. Remove immediately from the fire and serve at once. Serves eight.

TRIED-AND-TRUE CORN CHOWDER

1/3 cup diced salt pork	2 1/4 cups fresh corn, or 1 can
1 onion, sliced	corn, chopped
3 cups boiling water	1 1/2 teaspoons salt
3 cups diced potatoes	1/8 teaspoon pepper
2 cups hot milk	6 crackers, split

Try out the pork and cook the onion in the fat. Remove the pork and add the boiling water to the fat and onion. Turn into a chowder kettle, add the potatoes, and cook fifteen minutes. Add the corn, hot milk, and seasonings. Remove from the fire just before the chowder comes to a boil. Add the split crackers and serve at once. Serves six.

BROWN SOUP

6 pounds beef shin	1 large carrot
3 to 4 quarts cold water	1/2 turnip
1 stick cinnamon	1/2 cup celery
1 blade mace	1 tablespoon salt
6 whole cloves	1/2 teaspoon pepper
1 large onion	

Wipe the meat, remove from the bone, and cut the meat in cubes. Crack the bones and remove the marrow. Brown half the meat in the melted marrow fat and whatever additional fat is needed to keep the meat from burning. Put in a soup kettle with the bones and the rest of the meat. Bring to a boil and skim. Add the vegetables and seasonings. Cook slowly for three or more hours. Remove the bones and serve the soup with slices of lemon and toasted bread. A half wineglass of brandy added just before the soup is served adds to the flavor. Makes two and a half to three quarts.

Seasonings for brown soup may be varied according to taste. Most modern cooks replace the cinnamon, mace, and cloves of the old recipes with half a dozen peppercorns, bay leaf, marjoram, and thyme. Minced parsley is often added just before serving.

For Stock

When brown soup is made for stock, the vegetables are cooked only a short time. Strained, cooled, and fat removed, the stock is stored in a crock or clarified for a clear soup.

To Clarify Soup

Allow the white and the shell of one egg for each quart of soup stock. Beat the egg white slightly and break the shell into pieces. Add to the strained stock and bring to a boil, stirring constantly. Boil two minutes. Add one tablespoon of very cold water. Let stand ten minutes, and strain through double-thick cheesecloth.

BEEF SOUP WITH DUMPLINGS

5-pound beef shin, or bones from a large roast	1 onion
Salt, pepper, flour	8 potatoes
3 quarts water	Dumplings

If fresh meat is used, cut in pieces, and brown as for Brown Soup. Place in the bottom of a kettle and dredge with salt, pepper, and flour. Add the water and onion. Skim when it comes to a boil. Boil three hours, then add the sliced potatoes. Cook half an hour or until the potatoes are tender. Add the dumplings and cook ten minutes longer. Makes about two quarts.

Dumplings

2 cups flour	1 teaspoon sugar
1 1/2 teaspoons baking powder	Milk
1/2 teaspoon salt	

Mix the dry ingredients. Add milk until you have a dough stiff enough to roll. Cut in small rectangles and add to the boiling soup. (Some other kind of dumpling may be used, if preferred.)

JULIENNE SOUP

Jean Baptiste Julien, a native of France, opened the first public eating house in Boston in the latter part of the eighteenth century. Julien, known as "Prince of Soup," originated the vegetable soup which bears his name.

3 small onions	3 young carrots
2 tablespoons butter	1 stalk celery
3 quarts clarified beef stock	3 turnips
Salt, pepper, mace	1 pint green beans

Cut the onions fine. Put the butter in a soup kettle, stir until melted, and fry the onions until brown. Add the clarified beef stock, salt, pepper, and a dash of mace. Boil one hour. Add the remaining vegetables cut into thin strips about an inch and a half long. Boil two hours. Serves eight to ten.

CHICKEN SOUP

Cut a four-or five-pound fowl in pieces, cover with water, and bring to a boil. Add one bay leaf, eight peppercorns, one onion, salt, and pepper. Cook until tender. Remove the meat and strain the broth. Makes about one quart.

For a thicker soup, add one-half cup rice to the broth. Cook until the rice is tender, then add the dumplings and cook ten minutes longer.

MUTTON IRISH STEW

3 pounds mutton	2 teaspoons salt
8 large potatoes	3/4 teaspoon pepper
3 onions	1 tablespoon flour
4 turnips	4 cups water
6 carrots	

Cut the mutton in cubes, peel and dice the vegetables. Put a layer of vegetables in the bottom of a kettle, cover with meat, sprinkle with the salt, pepper, and flour. Add another layer of vegetables and so on until all are used. Add the water, cover tightly, and simmer for three hours. Serves eight.

POTATO IRISH STEW

Cut two pounds of beef stew meat in cubes, and dice one large onion. Brown in three tablespoons of fat. Add six large potatoes cubed and enough water to cover. Cook slowly, covered, adding water a little at a time as the potatoes absorb it, always keeping the meat and potatoes covered with liquid. Season with salt and pepper. Serves six.

CREAM OF VEGETABLE SOUP

1 cup diced celery	1 1/2 cups diced potatoes
1/2 onion, sliced	4 cups water
4 tablespoons butter	1/4 cup melted butter
1/3 cup sliced carrots	1 tablespoon flour
1/3 cup diced turnips, or	1 quart scalded milk
1/2 cup diced squash	Salt and pepper

Cook the celery and onion in the butter for ten minutes. Add the other vegetables and the water. Boil one hour. Beat with a fork. Add the flour to the melted butter and combine with the scalded milk. Mix with the vegetable pulp, season with salt and pepper, and cook fifteen minutes in a double boiler. Serves eight.

PEAS-PORRIDGE

Mrs. Hannah Glass, whose *Art of Cookery,* 1710, was used in most New England homes until the end of the eighteenth century, gives the following recipe for peas-porridge.

"Take a Quart of Green Peas, put to them a Quart of Water, a Bunch or dry'd Mint, and a little Salt. Let them boil till the Peas are quite tender, then put in some beaten Pepper, a Piece of Butter as big as a Wallnut, rolled in Flour, stir it all together, and let it boil a Few Minutes. Then add two Quarts of Milk, let it boil a quarter of an Hour, take out the Mint, and serve it up."

BEAN PORRIDGE

In the old days bean porridge was made very thick. It was molded and frozen and stored in the buttery. Then it was sliced, as needed. It was often used by people going on long journeys.

To make the modernized version of bean porridge, begin the day before it is to be served.

Use a four-pound shank bone with plenty of meat and fat on it. Cover with four quarts water, bring to a boil, and cook slowly until the meat falls from the bones. Strain and allow the liquor to cool until the next day.

Pick over and soak a pint of white beans overnight. In the morning put them on in fresh water and cook slowly over low heat until the skins crack. Remove the fat from the meat broth, and add the broth to the beans. There should be about four quarts of liquid in all. Moisten one-half cup corn meal with cold water. When the beans and broth have cooked about an hour, stir in the corn meal. Let cook until thick. Then put the kettle over low heat and allow to simmer until ready to use. Season to taste with salt and pepper, and add the cooked cut-up meat if desired.

BLACK BEAN SOUP

2 cups black beans	1/4 teaspoon mustard
6 cups water	4 tablespoons fat
2 medium onions, sliced	1 tablespoon lemon juice
1 clove garlic	1/4 cup sherry
1 1/2 teaspoons salt	1 lemon, sliced
1/4 teaspoon pepper	1 hard-cooked egg, minced

Soak the beans overnight. Drain. Add the water, onions, garlic, salt and pepper, and cook until soft. Strain through a coarse sieve. If too thick, dilute with warm milk. Add the mustard, fat, lemon juice, and sherry. Serve with a slice of lemon covered with minced hard-cooked egg floating in each bowl. Serves six to eight.

PEA SOUP

2 cups dried peas
4 quarts cold water
1 stalk celery, diced
1/2 onion

1 ham bone, or
    1 pound lean salt pork
Salt and pepper

Soak the peas overnight. Put in a soup kettle with the water, vegetables, and ham bone. Boil until the peas are tender. Strain, add salt and pepper to taste. Serve with croutons. Serves ten.

BAKED BEAN SOUP

The thrifty New England housewife never allowed baked beans to go to waste.

3 cups baked beans
4 cups water
1 small onion
1 stalk celery

1/4 cup diced salt pork
1 tablespoon flour
1 1/2 cups tomatoes
Salt, pepper

Let the beans, water, onion, and celery simmer for half an hour. Strain. Try out the salt pork, blend the flour with the pork fat, and add the tomatoes. Let cook one hour, season with salt and pepper, and serve. Serves eight.

POTATO SOUP

4 medium potatoes
1 quart milk
2 teaspoons salt
1/4 teaspoon pepper

1 small onion
3 tablespoons butter
1 tablespoon chopped parsley or
    chives

Cook the potatoes in boiling salted water until tender. Mash as for mashed potatoes. Scald the milk, add the potatoes, salt, and pepper. Mince the onion and fry it golden brown in butter. Add to the potatoes and milk. Add parsley or chives just before serving. Serves four.

CREAM OF SPINACH SOUP

2 cups spinach purée

2 tablespoons butter

1 tablespoon grated onion

2 tablespoons flour

1/8 teaspoon nutmeg

3/4 teaspoon salt

3 cups chicken stock

1 cup cream

Wash fresh spinach and cook it quickly with only the water that clings to it. Put through a sieve. Measure out two cups. Melt butter and sauté the onion until transparent. Add the flour mixed with the nutmeg and salt. Blend, add the chicken stock slowly, and put in the top of a double boiler. Add the spinach purée and cook uncovered for twenty minutes. Add the cream. Serves six.

MRS. LESLIE'S CORN SOUP, 1846

Cut whole grains from twelve ears of corn. Add one cup rich milk and cook until the corn is soft. Add two more cups milk, two tablespoons butter cut in pieces and dredged with flour, and salt to taste. Just before serving, add two well-beaten egg yolks. Serve with sugar and nutmeg or with cayenne pepper. Serves six.

THREE RIVERS TURNIP SOUP

From an old New Hampshire family comes this recipe for turnip soup.

Heat one pint milk in a double boiler. Add two tablespoons butter, one tablespoon flour, two cups grated turnip, and one grated onion. Cook slowly until the turnip is well done. Serve with minced parsley. Serves four.

BROWN ONION SOUP

6 onions

1/2 cup butter

2 tablespoons flour

1 quart chicken or brown stock

Salt and pepper

Buttered toast

Grated Parmesan cheese

Slice the onions thin. Cook slowly in the butter until a rich brown. Add the flour and brown slightly, stirring constantly to keep it from burning. Add the stock slowly. Blend well, and season with salt and pepper. Toast rounds of bread, spread them with butter, and sprinkle with Parmesan cheese. Set under the broiler to melt the cheese. Put a round of toast in the bottom of each bowl, and pour soup over it. Pass extra slices of toast and a bowl of grated cheese. Serves four.

LOBSTER STEW

Lobster stew should be rich, pinkish in color from the lobster and coral, the top floating with butter, and full of large pieces of tender lobster meat. Although the Maine poet, Robert P. T. Coffin, says lobster stew should be half lobster and half liquid, most people use a little more liquid.

Sauté two cups cooked lobster meat for two minutes in three tablespoons butter. Add the tomalley or liver and blend well. Add one and one-half cups scalded milk and one cup thin cream slowly. Add salt and pepper to taste and serve with toasted crackers. Serves four.

OYSTER STEW

Clean one quart oysters and cook in four tablespoons butter until the edges curl. Scald one quart top milk, add the oysters, one teaspoon salt, and one-fourth teaspoon pepper. Serve piping hot, but do not boil. Serves four to six.

OYSTER SOUP

1 quart oysters	3 tablespoons flour
1 cup chicken stock	3 cups scalded milk
1 tablespoon minced onion	1 tablespoon minced parsley
1 tablespoon minced celery	Salt and pepper
3 tablespoons butter	

Clean the oysters and chop them fine. Scald them in their own liquor, and add the chicken stock. Cook the onion and celery in butter until light brown. Add the flour, blend, and add the scalded milk. Bring to a boil, add the oyster mixture and salt and pepper to taste. Sprinkle with the minced parsley, and serve. Serves four to six.

CREAM OF SALMON SOUP

1/4 cup minced onion	1/2 cup light cream
4 tablespoons melted butter	1 quart rich milk
2 tablespoons flour	1-pound can salmon, or
1 teaspoon salt	2 cups flaked fresh salmon
3/4 teaspoon dry mustard	Parsley
1/4 teaspoon pepper	1/2 teaspoon Worcestershire sauce

Cook the onion in the butter until yellow, stir in the flour, salt, mustard, and pepper. Add the cream, milk, and salmon, and heat thoroughly. Just before serving, garnish with parsley, and add Worcestershire sauce if desired. Serves six.

TURTLE SOUP

4-pound veal knuckle	1/4 teaspoon marjoram
2 sliced onions	1 bay leaf
2 carrots	3 cups tomatoes
2 stalks celery	Meat from 1 turtle
3 quarts water	1 cup sherry
Salt and pepper	1 hard-cooked egg
1/4 teaspoon thyme	Lemon slices

Brown the veal in enough fat to keep it from burning. When it is a rich brown, add the vegetables, water, spices, and tomatoes. Cook slowly for three or four hours. Cut the turtle meat into pieces and cook fifteen minutes in sherry. Strain the veal broth and combine it with the turtle meat. Mince the hard-cooked egg, add it to the soup, and serve with slices of lemon. For a very thick soup, thicken with a little flour blended with an equal amount of butter. Serves ten to twelve.

MOCK TURTLE SOUP

1 calf's head	2 turnips
6 quarts water	3 tablespoons flour
12 cloves	1/4 pound butter
24 peppercorns	1 pint Madeira or sherry
Salt and pepper	6 hard-cooked eggs
2 onions	1 lemon, sliced
2 carrots	

Soak the calf's head in cold water and wash it clean. Add the water and boil the calf's head four hours. Strain off the liquid, cool, and remove the fat. Take out two quarts of the liquor, add to it the seasonings and the vegetables cut fine. Boil two hours. Add one cup calf's face meat cut fine, the rest of the stock, and bring to a boil. Add the flour browned in the butter, then add the wine. Mince the hard-cooked eggs and put them in a soup tureen with the sliced lemon. Add the hot soup and serve at once. Serves twelve or more.

Forcemeat for Mock Turtle Soup

Use equal amounts of minced calf's face meat and mashed calf's brains. Season highly with salt, pepper, cloves, and sweet herbs. Mix with beaten egg to hold together, shape into balls, and sauté in butter.

MRS. PUTNAM'S OXTAIL SOUP

Oxtail soup was another New England favorite.

1 oxtail	1 sliced carrot
1 quart water	1 diced turnip
2 cloves	1/4 head cabbage, or
Salt and pepper	1/2 cup celery
1 onion, sliced	1 teaspoon lemon juice
2 tablespoons butter	

Boil the oxtail in the water with the spices for two hours. Strain, cool, and remove the fat. Fry the onion in butter until brown, add the cut-up oxtail, and brown it. Add with the other vegetables to the stock, and cook until the vegetables are tender. Add the lemon juice, and serve. Serves six.

If a thicker and more highly seasoned soup is preferred, use one and one-half cups water and one and one-half cups tomatoes. Add one-fourth teaspoon cinnamon, one-eighth teaspoon thyme, one-eighth teaspoon marjoram, one bay leaf, and one-half bunch celery to the stock. The whole may be baked as a stew in a casserole. Two tablespoons sherry added just before serving improves the flavor.

5. BRICK-OVEN COOKERY

THE kitchen was the heart of the early New England home—a heart that pulsated day in and day out with activities around the great fireplace where good food was continuously in process of preparation. Even at night the fireplace did not wholly cease work. Things went on—at a more moderate tempo, to be sure—after the ashes were raked up and the fire banked. The warmth of the hearth bricks and the steady mild heat from the carefully guarded coals played a big part in turning out bountiful meals for the following day.

From the hearth came the warmth that helped raise the bread set in the big wooden dough trough and the buckwheat cake mixture in the earthen batter pitcher. The banked coals kept warm the breakfast porridge in the small kettle swinging from the crane, and held the meat in the great dinner pot at the point where it could quickly start bubbling and steaming when the morning fire was freshened.

The hearth was the place to keep conveniently at hand, and partly warmed, the iron cooking utensils—the gridiron, the three-legged spider, the long-handled skillet, the round baking pot with its tight cover, and the large and small kettles. These utensils were used every day, but there was another—a very important one indeed—that was put in operation once or at the most twice a week. This was the brick oven at the side of the fireplace and connected with the kitchen chimney. Into the huge cavern behind the iron door went dishes that required hours of slow cooking, the baked Indian puddings, the pots of baked beans, the chicken pies that helped stem hungry appetites during the long New England Sabbath from sundown on Saturday until Sunday evening. Into it too went myriads of pies, loaves of bread, dowdies, and cakes.

The pudding of all puddings associated with brick-oven cookery is baked Indian pudding. It was not only served at noonday dinner, but was an important item at Sunday breakfast when it came from the Saturday oven rich and red and wheyey. Apple pandowdy is another brick-oven dish served at Sunday breakfast.

Thanksgiving chicken pies were for special occasions. With their flaky built-up crusts browned to a turn they were masterpieces of Yankee ingenuity. They called for experience and patience but chicken pies that required less time to prepare were a routine part of the weekly Saturday baking.

The baked beans that came out of the old brick ovens—beans sweetened with maple sugar, subtly flavored with salt pork "streaked fat and lean," and enriched by hours of cooking that blended flavors and goodness to a perfect whole—established New England's reputation for its best-known dish. The earliest baked beans were not sweetened with molasses. This sweetening became popular with the development of the West Indies trade. But even after they began pouring the thick dark syrup into their Boston bean pots, our great-grandmothers kept a steady hand on the molasses jug. Too much molasses made baked beans tough, they said. They knew too just how deep in the mound of parboiled beans to bury the "hunk" of pork and how to arrange it so the scored rind would absorb oven heat to turn it golden brown and crispy.

You may own a traditional Boston bean pot, you may choose pea beans, "yellow eyes," kidney, or other horticultural beans, you may parboil them just right, flavor with the sweetest pork from the barrel, add sugar or molasses to taste, throw in an onion or leave it out, but if you do not give beans a long baking, you will not serve the dish that New Englanders relish for Saturday supper and Sunday breakfast.

Serve the pork and beans with piccalilli, cucumber pickles, or mustard pickles. Place a bottle of ketchup on the table. And be sure the beans are accompanied by thick slices of steamed brown bread with custard pie for dessert.

Poundcake was kept on hand for elaborate tea drinkings and calls from the clergyman. A light and dexterous hand was needed to get the velvety texture characteristic of poundcake at its best. A standard old-time recipe calls for a pound each of butter, sugar, and flour, ten eggs, and half a wineglass each of wine and brandy. Currants were put in one-fourth of the dough, blanched almonds pounded in rose water in another fourth, and the remaining half of the dough was left plain. The cake was baked in four small round tins.

Before the Civil War, Election Day, when the governor of a state was inaugurated, was a great event in New England. Weeks of preparation went into getting ready for this June celebration. It was a day of parades, speechmaking, and general jollification, of feasting and drinking, with tables groaning under the weight of meats and pastries, and punch and eggnogs by the gallon. But no matter how many rich viands were served, Election Day was not complete without its time-honored raised cake, stuffed full of raisins and thin slices of citron, and topped with a sticky coating of treacle.

We often confuse with election cake the simple bread-dough cake that came from New England brick ovens on the General Training Day in May. Genuine Hartford election cake was far more "elegant" than the bread-dough cake. Often two or three days were required to prepare the ingredients and allow for the risings and the brick-oven baking.

Many old New England houses have kept their brick ovens, and in some recently built summer homes such ovens have been installed. And here and there you will still find New England cooks who pride themselves on their knowledge of brick-oven cookery, though often they put it into execution only on special days like Thanksgiving and Christmas.

It takes time to get a brick oven ready for baking, but if you own one, do not be afraid to try it out. First, it is important to be sure that the draughts and the chimney are in perfect shape. Use dry pine wood, cut into four-foot sticks and split very thick, to heat the oven. It takes about four good armfuls for each heating. Pile the sticks crisscross in the oven, start a fire under them, and let them burn for about two hours. At the end of this time, the top and sides of the oven will be covered with black soot, which soon will burn off. When the top of the oven is white, it is heated right for baking.

But you still have a few things to do before you can slide your loaves of "ryaninjun" from the wooden peel—a long-handled shovel— into the cavern. First, you must rake the coals over the bottom of the oven and let them lie there a while. Then take a long-handled poker and pull them into a long pile toward the front. Take them out with an iron shovel into an iron pail and turn them into the fireplace. Now wet an old broom and brush the soot and any ashes that are left into a pile. If you follow the spirit of your great-grandmother's day, you will use a turkey wing to brush the pile into a pail.

Next, close the draught leading into the chimney and shut the iron door until you are ready to put in the dishes you prepared while the oven was heating. There is a definite routine for arranging the dishes on the oven floor. Put the loaves of rye and meal bread on the farther edge; then set in place the puddings, the pandowdies, and the baked beans, with the beans located so you can easily refill the bean pot. Then come the chicken pies, the sweetened pies, with the cakes directly in front.

If you do not have a brick oven, you can still make any of the dishes described here but we cannot promise that your food will have a real brick-oven flavor when it comes from the modern range. Still if you give the dishes the slow cooking called for in most of the recipes, they are bound to be satisfactory. We also have included other directions for making some of the old-time dishes, recipes in which the cooking time has been shortened to meet present-day conditions.

"Ryaninjun" is the standard bread for brick-oven cookery. No pans were used for the old-time bread; the dome-shaped loaves were baked on the oven floor. The original bread was made of equal parts of rye meal and corn meal mixed with milk, sweetened with stewed pumpkin, and raised with "emptyings." In some sections a bed of oak leaves was spread on the oven bottom before the "ryaninjun" was baked, to give the special flavor to the bread. Rhode Island housewives had a slightly different way of using the leaves. They spread them on the peel blade and set the loaves of molded dough on top. Then they put the shovel in the oven and with a quick turn of the handle deposited both leaves and bread on the bottom. "Going leafing" was a special autumn task for children. They gathered the leaves and strung them on sticks to keep them in order.

RYE AND INDIAN BREAD

Although the following recipe is very old, it is adapted to the use of present-day ingredients.

2 cups yellow corn meal	1/2 cup molasses
Boiling water	1/2 teaspoon salt
Cold water	1/4 teaspoon soda
1/2 cup yeast, or	2 cups rye meal
1 yeast cake	

Put the corn meal in a mixing bowl and scald with just enough boiling water to wet it. Let stand ten minutes. Then add enough cold water to make a soft batter. When lukewarm, add the yeast, molasses, salt, and soda, and stir in the rye meal. If you use a yeast cake, dissolve it in half a cup of lukewarm water. Beat well, and set the dough in a warm place to rise overnight. In the morning, stir it down and mold into dome-shaped loaves. Let them rise. Sprinkle flour over tops. Put the loaves on the blade of the peel, which has been floured, and place in the brick oven. Bake about two hours. If you bake the loaves in a range, put them in pans, and bake in a slow oven, 325 degrees F., for two hours.

THIRDED BREAD

4 cups white flour
4 cups yellow corn meal
4 cups rye flour
1 cup yeast, or
  2 yeast cakes

1 tablespoon salt
1/2 cup brown sugar
2 cups scalded milk
Lukewarm water

Mix the ingredients, adding enough lukewarm water to make a dough that can be molded. Let it rise until it cracks open. In the morning shape into loaves, place in brick-loaf pans, and let loaves rise for forty-five minutes. Bake in a slow oven, 325 degrees F., about one hour. This large recipe makes a number of loaves. (If you use yeast cakes, dissolve in one half cup of lukewarm water.)

DOWN-EAST BAKED BLUEBERRY PUDDING

A variation of plum pudding which was popular in berrying time called for blueberries or huckleberries instead of raisins.

2 cups dark bread crumbs
4 cups milk
4 eggs, separated
1 cup brown sugar
Grated lemon peel

Butter the size of an egg
1 1/2 cups blueberries
1/3 cup white sugar
Lemon juice

Mix the bread crumbs with the milk and let them set until soft. Beat the yolks of the eggs and add the brown sugar and the grated lemon peel. Soften the butter and beat it into the egg mixture, then combine with the softened crumbs. Turn the mixture into a buttered pudding dish with a wide top and bake until firm, about one hour in a slow oven, 325 degrees F., but not long enough to get watery. Remove from the oven and turn the blueberries over the top while the pudding is steaming hot. Let it set until cool. Top with a meringue made by beating the whites of the eggs until stiff and adding the white sugar. Flavor with a squeeze of lemon juice. Put the pudding in a slow oven until the meringue is golden in color but not brown. The combination of cooked and practically uncooked berries is especially delicious. Serves six.

WHITPOT

3 quarts milk
1 cup bolted corn meal
1 teaspoon salt

1/4 cup butter
1/2 teaspoon ginger
1 cup dark molasses

Put one quart of the milk in a saucepan set in a kettle of boiling water. When full of bubbles, sift the corn meal in slowly, stirring briskly all the time. When the mixture is a smooth mush, cover the saucepan, and cook for two hours. Stir it once in a while. Add the salt, butter, and spice. Turn the mixture into a deep baking dish large enough to hold the extra milk. When cool, add the second quart of milk and the molasses, and mix well. Cover and put in the oven and bake slowly at 325 degrees F. for one hour. Then remove the cover and turn in, without stirring, one cup of the third quart of cold milk. Repeat this at intervals of half an hour until you have added all the milk. Bake at least five hours. When done, the pudding should be rich red in color and with enough whey or juice to form a sauce. Serve with cream sweetened with shaved maple sugar. Serves eight to ten.

TASTY BAKED INDIAN PUDDING

Another equally good old-time Indian pudding is made of yellow corn meal.

1 tablespoon butter
1/2 cup boiling water
2 quarts milk
2 cups yellow corn meal

1 teaspoon salt
1 cup dark molasses
1/4 teaspoon ginger

Rub the butter around the bottom and sides of a deep kettle. When melted, add the boiling water. Then turn in one quart of the milk and let it boil up. Sift in the corn meal gradually, stirring constantly. Add the salt and set the mixture aside until cold. Then add the molasses, ginger, and the other quart of milk which should be very cold. Pour into a deep pudding dish, and cover. Bake for ten to twelve hours in a very slow oven, 275 degrees F. If you want the pudding for Sunday morning breakfast, put it in the Saturday afternoon oven and let it bake all night. Serve with thick cream. No extra sweetening will be needed. Serves eight.

BAKED INDIAN PLUM PUDDING

1 1/2 quarts milk
2/3 cup corn meal
2/3 cup molasses
1 cup huckleberries
1/2 teaspoon salt

1/2 teaspoon cinnamon
2 eggs, well beaten
Butter size of an egg
Cold water

Scald half the milk and stir the corn meal in slowly. Butter a baking dish and put the molasses and huckleberries in the bottom. Add the salt and cinnamon. Turn in the corn meal mixture. Add the cold milk, beaten eggs, and butter. Mix well. Bake five hours in a slow oven, 300 degrees F., adding half a cup of very cold water every hour while the pudding is baking. Do not stir it. Serves eight.

OXBOW INDIAN PUDDING

Only a three-hour baking is required for the next two recipes. The first one comes from and is named for the section of Vermont where the Connecticut River winds back and forth through the meadows in a great bow.

1 quart milk
1 cup corn meal
Salt
1/2 cup molasses

1/4 cup sugar
1 tablespoon butter
Cold milk

Heat the quart of milk and stir in slowly the Indian meal. Add salt to taste and the molasses and sugar. Turn into a two-quart baking dish. Add the butter and pour in enough cold milk to fill the dish. Do not stir the milk. Bake slowly about three hours in a very slow oven, 275 to 300 degrees F. Serve with maple syrup. Serves six.

FLO'S INDIAN PUDDING

Suet and raisins are added to the ingredients for this three-hour pudding. The recipe was the prized possession of a White Mountain cook noted for her lavish and bountiful hospitality.

1/2 cup corn meal	1/2 teaspoon salt
2 cups scalded milk	1/4 teaspoon ginger
1/2 cup suet, chopped fine	1/4 teaspoon cinnamon
1/2 cup molasses	1 cup cold milk
1/2 cup raisins	1/2 cup cold water
1 egg, well beaten	

Stir the corn meal into the scalded milk, and cook long enough to make a smooth batter. Add the chopped suet, molasses, raisins, egg, salt, and spices. Turn into a buttered baking dish. Pour the cold milk and water over the mixture, but do not stir them in. Cover the pudding and bake very slowly for three hours, 275 degrees F. Serve each portion topped with vanilla ice cream. Serves six.

BERRY FAMILY APPLE PANDOWDY

3 quarts sliced tart apples	Nutmeg
1 1/2 cups maple sugar	1 cup corn meal
1 1/4 cups cold water	1 cup white flour
2 tablespoons finely chopped	3/4 cup lard
salt pork	Cold water

Put the sliced apples in a large earthen pan. Mix the maple sugar with the cold water, and pour this over the apples. Dot with the bits of salt pork and sprinkle with nutmeg. To make the crust, mix the corn meal and white flour, and rub the lard into the mixture. Stir in just enough cold water to make a dough that can be handled. Roll out a crust that is large enough to cover the top of the pan. Place it on the apples, pricking it a number of times with a fork. Place the dowdy in the Saturday afternoon oven and let it stay in the brick oven overnight, 250 degrees F. In the morning remove the crust, place it in another large dish, and turn the apple mixture over it. It should be a rich red in color. Serve for Sunday morning breakfast with thick cream and shaved maple sugar or with maple syrup. Serves eight.

APPLE PANDOWDY WITH NUTMEG SAUCE

Tart apples, peeled and sliced
Salt
Butter

1 tablespoon flour
1 1/2 cups sugar
Rich biscuit dough

Fill a buttered baking dish with the sliced apples. Sprinkle with salt and bits of butter. Mix the flour with the sugar and turn it over the apples. Cover with a rich biscuit dough about three-fourths inch thick. Bake one hour in a slow oven, 325 degrees F.

Nutmeg Sauce

1 1/3 cups sugar
2 tablespoons flour
1 1/2 tablespoons butter
1 1/2 cups boiling water

Pinch of salt
1/2 teaspoon vanilla
1/3 teaspoon nutmeg

Mix the sugar and flour, and cream them with the butter. Stir quickly into the boiling water. Add the salt, vanilla, and nutmeg.

THANKSGIVING CHICKEN PIE

Filling

2 chickens

Boiling salted water

Disjoint chicken. Cover with boiling salted water, and cook until tender but not mushy. Let cool and then remove larger bones and cut chicken up into sizable pieces.

Crust

1 teaspoon salt   3/4 pound butter
Flour   1/4 cup milk
6 cups cream

Arrange the crust in "rims" placed one above the other around the inside of the baking dish. If possible, use a deep earthen dish with flaring sides. To make the crust, sift the teaspoon of salt with a cup of flour and stir vigorously into the cream. Continue to add sifted flour until dough is stiff enough to roll out easily. Turn the dough on a molding board. Cut off a piece, and, using a rolling pin, roll out a thin layer large enough to line the bottom and sides of the dish. Butter the dish and carefully arrange this thin crust in it. Prick with the tines of a fork to keep it from "humping" while baking. This lining crust serves as the background for attaching the strips of dough which form the rims.

Roll out the remainder of the dough to one-half inch in thickness. Dot with small pieces of butter, and sprinkle with flour. Fold the crust with the buttered side in, and roll out again. Repeat the process three times, adding bits of butter and sprinkling with flour each time. Then roll the crust out flat on the molding board until it is one-half inch thick. With your hands mold the crust into a "roll." Cut off the ends and roll out each one separately with the rolling pin, until it is from one and one-half to two inches wide. Do this again until you have four rims or strips of dough long enough to encircle the inside of the dish. (The number of rims needed depends upon the depth of the dish.) Moisten the crust lining with milk, using a small piece of clean cloth. Starting at the bottom of the dish, lay a rim around the inside. Arrange another rim above it and continue until you reach the top of the baking dish.

Place the pieces of chicken in the center of the dish. Season the water in which the chickens were cooked with salt and pepper to taste and pour over the pieces of chicken until they are nearly covered. Dot with small bits of butter. Roll out the remainder of the crust, making a circular lid to fit the top of the pie. Make curving cuts with a knife and turn them back to let the steam escape. Place a cup on top of the chicken to hold up the crust. Bake three hours in the brick oven or in a slow oven, 325 degrees F. Serves twelve.

SMALL FAMILY CHICKEN PIE

These two recipes for chicken pie are family heirlooms. The first comes from Rhode Island, the second from Maine.

1 large chicken	1 cup milk
1 tablespoon flour	1/2 teaspoon salt
Salt and pepper	1 teaspoon baking powder
1/2 cup lard	Flour

Cut up and boil the chicken. When tender, take out the largest bones. Thicken the broth with the tablespoon of flour dissolved in a little cold water. Season to taste. To make the crust, melt the lard and add it to the milk. Sift the half teaspoon salt and baking powder with one cup of flour, and add this to the liquid. Then add enough flour to make a dough, and roll out to half an inch thick. Line a deep dish with the dough. Put in the chicken and enough gravy to cover. Cover the pie with strips of dough in lattice form. Bake in a quick oven for twenty minutes, 400 degrees F. Then lower the heat and bake in a moderate oven for one hour, 350 degrees F. Serves six.

CHICKEN AND OYSTER PIE

1 fowl	Salt
Boiling water	Paprika
1 bay leaf	Chopped parsley
1 sliced onion	1 tablespoon flour
Sprig of thyme	Biscuit dough
1 pint oysters	1 egg, beaten
1/4 pound salt pork	Cold water

Cut the fowl as for fricassee. Cover with boiling water. Add the bay leaf, onion, and thyme. Boil until the chicken is tender. Remove from the fire. When the broth is cool, remove the fat. Scald the oysters in their own liquor. Dice the pork and fry until light brown. Arrange the chicken, oysters, and pork scraps in layers. Season with salt, paprika, and a little chopped parsley. Thicken the liquor in which the chicken was cooked with the flour dissolved in a little cold water. Prepare a rich dough, using the chicken fat for shortening. Roll thin and cover the top of the pie. Make several incisions to let the steam escape. Brush the top of the crust with the egg mixed with a little cold water. Bake in a moderately hot oven, 400 degrees F., until the crust is golden brown, about one hour. Serves eight.

BOSTON BAKED BEANS

This recipe is the standard rule for molasses-sweetened Boston baked beans.

1 quart pea beans	1/3 cup molasses
1 very small onion	1 teaspoon salt
1/2 pound salt pork	1/2 teaspoon dry mustard
1/3 cup sugar	Boiling water

On Friday night put the beans to soak in enough water to allow them to swell good and plenty. On Saturday morning drain off the water. Cover the beans with cold water and parboil them, skimming them often during the process. Test by removing a few beans in a spoon and blowing on them. If the skins crack, it is time to take the beans from the heat. Put a very little water in the bottom of a Boston bean pot. Add two cups of the beans and nestle the onion in them. Add more beans until the bean pot is about three-fourths full. Score the rind of the salt pork and lay the pork on top. Put in the rest of the beans and add the other ingredients. Cover with boiling water. Bake eight hours in a moderately slow oven, 325 degrees F. Keep the beans almost but not quite covered with water; do not have them too swimming. After the beans start to bake, put the cover on the bean pot, but remove it during the last half hour of baking in order to brown the pork. Serves eight to ten.

NORTH COUNTRY BAKED SOLDIER BEANS

1 quart soldier beans	1/2 teaspoon ginger
1 tablespoon white sugar	2 teaspoons salt
1/2 cup shaved maple sugar	1/2 pound salt pork streaked with
1 teaspoon mustard	lean
1/2 teaspoon pepper	Boiling water

Soak the beans overnight in cold water. In the morning drain and parboil them in fresh water until the skins wrinkle. Drain off the water and place the beans in a bean pot. Add the other ingredients and half bury the salt pork with the scored rind uppermost in the top of the beans. Fill the bean pot with boiling water. When the beans really begin to bake, cover the bean pot. Bake six hours in a moderately slow oven, 325 degrees F. Keep the beans almost covered with water during the baking. Uncover during the last half hour. Serve the beans in a large earthenware nappy. Cut the pork in slices and place on a small platter. Serves eight to ten.

BRICK-OVEN PAN PIE

This recipe is a genuine old-timer.

Pare and quarter enough tart apples to fill a deep earthen dish. Add one cup water and one cup shaved maple sugar. Cover with a thick crust of risen bread dough. Bake all night in the brick oven, 250 degrees F. In the morning, remove the pie from the oven, and take off the crust. Have two large pudding dishes ready. Cut the crust in slices and put them in the pudding dishes. Add one-half cup molasses, one teaspoon allspice, one teaspoon cinnamon, and one teaspoon salt to the apples, and mix well. Turn the apple mixture over the pieces of crust. Cover the pudding dishes with earthen plates and place the dishes in a moderate oven, 350 degrees F., for half an hour. Serve the pies with cream. Serves six.

POUNDCAKE

At least fifty years ago a famous New England cook adapted a very old recipe for poundcake, measuring the ingredients by cups instead of by pounds. All the mixing of this cake is done by hand. The cook's arm will ache before she finishes, but the end will justify the means.

1 cup butter, packed solid	5 eggs, unbeaten
1 2/3 cups granulated sugar	2 cups pastry flour
1/2 teaspoon mace	

Butter and flour a round tin, and have all the ingredients ready before you start. Cream the butter and sugar, and work them with the hand until very light. Add the mace and one egg at a time, stirring each one into the mixture with the hand until you do not see any of the yolk. It is this thorough blending of butter and sugar that helps to give the cake the desired velvety texture. But you must be careful not to overbeat the eggs. Mix in the flour and turn the mixture into a pan, nine by five by three inches. Bake slowly at 325 degrees F. for one hour.

HARTFORD ELECTION CAKE

This recipe has been simplified by measuring the ingredients by cups instead of pounds, but the method of making the cake remains the same as it was when our great-grandmothers drew the round sweet-smelling loaves from their brick ovens.

1 pint milk	1 teaspoon cinnamon
1 teaspoon salt	1/2 teaspoon nutmeg
1 yeast cake	4 eggs, well beaten
1/2 cup lukewarm water	2 cups raisins
5-6 cups flour	1/2 cup sliced citron
1 cup butter	Molasses
2 cups brown sugar	

The night before you plan to make the cake, prepare a soft dough as follows: Scald the milk and, when lukewarm, add the salt and the yeast cake dissolved in the lukewarm water. Add flour to make a soft dough. Let rise overnight. In the morning, cream the butter and sugar. Add the spices and well-beaten eggs. Combine with the first mixture. Flour the raisins and citron, and add. Let the dough rise until light.

Then cut the dough down and put it in two large round tins, filling them about two-thirds full. Let the loaves rise for about half an hour, or until light. Bake one hour in a moderate oven, 350 degrees F. Glaze with molasses and return to the oven for five minutes to set the glaze.

TRAINING DAY CAKE

1 cup bread dough
1 cup sugar
1/2 cup shortening
1 egg
1/2 cup milk
1 teaspoon baking powder

1 cup flour
1 cup raisins
1 teaspoon nutmeg
1/2 teaspoon lemon extract
Molasses

Cream the sugar and shortening. Add the egg and milk. Mix thoroughly with the cup of bread dough. Sift the baking powder with the flour and combine with the first mixture. Cut up the raisins and add with the nutmeg. Add the lemon extract. Knead thoroughly and shape into a round loaf. Place in a round tin and let rise until within one inch from the top of the pan. Bake forty-five minutes in a moderate oven, 350 degrees F. Glaze with molasses. Return to the oven for five minutes.

6. MAIN DISHES

THE white-tailed deer and the wild turkey furnished most of the meat supply of the early New England settlers. Wild turkeys disappeared from the region long ago, but deer are still hunted, though only during very short seasons and under rigid game laws. In Rhode Island and Connecticut, however, there is no open season for deer, and the animals may be killed only under special permits to landowners or their representatives.

Besides deer, wild ducks and ruffed grouse, quail, rabbits and black bears may be hunted in season. But the person who goes after them should be sure he is familiar with the state game laws and any federal laws that may apply. This is true of pheasants too which are not native New England birds, although most of the states are stocking and carefully protecting them. The first known introduction of pheasants into Rhode Island was in 1894.

For many years, hunting teal was combined with the job of getting the stacks of marsh hay from the frozen marshes. Some of the people who lived along the coast and on the islands preferred sea fowl with a "twang" and relished sea coots and even herons. But the inhabitants of old Hampton voted for teal. Many of the women who live in this section of New Hampshire are experts at cooking them by the old rules.

The early settlers did not do much about hunting partridges or ruffed grouse. But later, after breech-loading guns made sport shooting popular, the tasty birds were almost exterminated. They were considered a delicacy, and breast of partridge was a favorite banquet dish of the last century.

The bobwhite, or quail, is one of the finest game birds. For some time the number of bobwhites in New England was sadly depleted by unrestricted hunting and by winter snows. Now, under heavy protective laws, coveys are growing in number. Bobwhites are often called birds of the plough because they follow the cultivation of new lands, eating the weed seeds. And the old saying in New Hampshire is, "Don't plant corn until the bobwhite whistles."

Rabbits were not much hunted for food until within a comparatively recent time. If prepared properly by a cook who knows the tricks, wild rabbits make a delicious dish.

The black bear's contribution to the New England menu is steak. Some people like it very much; others find the meat too coarse and gamy. The black bear counted heavily in the scoring in the game hunts which were once held in many White Mountain towns. And at the big suppers put on by the losing side in the contest, the steak was served as a specialty.

We have collected a few recipes for cooking game, but have not attempted to get one for bear steak. Those who want to try it should go to northern New Hampshire or Maine and eat it first as prepared by the guides and woodsmen who know how to cook the steak to a turn.

Venison, though fat, is dry, and a roast must be basted often while cooking. Venison always should be ripened by hanging in the hide for at least a week before it is prepared for the table. North country cooks make use of every bit of the meat. All the scraps and tough parts are made into sausage and mincemeat. The liver is considered a great delicacy, and the tenderloin is something deer hunters give to their friends when they want to honor them.

Geese were not common in New England until well into the eighteenth century. After that, most country families kept flocks of the great squawking fowls. They fed on grass along the roadsides, wandered with the cows in barnyards and pastures, or took possession of the deep puddles in the rough dirt roads.

There are many delicious New England rules for cooking chicken. Daniel Webster's favorite dish, which his mother always cooked for him in "her own rare manner" whenever he visited her in New Hampshire, is included among those given here.

A New England farmhouse without a pork barrel in the cellar was something that just did not happen. Not only was salt pork used to season stews, vegetables, meat, and poultry, the barrel was a source of supply for main dishes when other things were not available. All good cooks knew how to prepare salt pork in many tasty ways.

Salt, smoke, and snow were the stand-by meat preservatives in New England for years. The brine of pork barrel and powdering tub, smoke from corncob fires under the smokehouse, and the icy chilliness of winter cold rooms helped to provide a variety of meat dishes for the family table. Pigs slaughtered at the annual pigsticking were salted down in brine and smoked into hams and bacons. Sausage making, in which everybody in the family engaged, was an accepted part of the yearly routine. Beef was salted down and corned, and when cold weather really set in, sides of a "beef creature" and mutton and pork were hung in the cold room to freeze solid.

Fresh meat was eaten little in the summer. But if you decided to kill a calf or a lamb in warm weather, you divided with your neighbors, fully expecting a return in kind before the end of September. Lawyers and physicians were glad to take part of their fees in roasts and steaks, and clergymen gratefully accepted gifts of meat from their country parishioners. Villagers bought meat from the butcher, who not only brought native meat to the door in his cart, but also regaled his customers with tidbits of neighborhood gossip. Down in Boston, many city folks sent to the stalls of the great Quincy Market for choice cuts, though some of them rebelled at paying twelve and a half cents a pound for steak.

BRAISED VENISON

Use a cut of venison of five and a half or six pounds from the lower end of the leg or shoulder clod. Wipe with a damp cloth, and lard it with slices of salt pork. Rub with well-seasoned flour, and sear it in half a cup of fat in the bottom of a deep heavy kettle. Cook until well browned on all sides, turning frequently. Add one-half cup hot water and one tablespoon vinegar. Cover the kettle and cook the meat for two to two and a half hours, or until tender. Watch the roast carefully and turn frequently, adding more water if necessary. About half an hour before the meat is done, cover it with one chopped apple, one chopped onion, one sliced carrot, one-half cup sliced celery, and one tablespoon lemon juice. Cook until the vegetables are done. Put the meat on a platter. If the gravy is cooked down, add more water. Turn it over the meat. Serve with elderberry and grape jelly.

BROILED VENISON STEAK

Venison steak is broiled like beefsteak, and is often served with currant jelly sauce.

Currant Jelly Sauce

Juice of 1 lemon	1 glass currant jelly
1 tablespoon butter	Salt and pepper
1/2 wineglass sherry	

Boil the ingredients and serve very hot. Serves eight.

WILD RABBIT IN CASSEROLE

As a general thing, rabbits may be cooked in the same way as chickens. Rabbit fricassee and rabbit pie are delicious. After the rabbits are properly cleaned and prepared, recipes for chicken pie and chicken fricassee may be followed. If you do not like the wild taste, soak the rabbit overnight in soda water and parboil it in salted water before you prepare the dish.

1 dressed rabbit	2 slices onion
2 teaspoons salt	1 slice lemon
1/4 teaspoon pepper	1 tablespoon ketchup
1 1/2 cups water	2 tablespoons butter
2 cloves	2 tablespoons flour
1/2 bay leaf	

Cut the legs from the rabbit. Separate the hind legs in two pieces at the joint. Cut the saddle into three pieces. Wash the rabbit thoroughly in warm water, then drain and dry. Combine all the ingredients except the butter and flour. Place the pieces of rabbit in a large casserole or covered pan and pour the mixture over them. Steam one and a half hours or until the meat is tender. Melt the butter and blend in the flour. Add the liquid from the pan and cook until thick, stirring all the time. Turn it over the rabbit, and serve. Serves six.

MRS. YORK'S ROAST TEAL

The following recipe for cooking teal comes from a New Hampshire family that has lived on the same land since the colonial wars.

Have the teal properly dressed, wash it inside and out, and wipe dry. Stuff, sew, and truss the bird. For the stuffing use crumbled stale bread, onions chopped fine, salt, pepper, sage, two eggs, a large piece of butter, and water to moisten. Mix like any stuffing. Put the bird in the roaster pan on top of the stove. Add enough water to cover about an inch of the bottom of the pan. Cook the teal until the skin begins to crack, then sprinkle with flour and a little salt. Put it in a moderate oven, 350 degrees F., and cook with plenty of whole onions. When the bird is done, the skin is brown, and the wings are loose. Serves two.

Another New England cook makes her stuffing for wild duck from equal parts of chopped tart apples, bread crumbs browned in the oven, and boiled onions. She seasons it highly with salt and pepper and a little sage, and moistens it with two or three tablespoons of melted butter. To get rid of the fishy taste, this cook puts a carrot inside each duck and parboils the bird before roasting it.

LARDED PARTRIDGE

Clean, wipe, and lard the breasts and legs of a brace of partridges. Rub with salt and soft butter, and dredge with flour. If you like the birds rare, roast twenty minutes in a quick oven, 450 degrees F. If you prefer them well done, roast for half an hour. Serve with bread sauce.

Bread Sauce

1/2 cup fine bread crumbs	1/2 teaspoon salt
2 tablespoons chopped onions	1/4 teaspoon pepper
2 cups milk	2/3 cup coarse bread crumbs
2 tablespoons butter	

Boil the fine bread crumbs and onion in the milk fifteen minutes. Add one tablespoon of butter and the salt and pepper. Fry the coarse bread crumbs in the other tablespoon of butter until brown. Pour the sauce around the birds, and sprinkle the browned bread crumbs over the whole. Serves four.

RHODE ISLAND ROAST QUAIL

Dress and truss each bird. Dust them with flour seasoned with salt and pepper. Prepare a slice of bread to a bird and put the slices in a roasting pan. Place the birds on the bread. Cover the breasts of the quail with thin slices of salt pork; or wrap fresh grape leaves over the breasts and hold them in place with slices of bacon. It is not always possible, however, to get grape leaves in the hunting season. Roast about fifteen minutes in a hot oven, 400 degrees F. Baste with melted butter at least three times during the baking. Serve with grape jelly or currant jelly. Allow at least one bird for each person and, if small, allow two.

ROAST PHEASANT

Rub the inside and outside of the pheasant with butter and salt. Cover the breast with slices of salt pork held on with toothpicks. Stuff with grapes, and sew together and truss. Put in a hot oven, 450 degrees F., and roast for fifteen minutes, basting every five minutes with the pan drippings. This is very important. When the bird is browned, reduce the heat to moderate, 350 degrees F. Cook one hour, basting every fifteen minutes. Remove the salt pork slices from the breast and place the bird on a hot platter. Pour one wineglass of tart grape juice in the pan and mix it with the drippings. Turn this over the pheasant. One pheasant serves two to four.

VERMONT TURKEY, ROASTED

And now we come to that once native but now more or less domesticated bird—the ruler of the New England Thanksgiving table.

Select a young medium-sized turkey with a rather short body. Have the bird well cleaned and singed, with the oil sac, lungs, and kidneys removed. Wash thoroughly and drain. Just before filling the bird with stuffing, rub the inside with salt. A good general rule to follow for the amount of stuffing needed is one cup to one pound of turkey. If you want the flavor of the stuffing to go through the bird, stuff the turkey the night before you roast it. In that case, the stuffing should be cold. But if you prefer to stuff the turkey just before it goes into the oven, use warm stuffing. Put enough stuffing in the bird's neck to round it out nicely, but do not overpack the body, as too much filling will crack the skin. Fasten the loose skin of the neck back to the body to keep the stuffing in. If you do not have the proper equipment to sew up the body vent, place an end crust of bread against the opening to hold the stuffing in place. Truss the bird by tying the wings and legs closely to the body.

Now place the turkey on a rack in a shallow pan without a cover and with no water in the pan. Brush the body with melted fat or lard it with thin slices of salt pork. Roasting at constant low heat gives the best results. A turkey which weighs from eight to fourteen pounds should be roasted in a slow oven, 325 degrees F. The time required for this size is from twenty to twenty-five minutes to a pound. Birds weighing under twelve pounds should be turned every forty-five minutes, and at the time of turning they should be basted with melted butter or pan drippings. Be careful not to break the skin in turning, so the juices will not escape.

When you think the turkey is done, remove it to a warm platter, and untie the wings and legs. A perfectly roasted turkey is tender, but is not cooked until the meat falls off the bones. Let the bird stand for about half an hour before serving so the meat can absorb the juices.

While the turkey is roasting, cover the giblets with boiling water and simmer for about one hour. Good gravy is important in serving good roast turkey. It should be made in the proportion of three tablespoons melted fat, three tablespoons flour, and two cups liquid. Drain the drippings, fat, and juices from the roasting pan, and skim off the three tablespoons of fat. Blend the flour thoroughly with the fat. If you need more liquid to make the required amount, use the water in which the giblets were cooked. Chop the giblets and add. Cook the gravy over low heat for five minutes, stirring constantly to prevent lumping. Season with salt and pepper. Serve the turkey with a large dish of cranberry sauce. Allow three-fourths to one pound of turkey for each person.

There are many ways to make stuffing for turkey, but here is one that adds a particularly fine flavor to the bird.

Oyster Stuffing

1 1/2 pints oysters	2 quarts bread crumbs, medium
3/4 cup butter	dry
1 tablespoon chopped parsley	1 teaspoon poultry dressing
1 tablespoon chopped onion	1/2 teaspoon celery seed
2 teaspoons salt	

Heat the oysters for a few minutes, drain off the liquor, and chop the oysters in small pieces. Melt the butter and cook the parsley and onion in it. Stir the seasonings into the bread crumbs. Mix the oysters with the butter. Combine the mixtures, stirring together thoroughly. Add a little of the oyster liquor, if the stuffing seems too dry.

ROAST GUINEA HEN WITH RAISIN STUFFING

Guinea fowl, the clattering-voiced creatures commonly known as farmers' watchdogs, are delicious eating. The small compact birds are all dark meat, which has a subtle flavor of its own, plus the gamy flavor of wild fowl. Guineas are at their best when about seven months old. You will need two birds to serve a family of six.

Prepare a guinea hen for roasting as you prepare other fowl. Stuff the bird and rub the outside with salt, pepper, and a little lemon juice. Cover the back with thin slices of salt pork held in place with poultry pins, and lay the bird in the roaster breast down. The following stuffing blends deliciously with the flavor of guinea fowl.

Raisin Stuffing

2 cups dry bread crumbs
1/3 cup seeded raisins, chopped
1/3 cup nut meats, ground
1 teaspoon salt
1/8 teaspoon pepper
1 teaspoon poultry seasoning
1/4 cup melted fat
1/3 cup hot milk

Mix the bread crumbs with the raisins and nut meats. Add the seasonings. Combine the fat and milk, and stir into the other ingredients. Cook very slowly, stirring often, for fifteen minutes over a low flame.

Fill the guinea hens with the stuffing. Roast for twenty minutes in a hot oven, 450 degrees F.; reduce the heat to 325 degrees and continue cooking, allowing about twenty minutes to a pound. Serve with currant or grape jelly.

ROAST GOOSE

Many New England cooks steam a goose the day before it is to be roasted. This is done to get rid of the oil. After steaming, the fat and oil are drained from the pan, and the goose is left uncovered overnight.

In the morning, the bird is filled with a stuffing made of equal parts of bread crumbs, chopped apples, and boiled onions, seasoned with salt, pepper, and sage. The goose is roasted in a very hot oven, 450 degrees F., for half an hour. Then the heat is reduced, and it is cooked in a slow oven, 325 degrees F., from two and a half to three and a half hours, or until the meat on the breast and legs is tender. Allow one pound for each person. Applesauce is the traditional accompaniment to roast goose.

ABIGAIL WEBSTER'S CHICKEN AND PORK

Disjoint and wash two chickens. Put in a stewpan with the skin side down. Sprinkle with salt and pepper, and place three or four slices of salt pork on top. Just cover with water and stew until tender. Remove the chicken and pork, and thicken the liquor with flour made into a smooth paste with cold water. Put the chicken back in the stewpan and cook for five minutes. Place thin slices of toast on a platter and turn the gravy over them. Arrange the chicken meat on the toast and gravy. Serves twelve.

SHAKER FRICASSEED CHICKEN

Cut up a chicken in large pieces. Put in a kettle with a perforated stand on the bottom. Turn in water enough to steam. Cook the chicken one hour. Add one teaspoon of salt. When the chicken is tender, remove from the kettle to a baking pan. Put in the oven and brown thoroughly. Add one cup of thick cream to the gravy in the kettle and thicken with a little flour which has been blended with butter. Season to taste. Serves six.

OLD-FASHIONED CHICKEN AND DUMPLINGS

Cut up a chicken as for fricassee. Sprinkle with salt and pepper and cover with water. About three-quarters of an hour before the chicken is done, add one small onion and one small potato for each person to be served. Use a large mixing spoon and push the vegetables under the chicken. Add only one or two at a time so the chicken will not stop boiling. When the onions are partly done, add the dumplings. Cover the kettle very tightly and do not lift the cover for twenty-five minutes. Serve at once. Serves six to eight.

NEW HAMPSHIRE FRIED CHICKEN WITH CREAM GRAVY

Disjoint and cut a chicken into pieces suitable for serving. Wipe as dry as possible and season with salt and pepper. Roll in flour. Use a very thick frying pan for cooking the chicken. Turn in enough fat to make half an inch deep on the bottom of pan. Put the thickest pieces of chicken in the pan first. Leave space for the fat to come up around each piece. Cook at moderate heat and turn when brown. Remove pieces of chicken from the frying pan before they are done and put in a baking dish. Finish cooking in a moderate oven. Put more pieces of chicken in the frying pan and continue as before. Serve with cream gravy.

Cream Gravy

2 tablespoons flour	1 1/2 cups milk
2 tablespoons pan drippings	Salt and pepper

Blend the flour and drippings, and add to this the brown bits in the bottom of the frying pan. Stir into the milk and cook until thick and smooth. Season to taste. Serves six.

ROAST CHICKEN WITH CORN-BREAD STUFFING

A four- to five-pound chicken is about the right size for roasting. Prepare and stuff as for roast turkey. Rub the chicken with soft butter and seasoned flour. Fasten strips of salt pork to the breast and back. Use a shallow uncovered pan with a rack in the bottom. Do not add water to the pan. Place the chicken on one side and, when the flour is brown, turn the other side up. At the time of turning, baste with melted butter and water or with pan drippings. Roast about two hours in a moderate oven, 350 degrees F. When the flesh is slightly shrunk beneath the skin and the joints are no longer stiff when worked, the bird is done. In season serve with corn on the cob. Serves six to eight.

Corn-Bread Stuffing

3/4 cup chopped celery	4 cups corn-bread crumbs
1/4 cup chopped parsley	1/2 teaspoon thyme
1 small onion, chopped	1 teaspoon salt
6 tablespoons fat	1/4 teaspoon pepper

Cook the celery, parsley, and onion in fat until the onion is light brown. Mix the corn-bread crumbs and the seasonings. Combine the mixtures. Add a little cream if more moistening is needed.

RIB ROAST OF BEEF

"The general rules [for roasting beef] are to have a brisk hot fire, to place the meat on a spit, to baste with salt and water, and allow one quarter of an hour to every pound of beef," says an old New England book. "Rare done is the taste of this age," the author adds.

"Rare done" continues to be the taste of this modern age. The secret of getting the roast to this preferred state of perfection is to start it cooking at a high temperature in order to keep the juices in.

Place a three-rib roast on a rack in a pan, and dredge all over with seasoned flour. Put in a very hot oven, 500 degrees F., and roast thirty minutes, or until light brown in color. When the flour is brown, reduce the heat, to 350 degrees, and continue cooking. For very rare meat, allow fifteen minutes to the pound, and twenty minutes for medium rare. Baste with melted fat two or three times while roasting. Serve with cranberry sauce and Yorkshire pudding. Serves six.

Yorkshire Pudding

About half an hour before beef is done, turn some of the drippings into an oblong pan. Beat three eggs until very light. Add one teaspoon salt and two cups milk. Pour half of this mixture on two-thirds cup sifted flour, and stir to a smooth paste. Add the rest of the egg and milk mixture, and beat thoroughly. Pour the batter in the pan under the rack, and bake. Cut the pudding in squares and serve around the beef. Some cooks prefer to bake the batter in gem pans, and baste the contents with the beef drippings.

BEEF À LA MODE

Lard a three-pound piece of top of the round with slices of salt pork. Rub the meat with salt, pepper, marjoram, thyme, cloves, mace, and nutmeg. Put a slice of onion and two bay leaves in a quart of claret and let stand for half an hour. Pour over the meat and put in a cool place overnight. In the morning, place a cracked knuckle of veal in the bottom of a pan. Put in the beef, cover with claret, and simmer two hours. Turn the meat over and simmer two hours longer. Add more claret, if necessary. Remove the meat to a baking dish. Brush with melted fat and sprinkle with bread crumbs. Brown in a hot oven. Strain the gravy into a saucepan. Remove the fat and reduce the liquid to one pint. Pour over the beef and serve. Serves six.

ALMA'S POT ROAST

The following recipe was the masterpiece of a White Mountain cook whose reputation for fine dishes brought many people to her door. This is the way she prepared pot roast for her summer boarders.

Put a four-pound piece of top of the round in an iron kettle without water. Let the meat sear, turning it often so all sides are a rich dark brown. Be careful not to burn it. Just cover with boiling water and cook slowly for three hours. Add one tablespoon cider vinegar during the last hour of cooking. Do not add more water unless necessary. Add salt fifteen minutes before meat is done. Thicken the liquor with flour mixed to a paste with a little cold water. If the meat is seared properly, the gravy will be nice and brown. Slice the meat while still warm and place bits of butter on each slice. Any preferred vegetables may be added while the meat is cooking, but it is delicious cooked without any. Serves eight.

PARKER HOUSE PLANKED STEAK

Have the steak cut one and a half inches thick and broil about eight minutes, turning four or five times during the process. Place the steak on a hot plank and arrange mashed potatoes around it. Place four boiled onions on the steak. Brush the edges of the potatoes and onions with beaten yolk of an egg diluted in a little water. Set in a hot oven, 425 degrees F., to brown. Serve with mushroom sauce.

NEW HAMPSHIRE PAN-BROILED STEAK

Heat an iron frying pan until it smokes. Put in slices of the top of the round. Turn almost immediately. The secret of pan-broiling a steak is to have the pan as hot as possible, but not to let it burn. Put the steak on a hot platter and dust with salt and pepper. Place a piece of butter on each piece. Turn about half a cup of hot water into the frying pan and let it come to a boil. When the water has absorbed the juices in the pan, turn it over the steak and serve at once.

OLD-FASHIONED BEEFSTEAK WITH ONIONS

Fry four slices of salt pork until brown. Remove the pork slices to a platter. Slice six onions very thin and fry in the pork fat. Take out all but a thin layer of onions. Lay the steak on this layer of onions. Cover with another layer of onions. Dredge with flour, salt, and pepper. Pour on enough boiling water to cover. Then tightly cover the pan and simmer until the steak is tender.

JANET'S STUFFED BEEFSTEAK

Take one pound of round beefsteak and spread with a bread-crumb dressing seasoned with sage and onions. This dressing should be one inch thick. Roll up the steak and tie it with a piece of string. Place in a baking dish and lay thin slices of salt pork on top. Pour a pint of water around the steak. Cover closely and bake in a moderate oven, 350 degrees F., for three and a half hours. Serves six.

MEAT LOAF

3 pounds bottom round	1 cup milk
1/2 pound salt pork	2 eggs, well beaten
1 small onion	2 teaspoons poultry seasoning
1/2 cup diced celery	1 teaspoon salt
8 crackers, rolled fine	1/2 teaspoon pepper

Chop together the meat, pork, onion, and celery. Add the cracker crumbs. Combine the milk and eggs, and mix thoroughly with the meat mixture. Add the seasonings and mix again. Form in a loaf and pack in one very large bread tin or in two smaller tins. If a large tin is used, bake the loaf one and a half hours in a moderate oven, 375 degrees F. If smaller tins are used, bake one hour. If necessary, raise the heat during the last fifteen minutes to brown. Serve with tomato sauce.

Tomato Sauce

1/2 cup butter	1 1/2 cups canned tomatoes
1/4 cup flour	1/2 teaspoon Worcestershire sauce
2 cups boiling water	Salt and pepper to taste

Melt the butter and blend in the flour. Gradually add the boiling water. Heat the tomatoes and strain. Add the Worcestershire sauce and seasonings. Pour over the meat loaf and serve very hot. Serves eight.

ROAST SPRING VEAL

Remove the bone from a fillet of veal and stuff the veal with highly seasoned moist stuffing. Tie into a round shape. Dredge with salt, pepper, and flour. Lay strips of salt pork over the top. Bake in a hot oven, 400 degrees F., for thirty minutes, then reduce heat to 300 degrees. Allow half an hour to a pound in roasting. When the flour has browned, turn a little water into the roasting pan. Baste often. Serve with asparagus, dandelion greens, and horseradish.

SCALLOPED VEAL AND CUCUMBER

Peel cucumbers and cut in pieces about an inch long. Boil them in salted water ten minutes, or until tender. Keep them warm. Cut veal in very small cutlets, and brown in butter. Remove from the pan to a platter and place the cucumbers on top of the veal. Put one cup of cream in the pan in which the veal was cooked. Add one-half teaspoon paprika, and salt and pepper. Boil, stirring constantly, for a few minutes. Pour this sauce over the veal and cucumbers. Serve very hot.

ROAST MUTTON WITH CURRANT JELLY GRAVY

Cut out the bone from a leg of mutton. Wash the meat and rub with salt. Fill the bone cavity with the following dressing:

2 quarts stale bread crumbs	1 teaspoon pepper
Cold water	1 tablespoon salt
1/2 onion, chopped fine	1 egg
1 tablespoon summer savory	Butter size of an egg

Soak the bread crumbs in cold water. Drain and mix with the onion and seasonings. Stir in the egg and melted butter. Mix well.

When the mutton is stuffed, fasten with a skewer and place in a roasting pan without water. Place skin side down and dredge with flour, salt, and pepper. Roast for about thirty minutes in a very hot oven, 500 degrees F. Reduce the heat to 325 degrees and continue roasting until the mutton is tender, allowing thirty-five minutes per pound. Do not cover the pan. Skim all the fat from the gravy, and thicken with flour in the proportion of one tablespoon for one cup of liquid. Put one tablespoon currant jelly in the gravy boat, and strain the gravy over it. Serve the mutton with mashed potatoes, boiled onions, mashed turnip, and currant jelly.

SWEET ROAST LAMB

Stick whole cloves into a leg of lamb as you do for baked ham. Sprinkle with three tablespoons brown sugar mixed with one tablespoon sweet marjoram. Roast like mutton. Serve with green peas and mint jelly.

ROAST PORK

"Some like it hot, some like it cold" is as applicable to roast pork as to pease porridge. Many people prefer second-day cold roast pork served in slices to the first-day hot roast. Fresh pork should be young and firm, the fat white, the lean a clear red, and the skin white and clear. It should be thoroughly cooked. This is very important. Select the chine, loin, or spareribs for roasting. Rub the roast with salt and pepper. Place in the roaster with fat side up. Cook uncovered without water. For the first fifteen minutes the oven should be hot, 500 degrees F. Then reduce the heat to 350 degrees. Allow thirty-five minutes to the pound. Baste often with the fat in the pan. Serve with gravy and applesauce. Parsnips are delicious when baked with roast pork.

PORK CHOPS AND APPLES

2 large pork tenderloin chops	1/4 teaspoon marjoram
1 cup bread crumbs	1/2 teaspoon minced onion
1 tablespoon melted fat	Salt pork strips
1/2 teaspoon salt	4 apples
1/4 teaspoon pepper	

Split the chops and stuff with dressing made of the bread crumbs, melted fat, and seasonings. Put the chops in a baking dish and lay strips of salt pork over them. Pare, core, and quarter the apples, and stew them with very little water until tender. Put in the baking dish with the chops. Sprinkle with sugar and dot with butter. Cover and bake slowly, 325 degrees F., about one hour, until the meat is tender and the apples are transparent. Serves two to four.

BAKED HAM WITH WINE RAISIN SAUCE

Boil a ten-pound ham for four hours. Remove the skin and score the fat side of the ham. Stick whole cloves in each square. Mix one cup brown sugar and two tablespoons dry mustard. Wet with some of the ham liquor to make a paste. Put this over the ham and bake one hour in a moderate oven, 350 degrees F. Serve with wine raisin sauce.

Wine Raisin Sauce

3/4 cup raisins	1/4 teaspoon cloves
1 cup white wine	1/4 teaspoon cinnamon
1/2 cup sugar	2 tablespoons cornstarch
1/4 teaspoon salt	3 tablespoons butter

Cover the raisins with half a cup of the wine. Simmer for five minutes. Add the rest of wine and other ingredients, and cook until thick. Stir constantly.

NEW BEDFORD STUFFED HAM

2 slices ham, one-inch thick	4 apples, sliced
Stuffing	1 cup water

Place one slice of the ham in a roaster and cover it with your favorite bread-crumb stuffing. Lay the sliced apples on top of the stuffing. Place the other slice of ham on top. Tie a string around the ham slices to keep them in place. Pour the cup of water into the bottom of the roaster. Cover and bake one hour in a moderate oven, 350 degrees F., turning once during the baking. Serves six.

OLD-FASHIONED CALVES' LIVER AND ONIONS

Fry enough bacon slices to serve two slices to each person. Remove the bacon to a platter, leaving about a quarter inch of fat in the bottom of the skillet. Slice the liver thin and pour boiling water over the slices. Pour the water off immediately, and roll the slices in seasoned flour. Fry in bacon fat until brown on both sides. Have ready about a bowlful of sliced onions. Remove the liver to the platter, and turn the onions into the skillet. Watch carefully and do not let them burn. When lightly browned, lower the heat, and cover for about five minutes. Return the liver to the skillet, placing it on top of the onions. Cover and reheat the liver. Be careful not to burn the onions. Sprinkle with salt and pepper, then turn the liver and onions onto the platter with the bacon.

LAMB KIDNEYS

12 lamb kidneys
Salt and pepper
3 tablespoons butter
4 teaspoons minced onion

1 tablespoon flour
1 1/2 cups hot stock
1 tablespoon sherry

Pare, trim, and slice the kidneys. Dust with salt and pepper, and sauté in the butter. Turn some of the butter into a small skillet and cook the onion in it. Add the flour, and blend. Then add the hot stock, and stir until smooth. Season to taste. Add the sherry, and pour the sauce over the kidneys. Serve at once. Serves six.

FRESH TRIPE IN BATTER

Fresh tripe
1 cup flour
1/4 teaspoon salt
1/2 cup cold water

1 egg, well beaten
1/4 teaspoon vinegar
1 teaspoon melted butter

Mix the flour and salt, and slowly add the water, stirring until smooth. Add the egg, vinegar, and melted butter. Cut fresh tripe into serving pieces. Dip in the batter and fry in deep fat.

PAN-FRIED PICKLED TRIPE

Turn boiling water over pickled tripe. Let it stand twenty minutes, then drain. Mix one teaspoon salt with one and one-half cups corn meal. Cut the tripe into serving pieces and roll them in the corn meal.

Meantime, try out salt pork until there is about a quarter inch of fat in the bottom of an iron skillet. When sizzling hot, put in the slices of tripe. Fry on one side until brown, then on the other. Remove the slices to a platter and put generous pieces of butter on them. Garnish with the pork scraps.

FRIED SALT PORK

Cut fat salt pork in thin slices. Pour hot water over them and drain. Beat two eggs, roll the pork slices in them, then roll in crumbs. Fry in deep hot fat. Serve with fried mush. Allow three slices for each serving.

PENTUCKET SALT PORK IN BATTER

1/2 pound salt pork	1/4 teaspoon cream of tartar
1/3 cup milk	1/8 teaspoon soda
1 egg, well beaten	5 tablespoons flour
Salt	

Cut the pork in slices a quarter inch thick and remove the rind. Pour boiling water over the slices. Let stand five minutes and drain. Make a batter of the milk, eggs, and other ingredients. Dip the slices of pork in the batter, and fry in pork fat in a skillet. Allow three slices for each serving.

FRIED SALT PORK WITH CREAM GRAVY

Fry slices of salt pork to a delicate brown. Put them in a deep dish. Remove part of the fat from the skillet, leaving about one tablespoon. Pour in one cup thick cream, and as soon as it is hot pour it over the pork slices. Allow three slices for each serving.

HOG'S HEADCHEESE

Take the gristly part of the pig's head, but not the fat, and the ears and feet. (Remove the hard part from the feet.) Scald. Soak in warm water and thoroughly scrape. Put in salt and water for ten hours. Scrape and clean again, and put a second time in freshly salted water, following the first procedure. When perfectly clean, put in a kettle, cover with cold water, and set over the heat. Skim the water when it begins to boil. Set the kettle over low heat and let simmer until the bones slip out easily. Skim out the meat, and remove the hard gristle, bones, and any fat that remains. Season with salt, pepper, and sage. Put in a strainer cloth and press out the fat. Pack in stone jars. Serve cold, or brown slightly in a frying pan. When vinegar is substituted for sage, the dish is known as souse.

JELLIED PICKLED PIGS' FEET

6 pigs' feet	1/2 red pepper
Bay leaf	1 teaspoon salt
1 large onion, sliced	1 bunch parsley
6 cloves	Vinegar

Cook the pigs' feet in boiling water until tender. Add all the other ingredients except the vinegar. Cook until the vegetables are in shreds and the meat drops from the bones. Take the pigs' feet from the kettle and remove every bit of bone. Skim the fat from the liquid, strain through a bag, and put back in the kettle over heat. Boil rapidly until reduced to about half enough to cover the meat. Add enough vinegar to make the liquid cover the meat. Mix the meat thoroughly with the liquid. Let stand twelve hours. Serve cold.

SAUSAGE AND APPLES

Core four apples and slice across in quarter-inch slices. Place sliced homemade sausage or link sausages on a rack in a dripping pan. Bake in a moderate oven, 350 degrees F., for half an hour, or until brown. Remove to a hot platter. Turn a little of the fat into a skillet and fry the apple slices in it. Brown them lightly on one side and then on the other. Arrange the apple slices around the sausages. Serves six. (The cooks of old Vermont and New Hampshire usually poured maple syrup over the apples before serving this hearty and delicious dish.)

FRICASSEED OXTAILS

Cut oxtails into pieces about three inches long. Wash thoroughly and soak in cold water one hour. Remove from water, wipe dry, and dredge in seasoned flour. Put some butter in a skillet and fry the meat until brown. Meantime, fry thin slices of onions, diced carrots, celery, and chopped turnip. Add to oxtails. Just cover with water and simmer until the meat is tender, about one hour.

FRIZZLED SMOKED BEEF

Pour boiling water over one quarter pound sliced smoked beef and let stand ten minutes. Put one tablespoon butter in a skillet and frizzle the beef in it. Add one cup cream. Beat one whole egg and the yolk of another, and add. Season with a little pepper. Cook two minutes and serve at once. Serves four.

VERMONT BEEF AND KIDNEY PIE

1 1/2 pounds round steak	1 1/2 tablespoons Worcestershire sauce
3 lamb kidneys	1/2 teaspoon salt
2 tablespoons butter	1/8 teaspoon pepper
2 tablespoons flour	1 1/3 cups boiling water
2 onions, sliced	Rich pie crust

Remove the excess fat from the round steak and cut the meat into cubes. Soak the kidneys, remove the skins, and slice them. Try out the trimmings from the beef and combine this fat with the butter. Blend with the flour. Add the beef and kidneys, and brown them. Add the onions, Worcestershire sauce, seasonings, and water. Cover the kettle and cook until the meat is tender. Put in a baking dish and cover with a rich crust which has been slit to allow the steam to escape. Bake in a hot oven, 400 degrees F., for thirty minutes. Serves six.

CASCO BAY OMELET SOUFFLE

6 eggs, separated   1/8 teaspoon pepper
6 tablespoons water   1 cup chopped cooked clams
1 teaspoon salt

Beat the egg yolks until light, then add the water, seasonings, and clams. Fold in the stiffly beaten egg whites. Put a piece of butter in a skillet and set over low heat. Turn the mixture into the skillet and cook slowly until bubbles show on the surface and the omelet is brown on the underside. Place in a slow oven, 325 degrees F., for about five minutes, or until the omelet is dry on top. Remove from the skillet and fold. Serve at once. Serves six.

BAKED EGGS, DOWN-EAST STYLE

3 egg yolks   1 tablespoon chopped chives
1/4 cup soft bread crumbs   2 sprigs parsley, chopped
2 tablespoons butter, melted   Salt and pepper
3 sardines, chopped   6 eggs

Mix the egg yolks, bread crumbs, melted butter, sardines, and seasonings. Spread the mixture in the bottom of a baking dish, and place in a very slow oven until set. Drop six eggs on top of the mixture, taking care to keep the eggs in shape. Dust with salt and pepper and bake in a moderate oven, 350 degrees F., for twenty to thirty minutes, or until the eggs are set. Place a small piece of butter on each egg before serving. Serves six.

BAKED CHEESE AND RICE

3 eggs, well beaten   3/4 cup milk
2 tablespoons butter, melted   2 2/3 cups cooked rice
3/4 cup cheese, grated   Salt and pepper

Combine the eggs, butter, cheese, and milk. Fold in the rice and season to taste. Turn into greased custard cups. Set in a pan of hot water. Bake forty minutes at 350 degrees F., or until set. Turn out of the custard cups and serve with tomato sauce or with thick cheese sauce.

Thick Cheese Sauce

4 tablespoons butter, melted   1 teaspoon salt
4 tablespoons flour   2 cups grated cheese
2 cups milk

Blend the butter and flour, and combine with the milk. Add the salt and cook until the mixture thickens. Add the cheese and cook until it melts. Serves six.

This sauce also may be used with cabbage, cauliflower, or broccoli.

7. GARDEN SASS

WHEN James Russell Lowell, writing on Yankee dialect in *The Biglow Papers,* said, "I cannot help thinking that the ordinary talk of the unlettered man among us is fuller of metaphor and of phrases that suggest lively images than that of any other people I have seen," he might well have been thinking of some of the early cookery terms. Gap and swallow pudding, tipsy parson, and garden sass all have the "native and puckery flavor" which Lowell felt was characteristic of New England speech.

Garden sauce and green sauce were old English terms dating from the time of Beaumont and Fletcher and perhaps before. Corrupted in New England to garden sass, it included all the vegetables raised in the garden. At one time some of the vegetables were classified as short sauce, others as long sauce, but these finer distinctions have been lost, and in northern New Hampshire and Maine, even today, garden sass is the accepted phrase for all green vegetables.

In the old days vegetables were actually served in sauce dishes and eaten with a spoon. Most of them were stewed, served with cream or the juice in which they were cooked. The dinner plate was for meat and potatoes only—great-grandfather and even grandfather did not like to have his food all mixed together in one plate. Serving vegetables in what used to be called bird baths is still a common practice in many New England hotels.

When we consider the poor soil, the short growing season, and the long hard winter in New England, the abundance of vegetables for garden sass in colonial times, is something to marvel at. Nearly all the vegetables and fruits which we grow were known to the housewife of that day.

From England the colonists brought seeds for cabbage, celery, cauliflower, asparagus, radishes, lettuce, turnips, carrots, parsnips, onions, and beets. From the Indians they learned which of the native vegetables to use, and the housewives soon improvised new ways of serving green corn, beans, pumpkins, and squash. Although only the more well-to-do seacoast families with their Irish and Scotch gardeners were able to cultivate all these vegetables, rural families always had a good supply of beans, peas, Indian corn, and the coarse vegetables, such as carrots, beets, turnips, and cabbage, to store for the winter.

When the colonists first came to this country they must have been astonished at the many varieties of beans grown by the Indians. In Europe only lima beans and broad beans were known, but in America they found beans of all colors, sizes, and shapes. Indian squaws taught the colonists how to bake beans in pots in the earth, how to cook them green in the summer and dry them for winter storage. It was not long before seafaring men, fur traders, and lumbermen realized the value of dried beans which could be kept so long and cooked so many ways.

The Indians also taught the early settlers that beans and corn have an affinity for each other. Some of the recipes in this chapter are adapted from the *Indian Meal Book*, a little-known cookbook published in London in 1846. Written by Eliza Leslie, an American, its purpose was to acquaint the English people with the uses of Indian meal and other foods of the new world to help overcome the food shortage caused by the failure of the Irish potato crop.

In New England the white potato was suspected for a number of years of being a forbidden fruit. It was said by some to be an aphrodisiac, by others to shorten life. When Parson Jonathan Hubbard of Sheffield, Connecticut, raised twenty bushels in one year, his parishioners thought he was trafficking with the devil.

Cabbage was one of the first vegetables planted by our forefathers in the new world. It was doubly welcome because it could be stored fresh and also pickled. New Englanders learned to like the Dutch sauerkraut, and making it became one of the important household tasks in the fall.

No one knows who cooked the first boiled dinner. No monuments have been raised or tablets engraved to the pioneering cook who first thought of the incomparable combination of meat and vegetables which ranks with baked beans, brown bread, and Indian pudding as one of New England's major contributions to American cookery. But we can imagine the first boiled dinner was as much of an accident as Charles Lamb's roast pig. One day perhaps, an unknown New England housewife took a hunk of corned beef brisket from the barrel in the cellar, put it in the big dinner kettle, covered it with water, and hung it over the fire to simmer. She brought vegetables up at the same time, washed the beets, turnips, and carrots, peeled the potatoes, and sliced the cabbage ready to cook.

But the day was not far along, so she decided to finish her weaving on the loom. Since the children were at school and the menfolk busy, the day went quickly and quietly. Suddenly she realized the morning was almost gone and no dinner ready so she threw all the vegetables into the kettle with the corned beef. After all, she thought, I can't take time now to heat water to boil them. And there was the pot of corned beef simmering gently just ready for the vegetables.

When dinnertime came, she sliced the corned beef on a platter, arranged the vegetables around it, and brought it to the table without a word. Her husband, sniffing the rich fragrance and looking at the pale pink cabbage and potatoes said, "Sarah, what's this?" She answered nonchalantly, "Just a boiled dinner." And later sipping his whisky toddy at the tavern, the man of the house said, "Sarah's a great hand with boiled dinners."

Neither of them had any idea that before many years, every Thursday noon, year in and year out, farm families in New England would have on their tables heaping platters of the meat and vegetables that became the traditional "bil'd dish."

To get the real flavor into a boiled dinner, only the best brisket was used, or if that was not available, a piece of salt-sparkling pork, deep pink with streaks of lean running through it. Although undiscriminating modern cooks often boil beets separately, the north country people of New Hampshire like to see the rich color of the beets all through the rest of the vegetables. In the old-time boiled dinner, too, only the potatoes and turnips were peeled before cooking; carrots, beets, and parsnips when they were used, had their skins left on.

Then when all the vegetables were cooked to perfection, the meat was sliced and placed in the center of the largest pewter platter in the pantry: sliced carrots at one end, sliced turnips at the other, beets on one side, cabbage opposite. Only the potatoes had a dish of their own. Vinegar, homemade horseradish, home-mixed mustard or mustard pickles were placed on the table for the meat, with a side dish of stewed pumpkin or pickled beets. For dessert, Indian pudding or apple pudding was boiled in a bag with the dinner.

No New England garden was considered a success if it did not furnish, a large mess of green peas for Fourth of July dinner. If the season were a late one, the whole family watched the rows of peas anxiously. If the season were early, the peas were left on the vine to be sure of enough to go with the fresh salmon and lemon sherbet. Served sometimes just with butter, at other times with milk sauce, each member of the family expected on that day to eat all the peas he could hold. Then at "the last of pea-time"—the New England expression for being hard up—when the scattered pods of large hard peas were picked, there were two special dishes to which all the family looked forward: peas and dumplings, and pea fritters. Recipes for both are given in this chapter.

GREEN BEANS AND SALT PORK

One of the oldest ways of cooking green beans was with salt pork. When the first new potatoes were dug, half a dozen or so were thrown in to cook with the beans and salt pork.

Snap the ends of fresh green beans and break into one-inch pieces. Put in a kettle with a good-sized piece of salt pork or bacon and a small amount of water. Cook until tender, twenty to thirty minutes. Add salt, if necessary, and pepper. Add the washed unpeeled potatoes when the beans are half done.

SUMMER SUCCOTASH

This is one of the recipes from Eliza Leslie's hundred-year-old *Indian Meal Book*.

Cut one-quarter peck of young string beans in one-inch pieces. Cook until tender, fifteen to twenty minutes. Cut the grains from twelve ears of corn, add to the beans with one teaspoon salt. Cook until the corn is tender, about ten minutes longer. Add butter and pepper. Boiled bacon, cut in small slices may be cooked with the beans, and salted or smoked meat is served with the succotash. Serves eight.

Our modern recipe for summer succotash calls for shell or horticultural beans. It is made the same way with a little cream added just before serving if the vegetables seem dry.

WINTER SUCCOTASH

Winter succotash in the old days was made with both dried beans and dried corn.

Soak equal amounts of dried beans and corn overnight. Put the beans on first with enough water to cover and cook until almost tender, about two hours. Add strips of bacon or cold pork and the corn. Cook until the corn is tender, about one hour longer, and season with salt and pepper to taste.

STEWED BEANS

Soak one cup of dried beans overnight. Cover with water and cook slowly one hour, or until tender. Add salt and pepper to taste, cover with sweet cream, and bring just to a boil. Serve in bowls or soup plates with hot johnnycake and baked ham. Serves four.

DRIED LIMA BEANS

Soak one cup of dried lima beans overnight. Drain and cook in boiling salted water one hour, or until tender. Drain. Put in a saucepan with two tablespoons of butter, and cook, stirring occasionally until browned. Serve with a sauce made of one tablespoon onion fried brown in one tablespoon butter, and one cup tomatoes. Bring to a boil, season with salt and pepper, and pour over the beans. Serves six.

JAGASEE

1 cup dried lima beans	1 green pepper, minced
3 slices salt pork	Salt and pepper
1 onion, minced	1 tablespoon rice
1/2 cup diced celery	

Cover the lima beans with water and cook until almost tender, about one hour. Try out the salt pork, add the onion, and cook until transparent. Add to the lima beans with the celery and green pepper. Season to taste with salt and pepper. Sprinkle the uncooked rice over the top, cover, and put over low heat to steam slowly until the rice is done, about one-half to three-quarters of an hour. Add a little water if necessary. Serves six.

GREEN CORN DUMPLINGS

4 cups grated green corn
1 cup flour
2 cups milk
6 tablespoons butter

1 teaspoon salt
1/2 teaspoon pepper
3 eggs, beaten

Mix the corn and flour, stirring smooth. Add the milk warmed with the butter and seasonings. Cool. Add the beaten eggs. Form the mixture into cakes, and fry them in hot fat. Serves eight.

THREE RIVERS BAKED SWEET CORN

1/3 cup grated cheese
1/4 cup milk
1 egg, beaten
2 cups grated corn

1/3 cup bread crumbs
Salt and pepper
1 tablespoon butter

Stir half the cheese into the milk, add the beaten egg, corn, and half the bread crumbs. Season to taste with salt and pepper. Pour into a buttered baking dish, and sprinkle with the remaining cheese and crumbs. Dot with the butter. Bake thirty minutes in a moderate oven, 350 degrees F. Serves four.

MAINE CORN PUDDING

2 cups corn
2 eggs
2 tablespoons drippings

1 teaspoon salt
1/2 teaspoon pepper
2 cups milk

Combine all the ingredients. Pour into a buttered baking dish, and bake in a moderate oven, 350 degrees F., for one hour. Serves six.

SOUR MILK CORNCAKES

8 ears corn
1 cup sour milk or buttermilk
2 eggs
1 teaspoon salt

1 teaspoon soda
1/2 teaspoon pepper
Flour

Cut the corn from the ears. Add the remaining ingredients and enough flour to make a thin batter. Fry on a hot griddle. Serves four.

PEAS AND MILK SAUCE

Cook two cups of shelled peas twenty minutes, or until tender (hard peas must cook longer) in very little water with a small piece of mint. Drain, add one tablespoon butter, one-half cup warm milk, salt and pepper to taste. Cream may be used in place of the milk, and the butter omitted. Serves four to six.

DOWN-EAST PEAS AND DUMPLINGS

Large, hard, end-of-the-season peas are used for this and the following recipe.

2 cups shelled peas
1/2 cup shortening
1 cup milk

1 cup flour
2 eggs
1 teaspoon salt

Cook the peas thirty to forty minutes, or until tender, in boiling salted water. Let the shortening and milk come to a boil, stir in the flour, and let cool. Add the eggs one at a time and the salt. Drop by teaspoons into the peas, cover and cook ten minutes. Serves six.

PEA FRITTERS

2 cups shelled peas
Salt, pepper
1 tablespoon butter
2 eggs, beaten

1 cup milk
1 teaspoon baking powder
1/4 teaspoon salt
1/2 cup flour

Cook the peas thirty to forty minutes, or until tender, and mash them while they are hot. Season with salt and pepper and the butter. The next day add the beaten eggs and the remaining ingredients, beating well. Fry like griddlecakes. Serves six.

PICKLED BEETS

Cover thin slices of cold boiled beets with vinegar to which a few cloves are added, or cover the beets with vinegar, salt, pepper, and a little sugar, and add a thinly sliced onion.

BAKED BEETS

In the early 1700s, beets were baked with the skins on. Just before serving, the skin was slipped off, and the beets were seasoned with salt, pepper, butter, and vinegar.

HARVARD BEETS

6 medium beets, cooked	1/8 teaspoon pepper
1/2 tablespoon cornstarch	1/4 cup water
1/3 cup sugar	1/4 cup vinegar
1/4 teaspoon salt	2 tablespoons butter

Slice the beets thin. Mix the cornstarch, sugar, salt, and pepper. Add the water and vinegar, and boil five minutes. Add the beets and heat through. Serves six.

GLAZED CARROTS

Cut six medium carrots in thin slices. Cook until tender, ten to twenty-five minutes, in boiling salted water. Drain, add one-fourth cup butter, one-half cup sugar, and one tablespoon chopped mint leaves. Let simmer until glazed. One-half cup maple syrup may be used in place of the sugar, and the mint omitted. Serves four to six.

BOILED TURNIPS

Pare and cube the turnips. Cook them in a small amount of boiling salted water to which half a teaspoon of sugar has been added, fifteen to thirty minutes, or until tender. Season with salt, pepper, and butter, or mash with a little sweet cream. One pound of turnips serves three or more.

LADIES' CABBAGE

Boil a small head of cabbage five to fifteen minutes, or until tender. Chop fine. Add two beaten eggs, one tablespoon butter, salt, pepper, and three tablespoons cream. Stir well together. Put in a buttered baking dish and brown. Serves six.

BOILED DINNER

Take four pounds of brisket corned beef, lean salt pork, or half brisket and half salt pork, cover with cold water and bring to a boil. Boil fifteen minutes and skim. Simmer over a low heat until the meat is tender, three to four hours. During the last hour of cooking, add six small beets, four peeled turnips, six scraped carrots, a small head of cabbage cut in quarters, and half an hour before serving add eight peeled potatoes. Although some recipes call for parsnips, they were not put in the original boiled dinner. In the spring, once in a while, two or three were thrown into the pot for good measure, but they did not really belong there. When ready to serve the boiled dinner, slip the skins off the beets. Serves six.

Old New England cooks, after skimming the fat from the water in which the boiled dinner was cooked, put the stock aside to moisten the hash next day.

RED FLANNEL HASH

To make red flannel hash, two things have to be watched. Sometimes it is necessary to cook extra potatoes, for the hash needs twice as much potato as other ingredients. Second, the vegetables should be chopped in a wooden bowl. No food chopper gives quite the right texture, for hash never should be soggy or too soft. Though all the flavors are blended, the vegetables must keep their shape and identity.

Use all the vegetables and meat left from the boiled dinner, and add twice as much cold boiled potato as you have beets. Chop the vegetables coarsely. Put a tablespoon of drippings or try out a good-sized slice of salt pork in a heavy spider. Turn the chopped vegetables into the spider and sprinkle with pepper and salt if needed. Moisten with the stock left from the boiled dinner. Smooth the hash to fill the pan, then cover it. Cook slowly until the hash is brown and crusted on the bottom. Fold over like an omelet and serve.

A beet hash is made the same way, using equal parts of beets and potatoes, and a vegetable hash the same way omitting the meat.

NEW HAMPSHIRE CORNED BEEF HASH

Freshly boiled or leftover corned beef make that choice breakfast dish—corned beef hash. Making hash is an art: it must not have too much fat; it should have just the right amount of potato. Above all, it should not be stirred. Cook the hash slowly in a heavy pan until the flavor of the meat goes through the potatoes, and the potatoes melt into the meat.

Take equal parts of corned beef and boiled potatoes. Chop coarsely in separate dishes, then mix with a fork. For two cups of meat and two cups of potatoes, add half an onion, ground, and salt and pepper to taste. Moisten with half a cup of milk or meat stock. Put one tablespoon of drippings in a heavy spider, add the hash, and smooth over the top. Cover and cook slowly until brown. Turn with a spatula and brown the other side. Serve with ketchup or chili sauce and poached eggs.

CORNED BEEF AND CABBAGE

Corned beef and cabbage was one of the standard dishes of New England families, served as often on Beacon Hill as along the docks.

Real corned beef and cabbage involves two days: one on which the meat is cooked, and the second on which the cabbage is cooked.

Take three pounds of brisket corned beef. Cover with water and bring to a boil in a good-sized kettle. Skim and cook slowly for three or four hours. During the last half hour of cooking, add three-fourths tablespoon brown or maple sugar and one teaspoon salt. When the meat is tender, remove to a platter, cover with a plate, and put a weight on top. Set aside to cool.

Reserve the water in which the corned beef was cooked. When cool, remove the fat. The next day, bring the meat stock to a boil, add ten unpeeled thoroughly washed potatoes and one onion, and lay two medium heads of cabbage, cut in quarters, on top of the potatoes. Cook slowly until the vegetables are done. Serve with sliced cold corned beef, home-mixed mustard, and horseradish. Serves eight to ten.

DANDELION GREENS

Dandelions are one of the strong-flavored potherbs. Although some people like the bitter flavor, many prefer to have some of the bitterness removed. To do this, cover with boiling water and drain twice. Boil one quarter pound salt pork in one quart water one hour and add greens. Cook until tender. One pound will make three servings.

Another method is to use young and tender greens. Cut off all the roots, remove the buds and coarse outside leaves. Cover with boiling water, drain, cover a second time, bring to a boil, and drain again. Then cover with clear water and cook fifteen to thirty minutes, or until tender. Drain well, chop, season with salt and pepper. Cook half an onion, minced, with one slice of bacon, minced, or with salt pork until both are brown. Pour over the greens and garnish with hard-cooked egg.

MOLDED BEET GREENS

Cook the beet greens with just the water that clings to them after washing thoroughly. Chop and season well with salt, pepper, and lemon juice. Pack in a buttered mold and set in a pan of hot water. Cook small beets, slip the skins, season with salt, pepper, and butter. Unmold the greens and serve with a ring of buttered beets. Allow one pound of greens for three servings.

TURNIP TOPS AND KALE

Turnip tops and kale may be cooked with salt pork or seasoned with minced onion and bacon as were dandelion, spinach, and beet greens.

CREAMED KALE

Cook two pounds of kale until tender in boiling salted water for fifteen to thirty minutes. Serve with a rich white sauce. Six onions may be boiled until tender and added to the white sauce before it is poured over the kale. Serves six.

BROCCOLI WITH EGG SAUCE

Boil a one-pound head of broccoli one-half hour, or until tender. Melt two tablespoons of butter with one teaspoon flour; blend in half a cup of water or stock, salt and pepper to taste, and one-half teaspoon lemon juice. Beat an egg into this sauce and pour over the broccoli. Serves four.

CREAMED BRUSSELS SPROUTS AND CHESTNUTS

Cook one quart of Brussels sprouts one-half hour, or until tender. Roast or boil chestnuts, using a pint of nuts to a quart of sprouts. Serve with a heavy cream sauce or with salt, pepper, and butter. Serves six to eight.

FRIED CAULIFLOWER

Cut a medium head of cauliflower into individual flowerets, and boil until almost tender, eight minutes. Mix two tablespoons flour, yolks of two eggs, and enough milk to make a thin batter. Add salt to taste, and fold in the well-beaten egg whites. Dip the cauliflower in this batter and fry in hot fat.

STEWED ASPARAGUS

After breaking off the coarse parts of the asparagus stalks, cut a two-pound bunch of asparagus in small pieces and cook fifteen to twenty minutes or until tender. Brown slightly one tablespoon of flour, and add one tablespoon of butter and half a cup of the water in which the asparagus was boiled. When thick, add salt and pepper to taste, and two tablespoons of sweet cream. Add to the asparagus and simmer a minute or two before serving. Serves six.

PARSNIP FRITTERS

Peel, boil, and mash three large parsnips. Remove the large fibers and woody parts. Add one beaten egg, one cup milk, one tablespoon butter, one teaspoon salt, three tablespoons flour. Shape into cakes and fry. Serves six.

PARSNIP PUFF

6 parsnips	1 tablespoon butter
3 large potatoes	1/2 teaspoon salt
1/4 cup cream	1/2 teaspoon pepper
1/2 teaspoon baking powder	1/4 cup grated cheese

Boil the peeled parsnips five minutes, add the potatoes, and cook until tender, about thirty minutes. Drain and mash. Add all the other ingredients except the cheese and beat well. Turn into a buttered frying pan, brown the mixture on the bottom, cover with the cheese, and run under the broiler until the cheese is melted. Serves six.

SALSIFY OR OYSTER PLANT

Scrape the roots of two pounds of salsify, dropping it into cold water immediately to keep it from turning brown. Cut into one-inch pieces, and cook in hot water twenty to forty minutes, or until tender. Drain, add cold milk to cover. Blend one tablespoon flour with one tablespoon butter, add to the salsify and milk, season with salt and pepper to taste. Bring to a boil and serve. Serves six.

MOCK OYSTERS

Mash two pounds of boiled salsify and remove the large fibers. Moisten with a little milk, add one tablespoon butter and one beaten egg for each cup of vegetable. Make into round cakes, dredge with flour, and fry brown. Serves six.

CONNECTICUT BAKED CELERY

Dice two cups of celery and cook in boiling salted water until tender. Put in a buttered baking dish, cover with rich cream sauce, sprinkle with grated cheese, and brown in a moderate oven, 350 degrees F. Serves six.

CELERY WITH MUSTARD SAUCE

Season cooked celery with two tablespoons butter to which one teaspoon prepared mustard has been added. Season to taste with salt and pepper.

FRIED CUCUMBERS

This old English recipe became popular in New England. This dish is still popular in the Great Bay region of New Hampshire.

Cut three large peeled cucumbers in half. Scoop out the seedy centers. Fry half a cup of sliced onions in three tablespoons butter until yellow. Season with salt and pepper. Fill the cucumbers with the onions and tie the halves together. Fry brown in the same fat used for the onions, adding a little more if necessary. When brown, add one tablespoon flour and one cup meat stock. Season with salt and pepper, and cook until the cucumbers are tender, about twenty minutes. Serves six.

BAKED CUCUMBERS

Cut the cucumbers in half lengthwise and remove as much of the pulp as possible. Chop the pulp with an equal amount of bread crumbs and cold chopped veal, ham, or chicken. Season highly with salt and pepper and minced onion, and moisten with milk. Stuff the cucumber halves, put in a buttered baking dish, and dot with butter. Bake in a moderate oven, 350 degrees F., thirty to forty minutes, or until brown.

CURRIED TOMATOES

6 green tomatoes   1 teaspoon curry powder
3 tablespoons butter   Flour, salt, pepper
3 tablespoons minced onion

Slice the tomatoes half an inch thick. Melt the butter and sauté the onion until light brown. Add the curry powder and mix well. Dredge the tomatoes in flour and brown on both sides. Sprinkle with salt and pepper. Pour the fat and onion over the tomatoes before serving. Serves six. This is a variation of the traditional curried dishes, and is very popular in New England during the late summer months.

STUFFED TOMATOES

6 tomatoes   1 onion, minced
1 cup minced veal, ham, or   Salt, pepper
    chicken   2 tablespoons melted butter
1 cup bread crumbs   1/4 cup salad oil
2 teaspoons chopped parsley

Slice the tops off the tomatoes and remove the pulp. Sprinkle with salt. Mix the meat, crumbs, parsley, onion, salt, pepper, and butter. Fill the tomatoes. Place in a buttered baking dish, add the salad oil, and bake twenty minutes in a moderate oven, 375 degrees F., or until the tomatoes are tender and browned. Serves six.

STUFFED ONIONS

6 large onions	Cream
1/2 cup ham, veal or chicken	1 tablespoon butter
1/2 cup bread crumbs	1/2 lemon, juice
1 beaten egg	4 tablespoons cream
Salt, pepper	1 tablespoon flour
Mace	

Parboil the onions until almost tender. Drain, remove the hearts, being careful not to break the outer layers. Chop the insides with the meat, mix with the bread crumbs, egg, salt, pepper, mace, and enough of the cream to moisten. Fill the onions and place in a buttered baking dish with enough hot water to cover the bottom of the dish. Dot with butter. Bake one hour in a moderate oven, 350 degrees F., basting occasionally. Remove to a serving dish. Add the lemon juice, cream, and flour to the juice in the pan. Bring to a good boil and pour over the onions. Serves six.

FRIED ONIONS

Slice six large onions thin. Cover with a quart of sweet milk and let stand thirty minutes. Drain and dry. Put one-fourth cup flour and salt and pepper in a paper bag. Add the onions and shake the bag until they are entirely covered with flour. Fry in butter or drippings until brown. Serves six.

MILTON ONIONS

12 small onions	1 tablespoon butter
Bread crumbs	3/4 cup white sauce
1/4 cup grated cheese	

Boil the onions until tender. Cover the bottom of a buttered baking dish with bread crumbs, cover with the onions, and sprinkle with the grated cheese. Dot with butter and cover with the white sauce. Brown in a hot oven, 400 degrees F. Serves six.

CAPE COD AU GRATIN POTATOES

2 cups diced potatoes
1 onion, diced
1 1/2 cups white sauce

Salt, pepper
Buttered crumbs
1/4 cup grated cheese

Boil the potatoes and onion five minutes in salted water. Drain, cover with white sauce, and add salt and pepper to taste. Turn into a buttered casserole and cover with buttered crumbs and the grated cheese. Bake forty-five minutes in a moderate oven, 350 degrees F. Serves four to six.

DUCHESS POTATOES

2 cups mashed potatoes
2 egg yolks, beaten
2 tablespoons butter

1/2 teaspoon salt
Egg white

Mix the potatoes, egg yolks, butter, and salt. Form into balls. Put in a buttered baking dish, brush with egg white, and bake in a hot oven, 425 degrees F., until brown. Serves four to six.

SARATOGA POTATOES

Saratoga potatoes are said to have been invented when one of the guests at the famous Saratoga House complained that the fried potatoes were soggy.

Soak peeled thinly sliced potatoes in cold water for twenty minutes. Drain and dry. Fry in deep fat a few slices at a time. Drain on absorbent paper and sprinkle with salt.

This recipe brought back by visitors from the famous New York watering place has become popular all over New England, and in other places as well.

HASHED BROWN POTATOES

Hashed brown potatoes were called "scootin' along the shore" by fishermen who often prepared them in the galley as they fished offshore.

1/4 cup bacon fat
1 cup sliced onions
4 cups diced raw potatoes

1 teaspoon salt
1/4 teaspoon pepper

Heat the fat very hot and add the onions and potatoes with the seasonings. Cover and cook slowly until the fat is absorbed and the potatoes are tender. Then uncover and brown. Serves six.

POTATO CAKES

Boil the potatoes and drain. Mash with a little milk, salt, pepper, and minced boiled onion. Make into small cakes and put in the pan with the roast half an hour before serving. When brown, drain and serve with the meat.

SCALLOPED POTATOES

Peel and slice thinly six medium potatoes. Put a layer of potatoes in a buttered baking dish; cover with salt, pepper, and flour. Add another layer of potatoes and seasonings. Fill the dish to the top with milk, and bake one to one and a half hours in a slow oven, 325 degrees F., until the potatoes are tender and the top browned. One slice of onion may be added. Serves four to six.

MASHED SWEET POTATOES

Boil sweet potatoes, drain, and mash. Season with salt, pepper, dash of nutmeg, butter, and milk. Beat well until smooth. The potatoes may be piled in a buttered casserole and covered with marshmallows, or just brushed with melted butter, and browned in a hot oven, 425 degrees F.

BAKED SWEET POTATOES

Cut cold boiled sweet potatoes in quarter-inch slices. Put in a buttered casserole, spread with butter, sprinkle with maple sugar or brown sugar, and salt and pepper. Bake in a slow oven, 325 degrees F., one hour, or until the potatoes are browned and the sugar is melted.

EGGPLANT FRITTERS

Pare and boil a medium eggplant fifteen minutes, or until tender. Drain and mash. Add one beaten egg, one teaspoon salt, and flour enough to make a dough that will drop from a spoon. Fry in hot fat. Serves six.

PORTUGUESE STUFFED PEPPERS

6 green peppers	1 teaspoon salt
1 cup mushrooms, sliced	1/4 teaspoon pepper
3 tablespoons butter	Dash of cayenne
2 cups bread crumbs	6 slices bacon
1 cup white sauce	

Dip the green peppers in hot water. Slip off the skins. Remove the top and seeds. Sauté the mushrooms in the butter, add the bread crumbs, white sauce, and seasonings. Stuff the peppers and place them in a buttered baking dish with a slice of bacon on each. Bake in a hot oven, 400 degrees F., thirty minutes or until tender. Serves six.

SAVORY APPLES

6 apples	1/4 teaspoon salt
1 cup bread crumbs	1/4 teaspoon paprika
1/2 teaspoon thyme	1/2 cup cream
1/2 teaspoon minced parsley	2 tablespoons butter
1 onion, minced	

Peel and slice the apples into a buttered baking dish. Add the seasonings, pour the cream over the apples, and dot with butter. Bake in a moderate oven, 350 degrees F., for half an hour or until the apples are tender. Serve with roast meat. When planned for roast lamb, use half a teaspoon of mint in place of the thyme. Serves six.

8. THE SALLET BOWL

Just as every English country house had its formal herb garden, every New England housewife planted marjoram, thyme, summer savory, sage, caraway, and other herbs to dry for winter use. In the shed chamber along with strings of onions and apples she hung bunches of sweet herbs and on the kitchen window sill kept pots of parsley and chives. Oil and vinegar with mixed herbs were used as a dressing for sallets of lettuce, chicory, watercress, dandelion, and other greens and vegetables. Although the word sallet literally means salted, as early as the seventeenth century it had become the name for greens used as a relish.

In many New England homes a bowl of pickled beets, a dish of onions or cucumbers sliced in vinegar and oil was as indispensable a part of the meal as the main dish. These simple salads of early times were displaced by elaborate concoctions in the form of butterflies, candles, and geometrical designs during the genteel 1860s when cooking schools and salad clubs first came into vogue. But to a real salad lover in New England, a bowl of mixed salad greens with a simple oil and vinegar dressing has no equal.

The basic rule for all green salads is to have the greens clean and crisp, with all hard or discolored parts removed. There was an ancient superstition that lettuce should be gathered only between dawn and sunrise when the witches that frolic in the fields at night had all disappeared, and before the little devils that lived in the plants during the day arrived. It is true that greens gathered early in the morning when the dew is on them keep their crispness longer.

In cutting greens for a mixed salad use kitchen shears so as not to bruise the leaves and make the salad soggy. Have the greens crisp and dry and cut them in medium-sized pieces that can be handled easily when eating, but not so small they will mush up. Add juicy vegetables like peeled ripe tomatoes last.

French dressing made with pure olive oil and wine vinegar is perfect for mixed salads. Excellent dressings can also be made with vegetable oils and mild vinegars. In dressing the salad, use just enough to lightly coat the leaves.

New England housewives made salad vinegar from cider or wine left over at mealtimes. They made herb vinegars of tarragon, parsley, mint, dill, and caraway, and in the old days, of sweet herbs like rose, elder flower, lavender, and rosemary. They also concocted mixtures of dried herbs for salads and seasonings. If you are fortunate enough to have an herb garden you may experiment with dried herbs; but you will find excellent combinations of them in most stores.

Grandmother also made sour cream dressing, mayonnaise, and boiled dressings of all sorts. Cream dressing made with either sour or sweet cream was the simplest of these and is excellent with either string beans or cucumbers. Today the art of making mayonnaise at home is almost lost, but many of us remember as children helping mother by stirring the salad oil drop by drop into egg yolk and worrying for fear the mixture would curdle and mother would scold. This dressing is properly made in small quantities. Gourmets say it should be used within two days if it is to be enjoyed at its best.

BASIC RECIPE FOR FRENCH DRESSING

1/3 cup vinegar	1/8 teaspoon mustard
1 cup olive or salad oil	1/2 teaspoon paprika
1/2 teaspoon salt	1/4 teaspoon sugar
1/4 teaspoon pepper	Mix all the ingredients and shake well.

HERB VINEGAR

Use the leafy tops of the plants just before they begin to flower. Pack loosely in a widemouthed jar, bruising slightly. Bring either cider or white wine vinegar to a boil and fill the jars to within an inch of the top. Cover tightly and leave for ten days in a warm place, shaking each day. Strain out the herbs, fill the jar with fresh herbs, and cover with the same liquid. Leave for another ten days, then strain.

The herbs used for making the vinegar may be covered with plain vinegar and kept to be cut up in salads during the winter.

If dried herbs are used for making vinegar, fill the jar one-quarter full, and fill to the top with boiled vinegar. Let stand ten days, then strain and filter.

CHEF'S SALAD

Lettuce	Cucumbers
Endive	Green pepper
Watercress	Radishes
Onion	Celery
Tomatoes	

Cut crisp greens in pieces and toss lightly with minced onion. Cut unpeeled tomatoes in eighths, slice either peeled or unpeeled cucumbers, cut green peppers in strips, slice the radishes, dice the celery, and arrange these on top of the chilled greens. Sprinkle with salt, add French dressing and salad herbs. Toss the salad just before serving at the table. For a more hearty supper salad, add julienne chicken, tongue, ham, veal, anchovies, or sardines.

MRS. HARLAND'S LETTUCE SALAD

Head lettuce

2 hard-cooked eggs

1/2 teaspoon salt

1 teaspoon sugar

1 teaspoon pepper

1/2 teaspoon prepared mustard

2 teaspoons salad oil

4 teaspoons vinegar

Clove of garlic

Clean and chill the lettuce. Rub the egg yolks to a powder, add the dry ingredients and the mustard and salad oil. Let the dressing stand five minutes, then beat in the vinegar. Rub a salad bowl with the garlic, add the chilled lettuce, the dressing, and the egg whites minced fine. Serves six.

SUMMER SALAD

Lettuce

2 teaspoons mustard leaves

Handful watercress

4 radishes, sliced

1 cucumber, sliced

3 hard-cooked eggs

2 teaspoons sugar

1 teaspoon salt

1 teaspoon pepper

1 teaspoon mustard

1/2 cup vinegar

2 tablespoons salad oil

Clove of garlic

Clean and chill the greens. Mix the dressing ingredients. Rub the salad bowl with the garlic, add the greens, sliced radishes, and cucumbers. Pour the dressing over the salad. Garnish with fennel heads and nasturtium blossoms, if these are available. Serves six.

LETTUCE SALAD WITH ROQUEFORT DRESSING

Rub the salad bowl with garlic. Cut a head of lettuce in pieces. Sprinkle with salt and half an onion, minced. Cover with Roquefort dressing.

Roquefort Dressing

1/2 pound Roquefort cheese	1 teaspoon Worcestershire sauce
1 teaspoon salt	2 cups olive oil
2 teaspoons paprika	2/3 cup vinegar

Mash the cheese and mix with the remaining ingredients. Makes about four cups of dressing.

WILTED LETTUCE OR SPINACH

To one shredded head of lettuce or one and a half pounds of fresh spinach, add half an onion, minced. Fry two or three slices of bacon, add one-fourth cup vinegar and enough salad oil to make half a cup. Season with one-half teaspoon salt, one teaspoon sugar (optional), one-half teaspoon mustard, and one-fourth teaspoon pepper. Pour hot over greens. A little sour cream may be added to the bacon fat instead of the salad oil. Serves six.

RAW VEGETABLE SALAD

For raw vegetable salad use any combination of salad greens and raw vegetables: lettuce, endive, watercress, spinach, carrots, tomatoes, cucumbers, green peppers, onion, cauliflower, and whatever else may be at hand. Mix and serve with French dressing. A good combination is one cup cauliflower, one cup carrots, one tomato, one cucumber, half a green pepper, half an onion, and one cup celery. Rub the salad bowl with garlic, add the mixed vegetables, and marinate a few minutes with French dressing. Serve on lettuce leaves with additional dressing.

MIXED VEGETABLE SALAD

Marinate two cups hot boiled potatoes in half French dressing and half mayonnaise for one hour. Season highly with salt and pepper. On a large platter arrange lettuce leaves, a ring of potatoes, and a ring of pickled beets. Fill the center with deviled eggs cut in eighths and small onions, sliced. Garnish with capers and minced parsley and pass extra French dressing. Serves six.

TOMATO SALAD

6 tomatoes	1 teaspoon mustard
2 hard-cooked eggs	2 teaspoons salad oil
1/2 teaspoon salt	1 egg, beaten
1/4 teaspoon cayenne	1/2 cup vinegar
1/2 teaspoon sugar	

Peel and chill the tomatoes. Rub the cooked egg yolks with the dry ingredients. Add the salad oil and the raw egg beaten to a froth, then add the vinegar. Serve over the chilled tomatoes. Serves six. The same dressing may be used for celery.

CREAM DRESSING

To half a cup of sour or sweet cream add one tablespoon vinegar, salt and pepper to taste, and one-fourth teaspoon dry mustard. Stir well.

STRING BEAN SALAD

Cut cooked string beans into one-inch pieces. To two cups of beans, add one tablespoon minced onion, one tablespoon minced green pepper, and salt and pepper to taste. Serve with either cream or French dressing. Serves four.

MAYONNAISE

Allow one and a half cups of salad oil for each egg yolk. Add the oil drop by drop, stirring with a fork or beating with a beater. When all the salad oil has been added, season with one teaspoon salt, three-fourths teaspoon mustard, one-half teaspoon sugar, one-fourth teaspoon cayenne, and two tablespoons lemon juice or vinegar.

POTATO SALAD

Potato salad, a favorite in the old days as it is now, deserves more attention than most cooks give it. In grandmother's day, the potatoes were boiled with their jackets on, peeled, and marinated in French dressing. Now many cooks prefer to use a marinade of half French dressing and half mayonnaise. The potatoes should be peeled rapidly and covered with the dressing while they are still hot. They may be peeled first and then cooked, but in this case great care must be taken not to overcook them or the salad will become mushy. Making salad of leftover potatoes is not so satisfactory because the dressing does not go through them as well as it should.

You might just as well leave the potatoes themselves out of the salad as try to make potato salad without onion. It does not need very much, but the onion flavor is essential. Mince the onion very fine—no one likes to take a big bite of raw onion—and mix it in well. Turn the potatoes over and over in the marinade, using a fork or a spoon, but being careful not to break the potatoes into small pieces. Each piece should be entirely covered with dressing. Then let the salad stand for several hours until the flavor goes through each piece of potato. Taste and add more salt if necessary. Then add more mayonnaise and other seasonings.

2 cups hot diced potatoes	1 cup celery
2 tablespoons minced onion	2 tablespoons minced green
French dressing	pepper
Mayonnaise	2 teaspoons minced parsley
	Salt and pepper

Marinate the hot potatoes and minced onion in half French dressing and half mayonnaise. When cool, add the remaining ingredients, salt and pepper to taste, and more mayonnaise. Serve either with or without lettuce. Serves four.

POTATO SALAD WITH BOILED DRESSING

2 cups hot boiled potatoes	1 dill pickle, diced
Boiled dressing	1 hard-cooked egg, diced
1/2 cup diced celery	Salt and pepper
1 tablespoon minced parsley	

Mix the potatoes with the boiled dressing and let stand one hour. Add the celery, parsley, pickle, and egg. Taste for salt and pepper, and add more dressing. Serve on lettuce leaves. Serves four.

MRS. WHITCHER'S BOILED SALAD DRESSING

1/2 cup vinegar

2 eggs

1 teaspoon salt

1/2 teaspoon mustard

1/4 teaspoon pepper

1 tablespoon sugar

Butter, size of an egg

Cream

Beat first six ingredients together in a bowl placed over a dish of cold water. Set mixture over low heat and cook until the cold water boils and the contents of the bowl thicken. Place butter on top of the hot dressing. When the butter melts, beat the dressing smooth with a rotary beater, adding cream until the consistency is proper.

MRS. HARLAND'S CABBAGE SALAD

Shred one small cabbage. Bring one cup vinegar, one tablespoon butter, and one tablespoon sugar to a boil. Pour over the cabbage and let cool. Add salt and pepper and two tablespoons sour cream just before serving. Serves six to eight.

EGG SALAD

Dice six hard-cooked eggs and shred half a head of lettuce. Mix these and serve with a French dressing to which an extra teaspoon of sugar has been added. Salt and pepper to taste. Serves six.

EGG AND WATERCRESS SALAD

Stuff six hard-cooked eggs by mixing the yolks with two tablespoons mayonnaise, one teaspoon curry powder, and salt and pepper. Rub a salad bowl with garlic, put in chilled watercress, stuffed eggs cut in quarters, and serve with French dressing. Serves six.

LOBSTER SALAD

Marinate two cups diced lobster meat in one-third cup French dressing. Drain, add salt and pepper to taste, and serve on lettuce leaves with mayonnaise. Serves four.

Lobster salad may have hard-cooked eggs and celery added, but no true New Englander likes to spoil the taste of lobster with foreign foods. Lobster salads are garnished with either the small lobster claws, capers, parsley, or perhaps slices of unpeeled tomatoes, celery curls, and olives. Sometimes the dressing in which the lobster is marinated is made with lemon juice instead of vinegar, and often the coral is mashed into the mayonnaise.

SHRIMP SALAD

Marinate three cups of fresh boiled shrimp or canned shrimp in French dressing. Drain. Arrange on lettuce leaves and serve with mayonnaise, garnished with parsley, celery curls, or hard-cooked eggs. Serves six.

Like lobster salad, shrimp salad has many variations none of which appeal to the old-timer who wants his shrimp salad to be just shrimp. For those who like to experiment, celery, cucumbers, or crushed pineapple may be added to the marinated shrimp, usually allowing three parts shrimp to one of other ingredients.

CRAB MEAT SALAD

Mix two cups flaked crab meat and one cup celery with mayonnaise. Serve on lettuce leaves with a spoonful of mayonnaise on top, and dust with paprika. Serves six.

MOLDED SALMON SALAD

1 cup cooked salmon	1/2 teaspoon salt
3/4 cup milk	1/4 cup vinegar
1 tablespoon flour	1 1/2 tablespoons sugar
1 egg, beaten	Cayenne
1 teaspoon mustard	1 tablespoon gelatin

Remove the bones from the salmon, and flake. Cook the milk, flour, egg, and seasonings in a double boiler until thick. Add the gelatin softened in cold water. When dissolved, add the salmon and turn into a buttered mold. Chill and serve with cucumber sauce.

Cucumber Sauce

1/2 cup cream, whipped
1/2 cup mayonnaise
1/2 teaspoon pepper

1/2 teaspoon salt
1 diced cucumber

Mix all the ingredients together well. Serves four.

HALIBUT SALAD

Rub a thick slice of halibut with salt and lemon juice and cook it in a court bouillon made of one and a half cups water, one carrot, one onion, two cloves, and six peppercorns. Remove the fish when tender, chill, and flake. Mix with one-half cup sliced radishes for each two cups fish, and marinate in French dressing. Serve on lettuce leaves with cucumber sauce. Serves four.

MAINE JELLIED SHRIMP AND EGG

1/2 teaspoon pickle spice
1 cup boiling water
1 package lemon gelatin
1 cup cold water
Juice 1 lemon
1 cup shrimps

1 green pepper, minced
1/2 cup minced celery
1/2 pimiento, minced
3 hard-cooked eggs
Parsley
Lettuce

Add the pickle spice to the boiling water, cook five minutes, and strain. Pour over the gelatin and stir well. When dissolved, add the cold water and lemon juice. Butter individual molds. Put a whole shrimp in the bottom of each. Quarter the rest of the shrimps and mix with the green pepper, celery, and pimiento. Fill the molds, cover with gelatin, and chill. Serve on lettuce leaves garnished with parsley and the hard-cooked eggs. Serves four.

RHODE ISLAND CHICKEN SALAD

Mix equal parts of cold diced chicken and celery. Make a dressing of three egg yolks, one cup salad oil mixed until smooth, one teaspoon sugar, salt to taste, one cup vinegar, one-half teaspoon pepper, and one cup whipped cream.

TONGUE SALAD

3 cups diced cooked tongue	3 dill pickles, diced
6 hard-cooked eggs	Mayonnaise
1 onion, minced	Salt and pepper

Mix the tongue, eggs, onion, and pickles. Add mayonnaise and salt and pepper to taste. For a more highly seasoned salad, add a little mustard and celery salt. Serves six.

ETHEL'S FRUIT SALAD DRESSING

1 egg	1/2 cup sugar
1 tablespoon vinegar	1 cup whipped cream

Cook the first three ingredients until thick. When slightly cool, fold in the whipped cream.

SOUR CREAM DRESSING FOR FRUIT SALAD

The secret of making this dressing lies in having the cream very cold and in not beating too long, or it will turn into butter. Whip one-half cup sour cream. Stir in one tablespoon sugar, one-fourth teaspoon salt, one-eighth teaspoon pepper, two tablespoons lemon juice.

APPLE SALAD

2 cups cubed apples   1 cup celery
Juice 1/2 lemon   Boiled dressing
1/2 cup walnuts, chopped

Sprinkle the apples with the lemon juice to keep them from turning brown. Mix all the ingredients with boiled dressing, and serve on lettuce leaves. Serves six.

APPLE AND CABBAGE SALAD

Shred a small cabbage, add two cups red apples, diced without peeling and sprinkled with lemon juice, one cup seedless raisins, and one-half cup French dressing. Serves eight.

JELLIED CRANBERRY SALAD

To one package lemon gelatin add the juice of one-half lemon, one-half cup diced celery, and one and one-half cups sweetened cranberry sauce. Chill and serve on lettuce leaves with mayonnaise. Serves four.

GRAPE SALAD

Peel and remove the seeds from Tokay or Malaga grapes. Place on chilled lettuce leaves and serve with a French dressing to which a few drops of Worcestershire sauce, one-fourth teaspoon horseradish, and one-half teaspoon sugar have been added.

MOCK CRAB

1/2 pound old cheese   1 teaspoon salt
1 hard-cooked egg   1 teaspoon sugar
1 teaspoon cayenne   1 tablespoon vinegar
1 tablespoon salad oil   1 teaspoon minced onion

Grate the cheese. Rub the egg yolk into a paste with the cayenne, oil, salt, and sugar. Add the vinegar and onion, and mix in the cheese. A cup of cold minced chicken may be added. Serve either on lettuce leaves as a salad or spread on crackers for cocktails. Serves four.

9. BREAD TINS AND GEM PANS

Y ou would be amused, my dear, if you could come in spirit to this large white house where I am staying for a few weeks," a visitor in a village in the Berkshires wrote to her sister in Dublin, Ireland, in the late eighties. "Twice a week, in the afternoon, Clara's aunt dons a long starched apron—lace trimmed, if you please—and with her mending sits in the kitchen to watch loaves of bread rise. She actually appears to enjoy it, and lets nothing interfere with what she evidently considers a pleasure, not a duty!"

Observant as the Irish guest was, she missed the point, not realizing the deep satisfaction her hostess felt when the bread was at last in the tins. She knew nothing of the work involved in baking bread for a large family before yeast cakes were sold at every country crosscorners.

Making yeast from hops and potatoes was a tedious task, but an improvement from the days when every capable New England housewife brewed beer and saved "good lively emptyin's" from the keg to raise bread.

There have been other forward steps in home breadmaking since that time, short cuts in sponging and methods of raising, and changes in flours. White flour was very scarce and so precious that it was saved for the finest pastries. It was ground at the moss-covered gristmill from wheat raised on the home place or purchased from a farmer. Barrels of bread flour did not roll into grandmother's kitchen until after the first fashion books reached the center table in her shuttered parlor.

But the gristmills with their water-driven granite grinding stones turned out corn meal of fine texture, unsurpassed flavor, and often as white as wheat flour. Corn meal was used in many delicious ways. For supper on a cold winter night there was nothing better than a spider corn-cake, crisply brown on top and bottom, with the center cooked to creamy custardlike perfection. Sometimes the recipes were rhymed, as in this one for Bay State Brown Bread:

> *"Three cups of corn meal,*
> *One of rye flour;*
> *Three cups of sweet milk,*
> *One cup of sour;*
> *A cup of molasses*
> *To render it sweet,*
> *Two teaspoons of soda*
> *Will make it complete."*

The old jingle tells us what ingredients our great-grandmothers used in making that legitimate descendant of "ryaninjun"—the steamed brown bread that always accompanies the Saturday night beans to New England tables. For the past century, brown bread has not been brown bread unless it has contained at least one cup of the whole wheat flour named for its advocate, Dr. Sylvester Graham.

In the north of England, brewis was a pottage made of crusts of bread with fat broth poured over them. In New England the term was applied to crusts of rye and Indian, or other bread, softened with milk and eaten with molasses, maple syrup, or sugar and cream.

An old-time bread that many of us know nothing about is still made at Three Rivers Farm in the coastal region of New Hampshire. Two or three generations ago, salt-rising bread was commonly served on New England tables. But the art of bringing the batter to the required light and foamy stage and keeping the stiffened dough warm enough to rise without the use of yeast is almost forgotten today.

The recipe for Bath buns was brought from England many years ago. These buns are still made on special occasions by the great-granddaughter of the woman who wrote the rule in spidery handwriting on a small piece of yellowed paper. The pounds and gills of the original recipe are now translated into cups and spoons.

Rusks, baked in cake tins, and broken or cut into wedges when served, are as popular today as they were when Lady Pepperell, wife of the hero of Louisburg, served them in the ancient mansion in Kittery, Maine. The same recipe used by the famous eighteenth-century hostess has survived the years. We give it here, with little idea that you will try to make rusks in such quantities. "To make rusks, take 1 pd. of flower, 1 pd. of sugar, 3 pints of milk, 20 eggs, half a pint of yeast. The butter and the sugar put into the milk and make it bloodwarm, the eggs and the yeast mix together and work it well, let it rise well, bake it." We have included a modern recipe for making rusks.

A rich yeast batter containing sugar and eggs formed the basis of the original Sally Lunn, the famous teacake, named for the woman who first made and sold it in Bath, England. But the American Sally Lunn is nothing more or less than a rich muffin or gem batter which is baked in shallow cake tins. Originally, the name muffin was given to batter made light by yeast and other leavening agents, while gems meant small cakes made from batter lightened by the expansion of air beaten into eggs. Today, the terms are applied interchangeably to the popular breakfast cakes that are baked in small tins.

In Chapter 1, there are directions for making some of the old corn breads and johnnycakes. The following recipes are of later date, but all are of New England origin. The first one is for a corn bread which is famous in Rockport, Massachusetts. The story goes that it was named for the woman who first made it. If she ever was away from home when her husband arrived, you could hear him booming, "Where am 'er, damn 'er?" Finally she was known as Amadama.

AMADAMA BREAD

1/2 cup corn meal	2 teaspoons salt
2 cups boiling water	2 yeast cakes
2 tablespoons shortening	1/2 cup lukewarm water
1/2 cup molasses	White flour

Stir the corn meal into the boiling water, and add the shortening, molasses, and salt. Soften the yeast cakes in the lukewarm water. When the corn meal mixture has cooled to blood-warm, stir in the dissolved yeast. Add enough white flour to make a dough you can knead, place in a greased bowl, cover with a clean cloth, and let the dough rise until double in bulk. Then cut the dough down and let it rise again for forty-five minutes. Turn it on a floured board and knead well. Shape into two loaves and put them in greased bread tins. Let them rise until very light. Bake in a hot oven, 425 degrees F., for fifteen minutes. Lower the heat to 375 degrees and bake forty-five minutes more. Take the loaves from the tins, brush the crusts with melted butter, and set the bread on a rack to cool.

CORN MEAL DODGERS

4 cups milk	2 tablespoons butter
4 cups corn meal	1/2 yeast cake
2 tablespoons sugar	1/4 cup lukewarm water

Scald the milk and turn it over the corn meal. Add the sugar and butter and the yeast cake dissolved in lukewarm water. Let the mixture stand overnight. In the morning, beat down and let it rise again. Heat a dripping pan and grease well. Drop the mixture a spoonful at a time, about one inch apart. Bake in a hot oven, 450 degrees F., for about twenty minutes. These cakes will be rough on top. They should be eaten piping hot.

AUNT HAT'S CORNCAKE

The recipes which follow are for corn breads and corncakes in which baking powders, or similar substances, are used for leavening agents. The first recipe comes from the White Mountains.

1 egg	1/2 teaspoon salt
1 cup sugar	1 cup flour
1 cup corn meal	1 cup milk
2 teaspoons baking powder	1 tablespoon melted butter

Mix the egg with the sugar and beat thoroughly. Add the corn meal. Sift the baking powder and salt with the flour, and turn into the mixing bowl with the other ingredients. Stir in the milk and beat until thoroughly mixed. Add the melted butter last, and beat until the dough is smooth. Bake in a moderately hot oven, 400 degrees F., for half an hour. Cut in squares and serve piping hot.

OLD-FASHIONED MOLASSES JONNE CAKE

1 egg	1/4 cup molasses
1/4 cup sugar	1 cup thick sour milk
1/4 teaspoon salt	1 cup white flour
1 teaspoon soda	1 cup corn meal

Beat the egg and sugar, and add the salt. Dissolve the soda in a little water and add to the molasses, stirring until it foams. Combine with the egg and sugar mixture. Add the sour milk, flour, and corn meal, and mix thoroughly. Bake like Aunt Hat's corncake above.

BAY STATE APPLE JOHNNYCAKE

2 tablespoons sugar	2 cups white meal
1/2 teaspoon salt	Milk
4 teaspoons baking powder	3 tart apples

Sift the sugar, salt, and baking powder with half a cup of the meal. Add this to the rest of the meal, which is not sifted. Mix with enough milk to make a soft cakelike dough. Pare and slice the apples and stir into the dough. Bake in a shallow tin in a moderately hot oven, 400 degrees F., for half an hour.

BLUEBERRY JOHNNYCAKE

1/2 cup shortening	1/4 teaspoon salt
1/2 cup sugar	1/2 cup white flour
1 egg, well beaten	1 1/2 cups blueberries or
1 cup milk	huckleberries
1 1/2 cups corn meal	Dash of nutmeg
3 teaspoons baking powder	

Cream the shortening and sugar, and add the beaten egg and milk. Stir in the corn meal. Sift the baking powder and salt with the white flour, and stir into the corn meal mixture gradually. Lightly flour the blueberries, and mix them into the batter without breaking the berries. Add the nutmeg last. Bake in a hot oven, 425 degrees F., for half an hour. Serve very hot with butter or cream.

PARKER HOUSE CORN ROLLS

1 1/4 cups wheat flour	1 tablespoon sugar
1/4 cups corn meal	2 tablespoons butter
2 teaspoons baking powder	1 egg
1/2 teaspoon salt	1/2 cup milk

Sift the dry ingredients and work the butter into them. Beat the egg and combine it with the milk. Stir into the first mixture. Turn quickly onto a floured board, roll out, and cut in rounds. Turn over like Parker House rolls, placing a small piece of butter under each turned-over piece. Brush with milk and bake in a quick oven, 400 degrees F., for fifteen to twenty minutes.

MOTHER'S SPIDER CORNCAKE

This recipe is a favorite with a family in Wells, Maine.

1 1/4 cups corn meal	2 cups sour milk
1/4 cup flour	2 eggs
1/4 cup sugar	1 1/2 tablespoons butter
1 teaspoon salt	1 cup sweet milk
1 teaspoon soda	

Sift together the corn meal, flour, sugar, and salt. Dissolve the soda in a little water and stir into the sour milk. Beat the eggs and add to the sour milk. Mix with the dry ingredients. Melt the butter in an iron spider which has been heated thoroughly. Pour the batter into the spider, and turn the cup of sweet milk over it. Do not stir. Put the spider in a hot oven, 450 degrees F. At the end of ten minutes, lower the heat to 350 degrees and bake forty minutes longer. Cut in wedges and serve piping hot with butter and maple syrup.

STEAMED BOSTON BROWN BREAD

1 cup corn meal	1 teaspoon soda
1 cup rye flour	1/2 cup molasses
1 cup graham flour	2 cups sour milk
1 teaspoon salt	1 cup raisins

Mix the dry ingredients. Dissolve the soda in a little water and stir into the molasses. Combine with the sour milk, and then mix the liquid into the dry ingredients. Lightly flour the raisins, and add to the mixture. Mix the batter thoroughly, and pour into two greased molds with tight covers. Put them in a kettle of boiling water and steam for three hours. Remove the loaves from the molds, and place them in the oven for ten minutes to form a crust. It is very important to remember that brown bread should never be cut with a knife, it should be sliced with the aid of a string.

STRAIGHT-DOUGH WHITE BREAD

2 cups milk

2 yeast cakes

1/2 cup lukewarm water

2 teaspoons salt

2 tablespoons sugar

2 tablespoons melted shortening

6-7 cups sifted flour

Scald the milk. When blood-warm, add the yeast cakes which have been dissolved in the lukewarm water. Add the salt, sugar, and shortening. Add enough flour to make a dough that will not cling to the bowl. Turn the dough onto a floured board, and knead in flour until the dough feels smooth and elastic. Grease a large mixing bowl and put the kneaded dough in it. Cover and put in a warm place to rise until the dough doubles in bulk. Cut the dough down and let it rise again. Then turn onto a board, and cut into two parts. Mold, and cut the dough again. Shape into four mounds. Put two in a well-greased loaf tin, and two in another tin. Brush the loaves with melted fat. Let them rise about one hour, or until double in bulk. Prick the tops with a fork two or three times. Bake for fifteen minutes in a hot oven, 400 degrees F. Then lower the heat to 350 degrees and bake forty-five minutes longer. Take the loaves from the oven and place on racks to cool.

RAISED GRAHAM BREAD

1 1/2 teaspoons lard

1 1/2 cups scalded milk

1/2 yeast cake

1/3 cup lukewarm water

3/4 teaspoon salt

1 1/2 teaspoons brown sugar

Pinch of soda

1 1/2 teaspoons molasses

2 cups wheat flour

2 cups graham flour

Put the lard in the scalded milk and, when lukewarm, add the half yeast cake which has been dissolved in the lukewarm water. Add the salt and brown sugar. Stir the soda into the molasses, and add to the liquid mixture. Then stir in the sifted wheat flour and graham flour. Let the dough rise overnight. In the morning, turn onto a floured molding board and knead quickly. Shape into two small loaves and let rise until double in bulk. Bake in a moderate oven, 375 degrees F., for 1 hour.

ALMA'S WHOLE WHEAT NUT BREAD

2 cups warm water	5 cups whole wheat flour
2 tablespoons shortening	2 teaspoons salt
4 tablespoons molasses	1 cup, or more, white flour
1 yeast cake	1/2 pound chopped nut meats

To the warm water, add the shortening and molasses. When blood-warm, crumble in the yeast cake and stir until dissolved. Stir in the whole wheat flour. Sift the salt with the white flour, and add. Turn the dough onto a floured board and knead it well. If sticky, add more white flour. Put the dough in a greased bowl and let it rise two and one-half hours. Turn again onto the board, knead lightly, and spread until the dough forms a thin sheet. Sprinkle the nut meats over it. Roll up like a jelly roll, fold over the ends, and knead again. Let it rise fifteen minutes. Mold into two loaves and put into well-greased pans. Let loaves rise to double their bulk, and bake in a moderate oven, 375 degrees F., for one hour.

BERWICK SQUASH BREAD

1 cup milk	1/2 teaspoon salt
1 1/2 cups sieved squash	1 yeast cake
4 tablespoons lard	1 cup lukewarm water
1/2 cup sugar	6 cups flour

Scald the milk and pour over the squash. Add the lard, sugar, and salt. When lukewarm, add the yeast cake dissolved in the lukewarm water. Stir in the flour. Turn the dough onto a molding board and knead well. Put in a greased bowl and let it rise overnight. In the morning, cut down the dough and let it rise again. Mold into two loaves, and let them rise until light. Bake one hour in a moderate oven, 375 degrees F.

RUTH'S WALNUT GRAHAM BREAD

1/2 cup sugar
1/2 cup molasses
1 teaspoon soda
1 cup sweet milk

1 cup white flour
1/2 teaspoon salt
1 1/2 cups graham flour
1/2 cup walnuts, chopped

Mix the sugar and molasses. Dissolve the soda in a little cold water and add to the milk. Sift the white flour with the salt and mix with the graham flour. Stir into the liquid mixture and beat well. Add the walnuts last. Turn into a loaf pan and bake in a moderate oven, 375 degrees F., for one hour.

JACK-O'-LANTERN NUT BREAD

1 teaspoon soda
1/2 cup molasses
1 teaspoon salt
1/2 cup sugar

1 cup white flour
2 cups graham flour
1 cup nut meats, chopped
2 cups milk

Dissolve the soda in a little warm water and mix with the molasses. Add the salt to the sugar and mix with the molasses. Sift the white flour and combine it with the graham flour. Stir in the nut meats. Then add the flour and nut mixture to the molasses alternately with the milk. Turn the mixture into a loaf tin and bake one hour in a moderate oven, 350 degrees F.

DOROTHY'S NUT BREAD

4 cups flour
4 rounded teaspoons
   baking powder
1 cup sugar

1 teaspoon salt
1 egg
1 scant cup milk
1 cup nut meats, chopped

Sift together the flour, baking powder, sugar, and salt. Beat the egg and add with the milk to the dry ingredients. Flour the nuts lightly and add. Mix thoroughly and turn into a greased loaf tin. Let stand twenty minutes. Bake one hour in a moderate oven, 350 degrees F.

BEA'S DATE NUT BREAD

2 eggs	1 teaspoon salt
1 cup sugar	2 cups milk
4 cups white flour	1 cup nut meats, chopped
4 teaspoons baking powder	1 package dates

Beat the eggs and add the sugar. Sift the flour with the baking powder and salt, and add to the egg and sugar mixture alternately with the milk. Add the chopped nuts and the dates cut in small pieces. Turn into two greased loaf tins. Let stand for three-quarters of an hour. Bake one hour in a moderate oven, 350 degrees F.

MOTHER'S BLUEBERRY BREAD

3 cups flour	2 eggs
4 1/2 teaspoons baking powder	2 tablespoons molasses
1 teaspoon salt	1 1/4 cups milk
3 tablespoons sugar	1/4 cup melted shortening
1 cup blueberries	

Sift the flour, baking powder, and salt. Add the sugar and blueberries. Beat the eggs and combine with the molasses, milk, and melted shortening. Stir into the other ingredients. Turn into a long bread tin. Bake one hour in a moderate oven, 350 degrees F.

QUICK CLOVER-LEAF ROLLS

Any good bread dough makes good rolls. But there are times when we want something special, rolls that are a little sweeter or a little richer than those we ordinarily bake.

3/4 cup shortening
1 cup boiling water
1 cup cold water
2 eggs, well beaten
3/4 cup sugar
2 yeast cakes

1/2 cup lukewarm water
1 tablespoon salt
7 cups flour
Melted butter
1 egg
Pinch of salt

Put the shortening into the boiling water. When melted, add the cold water. Beat the eggs well and add them to the liquid. Add the sugar and the yeast cakes which have been dissolved in the lukewarm water. Sift the salt and flour and stir into the other ingredients. Grease a large bowl and turn the dough into it. Put in the refrigerator. About three hours before you want to bake the rolls, turn the dough onto a floured breadboard, and mold it. Cut off small pieces of dough and shape them into balls about the size of a walnut. Roll them in melted butter. Butter muffin tins and put three balls in each tin. Let them rise two and one-half hours. Beat the egg and add a pinch of salt. Glaze the tops of the rolls with this mixture. Let them stand ten minutes. Bake at 425 degrees F., for twenty to twenty-five minutes. Makes one and a half dozen rolls.

WHITE MOUNTAIN ROLLS

1/4 cup shortening
1 cup scalded milk
1 yeast cake
1/4 cup lukewarm water

4 cups flour
4 tablespoons sugar
1 teaspoon salt
1 egg white, beaten stiff

Melt the shortening and add to the scalded milk. When bloodwarm, add the yeast cake dissolved in the lukewarm water. Sift the flour, sugar, and salt, and stir into the liquid mixture. Fold in the beaten egg white. Let the dough rise until light. Cut down, turn on a molding board, and shape into long rolls. Place on a greased pan. Let rise one hour or until light. Bake in a hot oven, 400 degrees F., for twenty-five minutes. Make one dozen long rolls.

GOLDEN-GLOW RAISED BISCUIT

1/2 yeast cake	3/4 cups brown sugar
1/2 cup lukewarm water	1 teaspoon salt
1/2 cup shortening	1 cup sieved cooked squash
1 cup scalded milk	6 cups sifted flour

Dissolve the half yeast cake in the lukewarm water. Melt the shortening in the scalded milk. When the milk is lukewarm, add the yeast. Mix the brown sugar and salt with the squash and stir into the milk. Add flour enough to make a dough that can be handled. Turn on a floured board and knead. Put the dough in a greased bowl and let it rise overnight. In the morning, knead again and roll to one inch thick. Use a round cutter to shape the biscuits. Set them close together on a round baking pan and let them rise until very light. Brush with melted butter and bake twenty minutes in a hot oven, 400 degrees F. Makes two dozen biscuits.

APPLE BISCUITS

1 cup milk	1/2 teaspoon salt
1 tablespoon butter	1 cup grated apple
1 tablespoon sugar	1/2 teaspoon soda
1/2 yeast cake	Butter
1/4 cup lukewarm water	Maple sugar
2 cups flour	

Scald the milk, add the butter and sugar. When lukewarm, add the half yeast cake dissolved in the lukewarm water. Sift one cup of the flour and the salt, and gradually stir into the liquid mixture. Beat until very light and let rise four to five hours. Stir in the grated apple, and add the second cup of flour sifted with the soda. Let rise one hour longer. Mold and shape into flat round cakes. Place them in a pan, and let rise until light. Bake twenty minutes in a moderate oven, 375 degrees F. Split the biscuits while hot, spread with butter, and sprinkle with maple sugar. Makes one and a half dozen biscuits.

BATH BUNS

3/4 cup sugar	1 tablespoon rum
1/2 teaspoon salt	1 tablespoon rosewater or vanilla
4 cups flour	8 eggs
1 yeast cake	2 tablespoons caraway seeds

Sift the sugar and salt with two cups of the flour. Soften the yeast cake in the rum and rosewater. Beat the eggs and add the dissolved yeast and the rest of the flour. Let the mixture rise two hours, then combine with the first mixture. Add one tablespoon of the caraway seeds and mix thoroughly. Drop by spoonfuls onto a greased baking tin and sprinkle with the other tablespoon of caraway seeds. Let the buns rise until very light. Bake twenty minutes in a hot oven, 400 degrees F.

HOT CROSS BUNS

This simple version of the famous hot cross buns is very delicious and is easy to make.

1/4 teaspoon salt	1 egg
3 cups flour	1/2 cup currants
1/2 yeast cake	Pinch of ground cloves
1 tablespoon lukewarm water	1/2 teaspoon cinnamon
1 cup lukewarm milk	1 teaspoon grated lemon peel
3 tablespoons butter	1 egg, beaten
1/2 cup sugar	

Sift the salt with the flour. Dissolve the half yeast cake in the lukewarm water and add to the lukewarm milk. Mix the dry and liquid ingredients and let the batter rise for two hours. Mix the butter and sugar until light and creamy. Add the egg and mix thoroughly. Work into the batter. Add the currants, spices, and lemon peel. Turn the dough onto a floured board and knead well. Add more flour if necessary, but be careful to keep the dough as light as possible. Too much flour makes the buns hard. Put the dough in a greased bowl, and let it rise until double in bulk. Cut down and turn onto the board and make into a long roll. Cut off pieces of the dough and shape them into round buns. Place on a buttered baking sheet and let them rise until light. Brush the tops with the beaten egg. Cut a cross on the top of each bun. Bake forty minutes in a hot oven, 400 degrees F. Another method of making crosses on buns is to glaze the tops with molasses ten minutes before the baking is completed. After the buns come from the oven and are partly cooled, make on top crosses of powdered sugar moistened with water.

KITTERY POINT RUSKS

1/2 yeast cake	2 tablespoons thick cream
1/4 cup lukewarm water	2 tablespoons butter
3 tablespoons sugar	1 cup scalded milk
1/2 teaspoon salt	1 cup raisins
Pinch of ground ginger	Butter
4 cups flour	2 tablespoons sugar
2 eggs, separated	1/2 tablespoon cinnamon

Dissolve the half yeast cake in the lukewarm water. Add one of the three tablespoons of sugar and let the mixture stand for fifteen minutes. Sift the remaining two tablespoons of sugar, the salt, and ginger with the flour. Beat the yolks of the eggs and the cream with two tablespoons of butter. Gradually add this mixture to the milk cooled after scalding. Then add the yeast and flour mixture and beat until very smooth. Beat the egg whites stiff and fold in. Let the dough rise until very light. Then cut it down and stir in the raisins cut in small pieces. When well mixed, spread the dough in a square pan, and let rise until light. Sprinkle the top with bits of butter and the sugar and cinnamon mixed. Bake in a hot oven, 450 degrees F., for half an hour. Serve hot with butter.

AMERICAN SALLY LUNN

4 cups flour	1 teaspoon salt
3 tablespoons sugar	Butter the size of an egg
2 teaspoons cream of tartar	2 eggs
1 teaspoon soda	2 cups milk

Sift the dry ingredients. Melt the butter and let it cool. Beat the eggs, and combine the butter, eggs, and milk. Stir into the dry ingredients. Turn into two well-greased round tins. Bake twenty-five minutes in a hot oven, 400 degrees F. Serve piping hot with plenty of butter.

RYE MUFFINS

1 cup rye flour	2 teaspoons cream of tartar
2 cups white flour	1 tablespoon shortening
1 cup sugar	1 egg
1 teaspoon soda	Milk
3/4 teaspoon salt	

Sift together the dry ingredients. Melt the shortening and let it cool. Beat the egg and add to half a cup of the milk. Pour this slowly into the dry mixture. Add enough milk so the batter will drop from a spoon. Before the mixture is thoroughly blended, pour in the melted shortening. Stir the batter, being careful not to overmix. It should look rough, not smooth like cake batter. Fill well-greased muffin tins two-thirds full. Bake in a hot oven, 400 degrees F., from twenty to twenty-five minutes. Makes one and a half dozen muffins.

CHEESE MUFFINS

2 cups flour	1/2 cup grated sharp cheese
2 teaspoons baking powder	1 egg, beaten
1/2 teaspoon salt	1 cup milk
1/2 teaspoon paprika	3 tablespoons melted shortening

Sift the dry ingredients and add the grated cheese. Combine the beaten egg, milk, and melted shortening. Add to the dry ingredients. Stir only enough to mix. Bake for twenty-five minutes in a hot oven, 400 degrees F. Makes one dozen muffins. These muffins are an excellent accompaniment to a green tossed salad.

CRANBERRY MUFFINS

2 cups flour	1 egg
4 teaspoons baking powder	1 1/2 cups milk
1/2 cup sugar	2 tablespoons melted butter
1 teaspoon salt	1 cup cranberries, cut in halves

Mix as for Rye Muffins. Lightly flour the cranberries and add them last. Bake twenty to twenty-five minutes in a hot oven, 400 degrees F. Makes one dozen medium-sized muffins.

BLUEBERRY MUFFINS

2 cups flour	1 egg
1/2 teaspoon salt	3/4 cup milk
2 1/2 teaspoons baking powder	1/4 cup melted fat
1/2 cup sugar	3/4 cup blueberries

Mix as for Rye Muffins. Lightly flour the blueberries and add them quickly, being careful not to break the berries in mixing. Bake in a hot oven, 400 degrees F., for twenty-five minutes. Makes one dozen medium-sized muffins.

GRAHAM BLACKBERRY GEMS

3/4 cup white flour	2 teaspoons shortening, melted
3 tablespoons sugar	1 egg, beaten
1/2 teaspoon salt	1 cup milk
2 teaspoons baking powder	1/2 cup blackberries
1 1/2 cups graham flour	

Sift the first four ingredients, then mix with the graham flour. Melt the shortening and mix with the beaten egg. Add to the milk and turn the mixture into a bowl with the dry ingredients. Do not stir until the blackberries are added. The berries should be firm and not mushy. Stir the mixture lightly and quickly. Turn into greased gem pans and bake twenty minutes in a hot oven, 425 degrees F. Makes about fifteen gems.

PEARL LAKE SQUASH MUFFINS

2 cups flour	1 egg
2 teaspoons baking powder	2/3 cup milk
2 tablespoons sugar	1 tablespoon melted shortening
3/4 teaspoon salt	1 cup sieved cooked squash

Mix and sift the dry ingredients. Beat the egg and mix with the milk, shortening, and squash. Pour the second mixture into the dry ingredients and mix just enough to blend. Bake in a hot oven, 450 degrees F., for twenty to twenty-five minutes. Makes one and a half dozen medium-sized muffins.

POPOVERS

2 eggs	1 cup sifted flour
1 cup milk	1 teaspoon salt

Beat the eggs and add the milk. Add the flour sifted with the salt, a little at a time, beating the flour in with a Dover egg beater. When bubbly, pour into heavy greased muffin tins or custard cups. Bake twenty minutes in a hot oven, 450 degrees F., then lower the heat to 350 degrees and bake twenty minutes longer. Serve immediately. Makes eight large cakes.

BAKING POWDER BISCUIT

2 cups flour	2 tablespoons shortening
4 teaspoons baking powder	3/4 cup milk
1/2 teaspoon salt	1 cup milk, for dipping

Sift the dry ingredients and rub the shortening into them. Add the three-fourths cup milk slowly and mix thoroughly but quickly. Turn the dough onto a floured molding board and pat it out lightly with floured hands to half an inch thick. Cut the biscuits with a round biscuit cutter. Have ready a cup of sweet milk and dip each biscuit in it. Place them on a greased pan and bake for twelve minutes in a hot oven, 475 degrees F. Serve immediately.

BLUEBERRY BISCUIT

Add three tablespoons of sugar and one cup lightly floured blueberries to the above recipe.

BUTTERMILK BISCUIT

4 1/2 cups flour	1 1/2 teaspoons salt
1 teaspoon baking powder	2 tablespoons lard
1 teaspoon soda	2 cups buttermilk

Sift the dry ingredients and work in the lard. Add the buttermilk. Turn onto a floured board and knead. Roll out half an inch thick. Cut in rounds and place on a greased tin. Bake fifteen minutes in a hot oven, 450 degrees F. Serve piping hot. These biscuits are rather thin and crackerlike.

MRS. PULSIFER'S CREAM-OF-TARTAR BISCUIT

This recipe for old-fashioned cream-of-tartar biscuit came from Campton, New Hampshire. It was given us by an eighty-five-year-old cook and was her husband's mother's recipe. We quote it as it was told to us. The biscuits are delicious.

Mrs. Pulsifer's daughter, who tested the recipe, found that the measurements for the cream of tartar and soda, when translated into modern cooking terms, are two level teaspoons soda and four level teaspoons cream of tartar.

"Take one quart of flour and sift with one heaping teaspoon of soda, two heaping teaspoons of cream of tartar, and one of salt. Mix thick sweet cream and sweet milk, half and half, and stir in enough to moisten the flour. Turn the dough on a floured board and pat out quickly. Cut these biscuits quite large and bake in a quick oven."

BREWIS

1 cup brown bread crumbs   1/4 teaspoon salt
1 cup milk   1 tablespoon butter

Crumble the brown bread, cover with the milk, and let stand five minutes. Add the salt, put over low heat, and cook slowly until the milk is absorbed. Remove from the fire, add the butter, and mix well. Serve with cold corned beef or cold boiled tongue. When used as a breakfast dish, serve with syrup or cream and sugar.

10. THE PIE CUPBOARD

Although the early settlers were amazed at the profusion of wild fruits in the New England woods, cultivated fruits were brought over from England almost immediately. In 1629, the first apple trees were planted. Crops for a few years were a great disappointment, small in number and distorted in shape, but gradually the trees became acclimated, and most of the modern varieties we now know are descended from these seedlings. Astrakhans, russets, pound sweets, "punkin" sweets, these and many others whose names are no longer familiar were the apples from which our great-great-grandmothers made their pies.

To the modern cook, apple pie means the ordinary two-crust pie made of raw apples, spiced and sweetened according to family taste. But to great-great-grandmother, baking apple pies meant choosing from one of a dozen or two recipes. In the fall of the year when apples were juicy, she made a plain apple pie in a deep dish. Following these first deep-dish pies baked something like our modern cobblers with only a top crust, the deep custard pie plates came into use. Then, with the crust built up around the edge like a wall, apples were put in in layers, each one sprinkled with mace or cinnamon, a grating of lemon rind, and dotted with a piece or two of butter. Covered with a top crust, they were baked in a slow oven until the crust was brown.

In some old recipes, whole cloves were used in the place of powdered spices, and molasses, maple syrup, and honey instead of sugar. Since sugar was scarce and expensive, the early pies were not as sweet as they are today. One eighteenth-century recipe called for only two ounces of sugar—one-fourth cup—to a peck of apples. Frequently when the filling was not very sweet, white sugar was sifted over the top of the pie just before it was served. A pork-apple pie similar to the deep-dish pie was made with "shavings of tender soft pork, so thin they wouldn't hold their shape" and only one crust. Ordinarily, however, apple was a two-crust pie with various flavorings.

Although the early settlers brought red garden currants to this country with them, they found a currant with firm sour berries growing wild, and a black currant which was used primarily for medicines because of its peculiar flavor. Cultivated garden currants were used for jams, jellies, and pies. In the middle of the eighteenth century it was considered fashionable to walk in the garden at the bottom of Boston Common to eat currants. The Boston *News Letter* in July, 1735, carried the following announcement: "Any person that has a mind to take a walk in the Garden at the Bottom of the Common, to eat currants, shall be kindly Welcome for Six Pence a piece."

Blueberries, huckleberries, raspberries, and the less-known amber-colored baked-apple berries and salmon berries were all used for pies. Authorities still disagree about the difference between blueberries, huckleberries, and whortleberries, all of which were the same color and about the same size. English botanists say the whortleberry or bilberry was similar to their huckleberry. Early blueberry pies were sweetened with one-third molasses and two-thirds sugar and served either hot or cold, but old-timers say, "There's but one time to eat blueberry pie—one-half hour out of the oven."

Custard pies with a flaky undercrust are very difficult to make, and even our grandmothers whose custard pies have never been equaled found that there were tricks to the baking. Often they put the crust for the custard pie in the pan the day before. After the crust dried out on the top, the custard did not soak in as easily. Sometimes they put the pies in a very hot oven and allowed the heat to go down gradually as the pies baked. The rapid cooking of the crust kept the custard from soaking in, but in this case there was danger that the oven would be too hot and the custard would whey.

In addition to pies of all sorts, turnovers and tarts were as much a part of the weekly Saturday baking as were beans and brown bread. Turnovers, oblong pieces of pastry with filling placed on one half and the other half folded over and pressed down, were always in demand for the children, who carried them to school in their lunch pails and munched on them between meals. Filled with stewed apples, mincemeat, or any pie filling, they ran cookies a close second in the list of family favorites.

Plain tarts were simple rounds of pastry, the lower one cut with a cooky cutter, the upper with a doughnut cutter, and the center filled with jam or jelly. But where plain tarts were an everyday affair, the little fluted ones, baked in patty pans were a company dessert. They were made of pastry so rich it melted in your mouth and were filled with fruits and custards, sometimes covered with strips of pastry, at other times baked without a top crust. Currant tarts always had a latticed top, plum tarts no top crust, although why no one but great-grandmother knows.

DEEP-DISH APPLE PIE

1 quart sliced apples	1 teaspoon salt
1/2 cup molasses	1/2 teaspoon black pepper
1/2 cup sugar	1 tablespoon diced salt pork
2 cups hot water	

Cover the parings and cores of the apples with water and simmer until soft. Strain the pulp, and add the liquid to the apples. Arrange the apples in a round twelve-inch baking pan. Mix the molasses and sugar with the hot water and pour over the apples. Sprinkle with the salt and pepper and bits of pork. Place in the oven and bake slowly at 325 degrees F. The apples should turn dark red while baking. One-half hour before time for serving, remove from the oven and cover with a crust.

Crust

1 cup yellow corn meal	3/4 cup clarified fat
1 cup flour	Cold water
1 teaspoon salt	

Mix the corn meal, flour, and salt with your fingers or with a pastry mixer. Rub in the fat. Stir in the cold water until the dough is of the consistency of pie crust. Roll, prick with a fork, and place lightly over the apples, tucking in the edges of the crust around the rim of the pan. Bake fifteen minutes in a moderate oven at 375 degrees F. During the last five minutes, if necessary, raise the temperature of the oven to 450 degrees to brown. Serve warm with sauce.

Caramel Sauce

3/4 cup maple syrup	1/3 teaspoon vanilla
1/4 cup light cream	

Combine the ingredients and stir until well mixed. Heat to the boiling point and cook three minutes. Pour two tablespoons of sauce over each serving of pie.

CARAWAY GREEN APPLE PIE

Make a sauce of sliced peeled green apples. Strain and sweeten to taste. Fill an unbaked pie shell, sprinkle with caraway seeds. Cover with a top crust. Place in a hot oven, 450 degrees F., for ten minutes. Then reduce the heat to 350 degrees and bake forty minutes, or until the crust is brown.

At the Isles of Shoals where this was a specialty, a little nutmeg was added to the applesauce. In Vermont, where there was an abundance of good rich cream, the top crust was carefully cut out just before serving and a cup of sweet cream poured in, stirred lightly, and the top crust replaced.

RHODE ISLAND GREENING PIE

10 greenings	Mace
3 cups sugar	1 wineglass wine
1 cup water	Egg white, beaten
1 lemon, sliced	Sugar

Halve and core the apples. Put in a pan the sugar, water, lemon slices, and a dash of mace, bring to a boil, and lay in the apples. Simmer until the apples are tender and slightly transparent. Take out the apples, keeping them as whole as possible. Boil the liquor down until there is only enough left to cover the bottom of the pies. Line two pie plates with crust, arrange the apples in the bottom, add the wine to the juice and pour over the apples. Brush the rim of the pie and the top of the apples with the egg white and sift sugar over the top. Bake in a hot oven, 450 degrees F., for ten minutes, then reduce the heat to 350 degrees, and bake forty minutes, or until the crust is brown. This makes two pies.

MARLBOROUGH PIE

6 tart apples	1 lemon, juice and grated rind
1 teaspoon butter	1 cup sugar
2 eggs, beaten	

Cook and strain the apples; add the butter, and cool. Add the eggs, lemon rind and juice, and sugar. Put in a deep-dish pie shell and bake in a moderate oven, 375 degrees F., for one hour, or until the crust is done. Garnish with small cakes of puff paste baked separately. Makes one nine-inch pie.

BOILED CIDER PIE

1/2 cup cider
1/2 cup maple sugar
2 egg yolks, beaten
1/4 teaspoon nutmeg

1/2 cup seeded raisins
1 tablespoon butter
2 egg whites
4 tablespoons powdered sugar

Boil the cider and maple sugar. Add the beaten egg yolks and stir until thick. Add the nutmeg, raisins, and butter. Turn into an unbaked pie shell, cover with top crust, and bake forty minutes in a moderate oven at 350 degrees F. The top crust may be omitted, and a meringue may be made of the beaten egg whites and powdered sugar. Brown in a moderate oven. Makes one nine-inch pie.

BLUEBERRY PIE

2 1/2 cups blueberries
1 tablespoon flour
1/2 cup sugar

1/8 teaspoon salt
1 tablespoon lemon juice

Clean the blueberries, mix with the flour and sugar. Add the salt and lemon juice. Put in an unbaked pie shell, cover with top crust, and bake in a moderate oven, 375 degrees F., for forty minutes, or until the crust is brown. Makes one nine-inch pie.

Blackberry pie made by the above recipe is excellent, but often our grandmothers added spices to blackberries—a dash of cloves or cinnamon. Because both blackberries and huckleberries are rather sweet, often a few fresh currants were used to take the place of lemon juice.

STRAWBERRY PIE

Fill a baked pie shell with three cups of strawberries, sliced and mixed with six tablespoons sugar. Cover with a meringue and brown in a slow oven, 325 degrees F., for ten minutes, or cover with one cup whipped cream sweetened with two tablespoons of sugar. Serve very cold. Makes one nine-inch pie.

GREEN CURRANT PIE

When currants begin to turn red, pick and wash them. Line a pie tin with crust, fill half full of currants, add plenty of sugar and cinnamon, and dot with butter. Add currants and sugar until the pie tin is full. Bake in a hot oven, 450 degrees F., for ten minutes, then reduce to 350 degrees, and bake forty minutes, until the crust is brown. This can be baked with either a top crust or with a lattice across the top. Most currant pies were latticed.

RIPE CURRANT PIE

1 cup sugar	1 1/2 cups currants
1/4 cup flour	2 egg whites, beaten
2 egg yolks	4 tablespoons sugar
2 tablespoons water	

Mix the cup of sugar, flour, egg yolks, and water. Add to the currants. Bake in one crust following directions for Green Currant Pie. When the crust is brown, cover with a meringue made of the egg whites and sugar. Brown in a slow oven, 325 degrees F., about ten minutes.

CRANBERRY PIE

1 1/2 cups cranberries	2 tablespoons flour or fine cracker
1 cup sugar	crumbs
2/3 cup water	1 tablespoon butter

Cook the cranberries and sugar in the water for ten minutes. They may be either strained or used whole for the pie. Mix with the flour and butter. Cool before putting into the crust. Cover with strips of crust and bake until crust is brown.

CHERRY PIE

1 quart cherries, stoned	1/8 teaspoon salt
1/2 cup sugar	1 tablespoon lemon juice
1 tablespoon flour	

Fill an unbaked pie shell with the cherries, sprinkle with the sugar, flour, and salt sifted together. Add the lemon juice. Cover with an upper crust. Bake in a hot oven, 425 degrees F., for forty minutes.

Cherries have so much juice that it is wise to put a vent in the center of the top crust. Many people like a few drops of almond flavoring in place of lemon juice.

RHUBARB PIE

2 1/2 cups diced rhubarb
1 cup sugar
2 tablespoons flour

1 egg, beaten
Dash of salt

Do not peel the rhubarb unless the stalks are unusually large and stringy. The pink skin, when it is tender, gives rhubarb its lovely color. Mix the diced rhubarb with the sugar, flour, beaten egg, and salt. Put in an unbaked pie shell, cover with crust, and bake in a moderate oven, 375 degrees F., until the crust is done, about fifty minutes.

FLO'S PUMPKIN PIE

Peel the pumpkin and cut in cubes, rejecting the seeds and soft fibers. Put in a kettle with very little water. Simmer until tender, pressing down into the water occasionally. Mash, press through a sieve, and cook until dark and dry. With one cup cooked pumpkin, mix one-half cup brown sugar, one-half cup molasses, one-half teaspoon each cinnamon and ginger, a pinch of salt, one beaten egg if desired, and two cups milk. Mix, bring to a boil, and partly cool. Fill an unbaked pie shell. Put in a hot oven, 400 degrees F., for fifteen minutes, then lower the heat to 325 degrees and bake thirty minutes longer or until the custard is firm and the crust brown.

SQUASH PIE

Most recipes for pumpkin pie may be used for squash pie also. The following modern version of squash pie calls for more spices than are used in older recipes.

2 cups strained cooked squash
2 cups milk
2 eggs
1 cup sugar
1/2 teaspoon ginger

1/2 teaspoon allspice
2 teaspoons cinnamon
2 tablespoons flour
1/2 teaspoon salt

Mix the squash, milk, and eggs. Sift the dry ingredients and stir into the squash mixture. Pour into an unbaked pie shell and bake in a moderate oven, 350 degrees F., until the crust is brown and the filling is set, about fifty minutes.

MRS. HARLAND'S MINCEMEAT

2 pounds lean beef, boiled
1 pound suet
5 pounds apples
3 pounds raisins
2 pounds currants
3/4 pound citron
2 tablespoons cinnamon
2 1/2 pounds brown sugar

1 nutmeg, grated
2 tablespoons mace
1 tablespoon cloves
1 tablespoon allspice
1 tablespoon salt
1 bottle sherry
1 pint brandy

Chop the beef, suet, apples, raisins, currants, and citron. Mix with the other ingredients. Put in a crock in a cool place. When pies are baked, add more sherry or brandy.

APPLEDORE SUMMER MINCEMEAT

2 soda crackers
1 cup molasses
1 cup brown sugar
1 cup cider
1 cup raisins
1 wineglass brandy

2 eggs, beaten
1 teaspoon cinnamon
1 teaspoon nutmeg
1 teaspoon cloves
1 teaspoon salt
1 teaspoon black pepper

Roll the crackers fine. Mix with the other ingredients. Makes two pies.

GREEN TOMATO MINCEMEAT

1 peck chopped green tomatoes   2 teaspoons cinnamon
3 pounds brown sugar   1 teaspoon cloves
2 pounds raisins, chopped   2 teaspoons nutmeg
1 cup suet   1 lemon, grated rind
2 tablespoons salt   3 lemons, juice and pulp
1/2 cup water   3 cups chopped apples

Sprinkle the green tomatoes with salt, let stand one hour, and drain. Cover with cold water, boil five minutes, and drain again. Add the sugar, raisins, suet, salt, and half cup of water. Simmer twenty minutes, add the spices, lemon, and apples, and cook rapidly until thick.

OLD-TIME LEMON PIE

1 1/2 cups sugar   1 teaspoon grated lemon rind
3/4 cup flour   1 cup cold water
1/2 cup peeled lemon, sliced thin   2 tablespoons butter

Blend the sugar and flour. Line an eight-inch pie tin with pastry. Sprinkle half the sugar and flour mixture over the crust, cover with the sliced lemon and rind, and spread with the remaining sugar and flour mixture. Add the cold water and butter. Cover with strips of pastry. Bake ten minutes in a hot oven, 425 degrees F., reduce to 350 degrees, and continue baking twenty to thirty minutes longer.

THREE-CRUST LEMON PIE

2 lemons, juice and pulp; grated   1/4 teaspoon salt
    rind of one   2 eggs, beaten
1 1/2 cups sugar

Mix the ingredients in the order named. Line a pie tin with rich pastry. Cover with half of the filling, cover with a second layer of pastry, add the rest of the filling, and cover with a top crust. Bake in a moderate oven, 375 degrees F., for thirty minutes. Makes one nine-inch pie.

LEMON MERINGUE PIE

4 tablespoons flour
1 cup sugar
1/4 teaspoon salt
2 tablespoons butter
2 egg yolks, beaten

2 cups water
1/2 lemon, grated rind
1/3 cup lemon juice
2 egg whites
4 tablespoons sugar

Mix the flour, cup of sugar, salt, and butter with the beaten egg yolks. Add the water and boil until thick. Add the lemon rind and juice. Cool. Pour into a baked pie shell and cover with a meringue of egg whites beaten stiff with the four tablespoons sugar. Brown in a slow oven, 325 degrees F., for ten minutes. Makes one nine-inch pie.

TRANSPARENT PUDDING

1/2 cup butter
2 cups sugar
6 eggs, separated

1 wineglass brandy or sherry
2 lemons, grated rind; juice of one
Dash of nutmeg

Cream the butter and sugar. Add the egg yolks and the remaining ingredients to the butter and sugar mixture. Fold in the stiffly beaten egg whites. Bake in one crust in a moderate oven, 350 degrees F., until the crust is brown, about forty minutes. Makes two eight-inch pies.

Just three of the egg whites may be folded into the filling and the other three beaten with six tablespoons sugar for a meringue. Either brown or white sugar may be used for this pie, and for those who do not care for the flavor of lemon rind, four tablespoons of tart jelly may be substituted.

CUSTARD PIE

3 cups milk, scalded
3 eggs, beaten
5 tablespoons sugar

1/4 teaspoon salt
1 teaspoon vanilla
Grated nutmeg

Stir the scalded milk into the beaten eggs. The eggs should not be foamy. Add the sugar, salt, and vanilla. Cool slightly, pour into an unbaked pie shell, and sprinkle with nutmeg. Bake in a slow oven, 325 degrees F., until the custard is set and the crust is brown, about one hour. Makes one nine-inch pie.

OLD-FASHIONED COCONUT CUSTARD PIE

3 egg yolks
1 egg white
2/3 cup sugar
Pinch of salt
1/2 cup shredded coconut

1 teaspoon vanilla
2 cups heated milk
2 egg whites
4 tablespoons sugar

Beat the egg yolks and the one egg white, add the sugar, salt, coconut, and vanilla. Stir in the heated milk and pour into an unbaked pie shell. Put in a hot oven, 400 degrees F., and allow the heat to decrease to 325 degrees. Bake until the custard is set, about one hour. Beat the two egg whites into a meringue with the four tablespoons of sugar and brown. Makes one nine-inch pie.

RASPBERRY CUSTARD PIE

Add one cup of raspberries to the Custard Pie recipe and increase the sugar to one-half cup.

RAISIN PIE

2 cups raisins
1/2 cup sugar
3 tablespoons flour

1 lemon, juice
1 tablespoon lemon rind
1 cup chopped nutmeats

Cook the raisins in boiling water to cover five minutes. Add the sugar mixed with the flour and cook until thick. Add the lemon rind and juice and the chopped nuts. Pour into an unbaked pie shell, cover with a top crust, and bake in a moderate oven, 375 degrees F., until brown, about forty-five minutes. Makes one nine-inch pie.

CHOCOLATE CREAM PIE

4 tablespoons flour	2 eggs, beaten
3/4 cup sugar	2 cups milk
4 tablespoons cocoa	Pinch of salt
1 tablespoon butter	1 teaspoon vanilla

Mix the flour and sugar with the cocoa, add the butter and beaten eggs, milk, and salt. Cook in a double boiler until thick. Add the vanilla, cool, and pour into a baked pie shell. Serve with sweetened whipped cream. Makes one nine-inch pie.

The egg whites may be reserved and made into a meringue with four tablespoons of sugar.

COCONUT CREAM PIE

3 tablespoons flour	2 cups milk
1/2 cup sugar	1/2 lemon, juice
1/8 teaspoon salt	1/2 cup coconut
1 tablespoon butter	2 egg whites, stiffly beaten
2 egg yolks, beaten	4 tablespoons sugar

Mix the flour, sugar, and salt with the butter. Add the beaten egg yolks and milk. Cook in a double boiler until thick. Add the lemon juice and coconut. Cool and pour into a baked pie shell. Cover with a meringue of the egg whites beaten stiff with the four tablespoons sugar. Sprinkle with coconut and brown in a slow oven, 325 degrees F., for ten minutes. Makes one nine-inch pie. This is a favorite dessert for New England Sunday dinners. Originally it was made with fresh coconut out of the shell. Today either the fresh or packaged product may be used.

OLD-FASHIONED WASHINGTON PIE

1 1/2 cups sugar
1 cup butter
6 eggs
4 cups flour
1 cup cream

1/2 teaspoon soda
1 teaspoon vanilla, or 1/2 teaspoon
    lemon extract or almond, or
    2 tablespoons brandy

An electric beater is essential in making this cake, for our grand-mothers always creamed the sugar and butter and then added the eggs one at a time, beating for fifteen or twenty minutes after each egg was put in. Then the flour and cream, mixed with the soda were lightly folded in. Since it has no baking powder, this makes a dense moist cake. Bake it in thin layers in a moderate oven, 350 degrees F., for twenty-five minutes. Cover each layer, when baked, with jelly as thick as the cake, and ice or sprinkle with powdered sugar.

BOSTON CREAM PIE

1 cup sugar
1/3 cup butter
2 eggs, beaten
2/3 cup milk

2 cups flour
1/2 teaspoon salt
2 teaspoons baking powder

Cream the sugar and butter, add the beaten eggs, the milk, and the flour sifted with the salt and baking powder. Bake in two layers in a moderate oven, 375 degrees F., for twenty to thirty minutes. Make a cream filling for between the layers. (If desired, grated coconut may be sprinkled over the top and also added to the cream filling.)

Cream Filling

1 cup milk
1/2 cup sugar
1 egg, beaten

1 tablespoon flour
1 teaspoon vanilla

Cook the first four ingredients in a double boiler fifteen minutes, adding the vanilla when the mixture is removed from the fire. Cool and spread on cake layers.

LAFAYETTE PIE

1 cup sugar	1 cup flour
3 tablespoons butter	1 teaspoon cream of tartar
4 egg yolks	1/2 teaspoon soda mixed with
4 egg whites	cold water

Cream the sugar and butter. Add the egg yolks one at a time, beating well. Add the flour sifted with the cream of tartar. Add the soda. Fold in the egg whites beaten stiffly. Bake in two thin layers in a moderate oven, 350 degrees F., for thirty minutes. Cover with lemon cream filling. This makes a dense moist cake something like spongecake.

Lemon Cream Filling

2 tablespoons butter	1/2 cup water
2 tablespoons flour	1/2 cup sugar
1/2 cup lemon juice	2 egg yolks, beaten

Melt the butter, add the flour, and blend well. Add the lemon juice, water, and sugar. Cook in a double boiler until the mixture begins to thicken, then add the beaten egg yolks, cook one minute, and cool.

VINEGAR PIE

1 cup water	1/2 cup vinegar
3 common crackers	1/2 teaspoon cinnamon
1/2 cup molasses	1/4 teaspoon nutmeg
1/2 cup sugar	1/4 teaspoon cloves
1 cup raisins	

Pour the water over the rolled crackers, add the remaining ingredients, mix well, and bake in two crusts. Put in a hot oven, 450 degrees

F., for ten minutes, then reduce to 350 degrees and bake forty minutes more.

MOLASSES PIE

1/2 cup sugar	2 eggs, beaten
1 cup molasses	1 tablespoon butter
1/4 cup flour	Dash of nutmeg

Mix all the ingredients well. Pour into an unbaked pie shell and bake in a slow oven, 325 degrees F., until the filling is set and the crust is brown, about one hour. Serve with unsweetened whipped cream.

CURRANT AND RASPBERRY TARTS

Stew three cups of currants and one cup of raspberries together. Sweeten to taste. Fill unbaked tart shells, put strips of crust across the top, and bake in a moderate oven, 375 degrees F., for thirty minutes, or until brown.

GOOSEBERRY TARTS

"Top and tail" the gooseberries, being sure to get off all the stem and blossom ends. Stew in a little water, and strain. Add sugar to taste, and cool. Pour into unbaked tart shells, cover with strips of pastry, and bake in a moderate oven, 375 degrees F., until brown, about thirty minutes.

BARBERRY TARTS

Boil one pound of barberries with three-fourths pound of sugar in an agate pan for fifteen minutes. Strain and pour into unbaked tart shells. Bake in a hot oven, 400 degrees F., until the crust is done, about thirty minutes.

OLD-TIME LEMON TARTS

6 ripe lemons	2 cups sugar
1/2 teaspoon salt	2 oranges, juice
6 apples	Powdered sugar
2 cups water	

Cut the lemons in thin slices, add the salt, cover with water, and cook until transparent. Pare and core the apples, cut in slices, and stew in the two cups of water with the sugar until tender. Strain out half of the apples, and add the other half with all the juice to the lemons. Boil until thick, then add the orange juice. Add more sugar if the lemon mixture seems too sour. Fill unbaked tart shells two-thirds full of the lemon mixture, and fill up with apple. Sprinkle with powdered sugar and bake thirty minutes in a moderate oven, 375 degrees F.

11. PUDDING BAGS AND
CUSTARD CUPS

COME for dessert," you casually say to your friends, knowing that they will appear at the end of the meal for a pleasant hour of conversation over the coffee cups. But a century and a half ago the invitation, "Come at pudding time," was a way of saying, "Come in time for dinner." You might have served the pies, the cakes, the fruit at the end of the meal, but the fragrant steaming pudding invariably preceded the main dish.

It was an ancient custom to bring in the pudding first, but it continued well into the nineteenth century. The dinner of succotash, oysters, clams, codfish, a haunch of venison, and seafowl served in Plymouth at the first Forefathers' Celebration started with a huge baked Indian whortleberry pudding. Years later, puddings of Indian corn, butter, and molasses, brought to the table before the meat and vegetables, were fea-

tured at Sunday dinners in the home of John Adams. And the place of
the pudding on the bill of fare even entered into the local political life
of old Salem. The Federalists ate their puddings first, but the Demo-
crats began their dinners with meat!

Many of these hearty puddings were boiled in bags which were not
actually bags but large flat strips of stout cloth with no sewing to give
them shape. Boiled bag puddings are still on the New England dessert
list. They do not appear frequently, but they make a fine addition to a
midwinter dinner, particularly when the meat course is a little light.

In making a bag pudding, first dip the cloth in boiling water and
wring it out. Then spread it over a deep bowl and sprinkle it liberally
with flour. Next turn the batter into the center of the cloth. The weight
of the batter will push the cloth to the bottom of the bowl. Gather the
loose edges of the cloth to form a bag and deftly tie it with "the pud-
ding-bag string." Then set the bag of pudding on a trivet in a kettle
of boiling water and let it cook hard for three or four hours.

The first rule given in this chapter for making boiled Indian pudding is very old, but it works as well now as it did a hundred years ago.
It is a down-East recipe, and the woman who gave it to us says she
serves it with boiled dinner or mutton stew as her mother and grandmother did before her. We think that you will like the boiled blueberry
pudding from New Hampshire. It is tasty when the portions are covered with thick cream, and it is what the people of the Granite State
call "real prime eating" when served with old-fashioned molasses sauce.
"Everyone who's eaten this sauce on puddings—from hired hands to
unexpected Sunday dinner guests—smacks his lips and rolls his eyes
when it's mentioned," says the daughter-in-law of the Kensington cook
who contributed the recipe.

We can't give you our word of honor that rich boiled puddings made
from the third ancient recipe were set before Elias Derby and Joseph
Peabody, whose staunch ships brought spices and "confections" and
hogsheads of blue Canton china to gladden the hearts of New England housewives. All we can say is that the "receipt" is of Salem origin
and the pudding could well have appeared on the tables of wealthy
merchants of the East India trade.

First cousin to the boiled bag pudding is the heavy dessert made of cakelike dough or of softened crumbs steamed in a covered mold or in cups. Foremost in this category are the molasses-sweetened batters, highly flavored with spices and enriched with currants, raisins, and other dried fruits. But sugar-sweetened batters less highly spiced and flavored make equally good steamed puddings. Most present-day New England cooks follow in their grandmothers' footsteps and liven their puddings by adding blueberries, cranberries, apples, or other native fruits. They send them to the table with brimming bowls of delicious tart sauces or pitchers of thick cream sweetened with maple sugar. The proof of the pudding may be in the eating, but a tasty pudding sauce has a lot to do with it.

Originally, the word duff meant the steamed pudding served for Sunday dinner on Yankee sailing vessels. Genuine duff is nothing more or less than gingerbread dough which is steamed instead of baked. The recipe for sailor's duff from Nantucket includes a family pudding sauce that is the making of the dessert.

The recipe for "second-day pudding" comes from Nantucket too. It was an heirloom in the family descended from Tristram Coffin, who, according to his relatives, "invented the island." Second Day was an important feature of wedding plans in the early nineteenth century. The groom's family entertained for the young couple, and the bride's trousseau included a special gown for the occasion. The celebration was quite likely to take the form of an evening reception with music and dancing. But dancing or not, there always was an elaborate collation in which a rich cracker plum pudding had a place of honor.

Batter puddings date from the eighteenth century. They are easy to make, and the ingredients are those most cooks have on hand. A batter pudding should be put in the oven just half an hour before you plan to eat it and served directly from the oven. It will not fall if properly baked, though we confess it will not make a very creditable appearance on a second journey from the kitchen.

Dumplings may be boiled or steamed, but most people prefer them baked. Every cook has her own ideas about the spices and sweetening that she believes add just the right touch to the quartered or whole apples encased in dough. The recipe we give comes from Massachusetts and gets its distinctive name because the dumplings are "gilded" with a sauce that makes them shine like the dome of the State House on Beacon Hill.

At times the debate on biscuit dough versus cake batter for strawberry shortcake is as spirited as the discussion on the pros and cons of using tomatoes in clam chowder. But all New Englanders know that strawberries piled on spongecake and topped with whipped cream do not constitute a real shortcake. It may be be delicious, but they want it called "strawberries on spongecake." New England shortcake is made of biscuit dough baked or cut in layers and drenched with berries mixed with sugar to form a rich concoction that drips in rivulets down the sides of the cake. There is one exception: the old-fashioned Nantucket shortcake made of well-risen bread dough to which sugar, butter, and eggs are added. A New England shortcake is not served with whipped cream; it is sent to the table so piping hot that the butter spread on the layers melts the minute it touches them. A large pitcher of pan cream and an extra bowl filled with sweetened sliced berries go with it.

Raspberry and blackberry shortcakes are made the same as strawberry shortcake, but blueberry shortcake is more delicious if the berries are stewed a little and sweetened before they are turned over the biscuit-dough layers.

The word grunt in Massachusetts and particularly on Cape Cod was another name for dumpling. Both the grunts and the slumps were transition desserts, halfway between the boiled and baked puddings but simpler to make. For the grunts, rich biscuit dough dropped on stewed fruit was covered tightly and steamed for several hours. For the slumps, drop dumplings of baking powder biscuit dough were dropped either on top of the fruit or in fruit juice and cooked on top of the stove. When served, the dumplings were put in a deep sauce dish, covered with fruit and syrup, and served with pudding sauce or pan cream. Fruit dumplings were much like the slumps.

In addition to the boiled and baked puddings, New England housewives were noted for their lighter desserts: all kinds of baked and boiled custards, whips, and trifles were made for everyday and festive occasions. Every New England home had its glazed brown pottery custard cups cracked by age and heat. Few if any housewives allowed a week to go by without making a dozen or two cup custards when the beans were baking.

With a boiled custard and a few pieces of stale spongecake the New England housewife was ready for anything. An old English dish, tipsy pudding, was one of her stand-bys. A spongecake or sunshine cake at least four days old and perhaps older was necessary. One cup of sherry was allowed for a quarter of a large cake. After the cake had soaked an hour, a rumflavored custard was poured over it. The trifles, another delectable dessert, differed from the tipsy puddings only by having jelly or fruits added to them. The fools were English desserts transplanted to this country. They too were made of boiled custards combined with fruit instead of cake.

Two kinds of syllabubs were popular in New England: the thin served as a drink, and the thick served in sherbet glasses as a dessert. The thick syllabubs were also called whips.

BOILED INDIAN PLUM PUDDING

2 cups milk	1 teaspoon salt
1 cup corn meal	2 eggs, well beaten
1 cup molasses	1/4 cup raisins
1 cup chopped suet	

Scald the milk and add the corn meal slowly, stirring constantly. Boil for five minutes. Remove from the fire and add the other ingredients. Mix thoroughly and turn into a pudding bag. Boil four hours. Serve with Lemon Sauce. Serves six or more.

BOILED BLUEBERRY PUDDING

1 cup butter	1 cup sour milk
2 cups sugar	4 cups flour
5 eggs, well beaten	1 quart blueberries
1 teaspoon soda	

Cream the butter and sugar and add the beaten eggs. Dissolve the soda in the milk and stir into the first mixture. Sift the flour and stir in, and add the blueberries last. Turn the batter into a pudding bag and boil for four hours. Serve with the following sauce.

Mrs. York's Molasses Pudding Sauce

2 cups molasses	1/2 pound butter
4 teaspoons vinegar	1 cup water

Cook the ingredients until the mixture boils up. Serve very hot. Makes four cups of sauce. Serves ten or more.

SALEM BOILED PUDDING

3 cups flour	1 cup molasses
1 teaspoon salt	1 cup milk
1 teaspoon cinnamon	1 cup chopped suet
1/2 teaspoon ginger	1 cup raisins, chopped fine
1 teaspoon soda	

Sift the flour with the salt and spices. Dissolve the soda in a little water and stir into the molasses. Mix the molasses and the milk with the dry ingredients, add the suet and raisins, and stir in thoroughly. Turn into a pudding bag and boil four and one-half hours. Serves eight or more. Serve with the following sauce.

Mrs. Lincoln's Foamy Sauce

1/2 cup butter	2 tablespoons wine or fruit juice
1 cup powdered sugar	1/4 cup boiling water
1 teaspoon vanilla	1 egg white, beaten to a foam

Cream the butter; add the sugar, vanilla, and wine. Just before serving add the boiling water and stir well. Then add the egg white and beat the sauce until foamy. Makes about one and a half cups of sauce.

SAILOR'S DUFF

1 egg, well beaten	1 1/2 cups flour
2 tablespoons sugar	1 teaspoon soda
2 tablespoons butter	1/2 cup boiling water
2 cups molasses	

Mix in the order given and steam one hour. Serves six or more. Serve with the following sauce.

Nantucket Sauce

2 egg yolks	1 cup thick cream
1 cup sugar	1 teaspoon lemon juice

Beat the egg yolks and add the sugar. Whip the cream and fold into the mixture. Flavor with the lemon juice. Serves six or more.

WEBSTER PUDDING

1 cup molasses	Flour
1 cup milk	1 teaspoon cinnamon
1/2 cup melted butter	1/2 teaspoon cloves
1/2 cup brandy	1/2 teaspoon nutmeg
1 teaspoon soda	1 teaspoon salt

Mix the molasses, milk, melted butter, and brandy. Dissolve the soda in a little water and add to the mixture. Sift two cups of flour with the spices and salt, and stir in. Add more flour if necessary. The batter should be like poundcake. Turn into a buttered mold and steam two hours. Serves six or more. Serve with the following sauce.

Old-fashioned Cold Sauce
(Hard Sauce)

2 cups powdered sugar	Grated rind and juice of 1 lemon
1 cup butter	

Cream the sugar and butter and gradually stir in the lemon juice. Add the grated lemon rind last. Makes about two cups.

OLD-FASHIONED STEAMED BLUEBERRY PUDDING

1 teaspoon soda	1 teaspoon cloves
2 cups molasses	1/4 teaspoon nutmeg
1 1/2 teaspoons salt	Flour
1 tablespoon cinnamon	1 quart blueberries

Dissolve the soda in a little cold water and mix with the molasses. Sift the salt and spices with one cup of flour. Stir into the molasses mixture. Add enough flour to make a batter of cake consistency. Add the blueberries one cup at a time. Turn the pudding mixture into a covered mold and steam for three hours. Serves eight. Serve with the following sauce.

Currant Wine Sauce

1/4 cup butter	2 egg whites
1 cup sugar	1 cup currant wine

Cream the butter and sugar. Beat the egg whites stiff and fold in. Add the wine gradually. This sauce does not blend and must be stirred before turning over the servings of pudding. Blackberry wine may be substituted for the currant wine. Makes about two cups of sauce.

STEAMED CHERRY PUDDING

2 cups cherries, stoned	1 cup milk
1/2 cup sugar	3 teaspoons baking powder
2 eggs	2 cups flour
	1/2 teaspoon salt

Sprinkle the cherries with the sugar and let them stand for an hour. Drain, saving any juice for flavoring the sauce. Beat the eggs and add the milk. Sift the dry ingredients. Combine the mixtures and stir well.

Stir in the cherries. Turn into a greased covered mold and steam one and one-half hours. Serve with Mrs. Lincoln's Foamy Sauce. Serves six.

STEAMED BLACKBERRY PUDDING

1 cup butter	1 cup sour milk
2 cups sugar	4 cups flour
5 eggs, well beaten	1 quart blackberries
1 teaspoon soda	

Cream the butter and sugar and add the eggs. Stir the soda into the sour milk and combine with the mixture. Sift the flour and stir in. Add the blackberries last. Pour the batter into a buttered mold and steam for three hours. Serve with any desired sauce. Serves six.

STEAMED CRANBERRY PUDDING

1 cup flour	1/2 cup sugar
1 1/2 teaspoons baking powder	2/3 cup finely chopped suet
1/2 teaspoon salt	1 cup chopped cranberries
1/2 cup cracker crumbs	1/2 cup milk
1 egg, well beaten	

Sift the flour, baking powder, and salt. Add the cracker crumbs and the well-beaten egg. Add the other ingredients in the order given. Mix well. Steam two hours. Serve with Nantucket Sauce. Serves six.

QUAKING PUDDING

4 cups bread cubes	6 eggs
Raisins	1 teaspoon salt
6 cups milk	1/4 teaspoon nutmeg

Put alternate layers of bread cubes and large raisins in a buttered mold. Beat the milk and eggs together and add the salt and nutmeg. Pour this over the bread and raisins. The mold should be two-thirds full. Steam for two hours. Serve with Currant Wine Sauce. The raisins furnish the sweetening in this pudding. Serves eight or more.

STEAMED STRAWBERRY BREAD PUDDING

1/2 cup butter	1 cup sour milk
1 cup sugar	1 cup flour
2 eggs, well beaten	1 teaspoon cinnamon
2 cups bread crumbs	1/2 teaspoon salt
1 teaspoon soda	3/4 cup strawberry preserves

Cream the butter and sugar and add the eggs. Soak the bread crumbs in water, and when soft, drain, and add to the mixture. Dissolve the soda in a little cold water and stir into the sour milk. Stir this liquid into the bread-crumb mixture. Sift the cinnamon and salt with the flour and stir in. Add the preserves last. Turn into a greased mold and steam two hours. Serve with sweetened whipped cream flavored with vanilla and strawberry syrup from the preserves, or with Lemon Sauce. Serves six to eight.

RAISIN PUFFS

1/4 cup butter	3 teaspoons baking powder
2 tablespoons sugar	1/2 teaspoon salt
2 eggs, well beaten	3/4 cup milk
2 cups flour	1 cup chopped raisins

Cream the butter and sugar and stir in the eggs. Sift the flour with the baking powder and salt, and stir into the first mixture alternately with the milk. Dust the raisins with a little flour and add last. Butter eight cups and fill two-thirds full. Set the cups in a saucepan of hot water and cover. Steam half an hour. Serve with the following sauce.

Maple Country Sauce

1/2 cup butter	1/3 teaspoon salt
1 cup shaved maple sugar	1/4 cup cream
1 teaspoon vanilla	

Cream the butter and sugar until smooth. Add the vanilla and salt. Add the cream a drop at a time stirring it in well. Makes about one and a half cups of sauce.

WELLESLEY BREAD AND BUTTER PUDDING

1 small loaf of bread	3 tablespoons sugar
1/4 pound butter	1 quart milk
Currants	1/2 teaspoon salt
Nutmeg	1 teaspoon vanilla
4 eggs	

Slice the bread, butter the slices, and cut them in small squares. Line the bottom and sides of a deep pudding dish with some of the squares. Sprinkle with a handful of currants and a little nutmeg. Cover with another layer of bread squares and sprinkle with more currants and nutmeg. Beat the eggs, add the sugar, milk, salt, and vanilla, and turn the mixture into the pudding dish. Bake like custard in a slow oven, 325 degrees F., about one hour. Serves eight. Serve hot with the following sauce.

Wellesley Lemon Sauce

1 egg, separated	Juice and grated rinds of 2 lemons
1 cup sugar	

Beat the egg white until stiff. Beat the yolk separately, stir in the sugar, and fold into the beaten egg white. Set the bowl over the steam of a boiling teakettle and stir slowly until the mixture begins to thicken. Remove from the heat and slowly add the juice and grated rind of the lemons. Makes about three-fourths cup of sauce.

QUEEN OF PUDDINGS

2 cups fine bread crumbs	1 teaspoon salt
1 quart milk	1/4 teaspoon nutmeg or cinnamon
1 tablespoon butter	3/4 cup jam
1/4 cup sugar	2 tablespoons sugar
4 eggs, separated	Pinch of baking powder

Soak the bread crumbs in the milk one hour. Cream the butter and sugar, and add the well-beaten egg yolks. Combine with the bread-crumb mixture and add the salt and spice. Stir well and turn into a deep buttered pudding dish. Bake in a moderate oven, 350 degrees F., about half an hour, or until firm. Cool the pudding and spread the top with jam. Beat the egg whites stiff and add two tablespoons of sugar and a pinch of baking powder. Pile this on the jam and return the pudding to the oven. Remove as soon as the top of the meringue whirls turn a delicate brown. Serves six.

APPLEDORE PUDDING

Butter a pudding dish and line it with strips of stale cake. Fill the dish within three inches of the top with blueberries, blackberries, or currants. Add one-half cup of sugar to each quart of berries, or one cup to each quart of currants. Cover with slices of cake wet with half a tumbler of sherry wine. Bake in a moderate oven, 350 degrees F., for half an hour. Cover with egg-white meringue and set in the oven again until light brown. Serves six to eight.

NEW ENGLAND CRACKER PUDDING

8 Boston crackers	2 eggs, slightly beaten
2 tablespoons butter	1/2 teaspoon salt
1/2 cup raisins	Extra milk
2 cups milk	

Split the crackers and spread the split sides with the butter. Put a layer of crackers in the bottom of a well-buttered deep dish, arranging them butter side up. Sprinkle with raisins. Cover with another layer of crackers and another of raisins. Mix the milk with the eggs and the salt and pour over the crackers. Let the mixture stand in a cool place for two hours. Add more milk and bake in a hot oven, 425 degrees F., for twenty minutes or until the crackers are brown. Serves six. Serve with the following sauce.

Yellow Sauce

1/4 pound butter

1/4 pound brown sugar

1 egg yolk, well beaten

1/2 cup sherry or fruit juice

1/4 teaspoon nutmeg

Cream the butter and brown sugar and stir over hot water until the butter melts. Add the egg yolk and stir until the mixture thickens. Add the sherry and nutmeg, and serve at once. Makes about one cup.

BROWN BETTY

This pudding is one form of brown Betty, the apple dessert that is as well known as the New England hills. Usually bread or cracker crumbs are used, but this modern version made with corn flakes has superseded the old Betty to a great extent.

2 tablespoons butter

2 cups corn flakes

1/2 cup sugar

1/4 teaspoon nutmeg

1/4 teaspoon cinnamon

Grated rind and juice of 1 lemon

3 cups chopped apples

1/4 cup water

Melt the butter and add the corn flakes. Mix together the sugar, spices, and lemon rind. Put a layer of corn flakes in the bottom of a buttered pudding dish and cover with about half of the apples. Sprinkle with half the sugar mixture. Add another layer of corn flakes and one of apples and the rest of the sugar mixture. Sprinkle the lemon juice over this and cover with the remainder of the corn flakes. Add the water. Cover and bake in a moderate oven, 350 degrees F., for forty-five minutes. Remove the cover, turn up the heat, and let the top of the Betty brown quickly. Serve with sugar and cream. Serves six.

ANNA COFFIN'S SECOND DAY WEDDING PUDDING

11 ounces cracker crumbs

3 pints boiling milk

1/2 pound butter

1/4 pound sugar

1 teaspoon salt

1/2 teaspoon nutmeg

10 eggs, beaten

1 pound boiled raisins

Pound the crackers and cover with the boiling milk. Cream the butter
and sugar. Add to the milk with the salt and nutmeg. When cold, add
the beaten eggs and raisins. Pour into a buttered pudding dish and
bake one and one-half hours in a moderate oven, 350 degrees F. Serves
six to eight. Serve with Brandy Sauce, Currant Wine Sauce, or Yellow
Sauce.

NANTUCKET CORN PUDDING

6 ears corn	1/4 pound sugar
1 pint milk	Nutmeg and mace
1/4 pound butter	4 eggs

Boil the corn and scrape the kernels from the cobs. Turn the milk
over the corn. Cream the butter, sugar, and spices. Beat the eggs and
fold into the butter mixture. Combine with the milk and corn and
turn into a buttered baking dish. Bake in a moderate oven, 350 degrees
F., until set like custard, about thirty to forty minutes. Serve with
butter and sugar or with sugar and cream. Not good cold. Serves six.

RHODE ISLAND HONEYCOMB PUDDING

1/2 cup milk	1/2 cup sugar
1/2 cup butter	1 cup flour
1 teaspoon soda	4 eggs, well beaten
1 cup molasses	

Warm the milk and melt the butter in it. When cool, add the soda,
dissolved in a little water, and the molasses. Mix the sugar and flour
and heat in the oven. Combine the two mixtures and add the eggs.
Beat thoroughly. Turn into a buttered pudding dish. If stringy, strain
through a sieve. Bake one and a half hours in a slow oven, 325 degrees
F. Cover the dish for the first half hour of baking. Serves six. Serve
with the following sauce.

Brandy Sauce

1/2 cup butter	2 tablespoons brandy
1/2 cup maple sugar	2 tablespoons thick cream

Mix all the ingredients thoroughly. Place over boiling water and beat until light and creamy. Makes about one cup of sauce.

APPPLE BATTER PUDDING

3 apples	2 1/2 cups flour
1/4 cup chopped nuts	1/2 teaspoon salt
1/4 cup chopped raisins	3 teaspoons baking powder
2 tablespoons brown sugar	2 tablespoons shortening
1/2 teaspoon cinnamon	1 cup milk
1 cup white sugar	2 eggs, well beaten

Pare and core the apples and place them in a buttered shallow baking pan. Fill the cavities with the nuts, raisins, brown sugar, and cinnamon. Sift the white sugar with the flour, salt, and baking powder. Melt the shortening and add to the milk and stir in the eggs. Combine the two mixtures and turn the batter over the apples. Bake twenty minutes in a moderate oven, 375 degrees F. Serves eight. Serve with the following sauce.

Vinegar Sauce

1 cup sugar	1 1/2 tablespoons cider vinegar
1 tablespoon cornstarch	1/8 teaspoon nutmeg
1 cup boiling water	Pinch of salt
2 tablespoons butter	

Thoroughly mix the sugar and cornstarch. Stir into the boiling water, adding only a little of the sugar mixture at a time, stirring constantly. Boil five minutes. Remove from the fire and add the butter, vinegar, nutmeg, and salt. Makes about one cup of sauce.

STATE HOUSE DOMES

Prepare rich biscuit dough. Turn on the molding board and roll out to about one inch thick. Cut in six-inch squares and spread with two tablespoons softened butter. Peel and core six apples and place one on each square. Mix one-half cup sugar with one teaspoon cinnamon and one-half teaspoon nutmeg, and fill the holes in the apples with the mixture. Turn up the corners of the squares of dough and twist them together over the apples. Prick the tops of the dumplings with a fork and put them in a buttered baking pan. Mix one-half cup sugar with one cup water and pour over the tops. Put the dumplings in a hot oven, 400 degrees F. Meantime, mix two cups boiling water with one tablespoon butter and one cup sugar. When the dumplings have been in the oven ten minutes baste with this mixture. Baste again in ten minutes. Bake twenty-five minutes in all. Then baste a third time and return to the oven five minutes longer. Serves six.

FRANCONIA BAKED STRAWBERRY DUMPLINGS

This recipe is the prized possession of a lifelong resident of the White Mountains. She serves it on very special occasions during the strawberry season, and for the first time has given the recipe away.

Make a rich biscuit dough. Roll out about half an inch thick and cut in three-inch squares. In the center of each square put about two tablespoons of wild or cultivated strawberries cut in pieces. Cover with one-half tablespoon of sugar and add a tiny pinch of salt. Fold the squares over to form dumplings and brush the tops with a little milk. Bake in a hot oven, 400 degrees F., about fifteen minutes. Serve piping hot with the following sauce.

Strawberry Butter Sauce

1 cup strawberries   1 cup sugar
1/2 cup butter

Mash the strawberries thoroughly. Cream the butter and sugar and mix with the berries. This sauce should be turned over the dumplings while they are hot enough to melt the butter. Serves six.

Strawberry butter sauce is also delicious on hot popovers and hot rice. In season, raspberries and blackberries may be substituted for the strawberries.

STRAWBERRY SHORTCAKE

Rich biscuit dough   Sugar
1/4 pound butter   Thick cream
1 1/2 quarts strawberries

Pat out the biscuit dough and cut in two parts, putting each section in large buttered round tins. Bake in a hot oven, 450 degrees F., ten to fifteen minutes. Reserve one cup of whole berries, but slice the rest and sweeten them to taste. Plan to serve the shortcake as soon as it comes from the oven. Turn a cake on a round platter and butter it lavishly. Heap berries on the layer and top with the other generously buttered cake. Turn berries over the second layer and arrange whole berries on top. Serve at once with cream. Serves six.

BERRY GRUNT

2 cups berries   3 teaspoons baking powder
1 cup water   1/4 teaspoon salt
1/2 cup sugar   1 tablespoon butter
1 1/2 cups sifted flour   1/2 cup milk

Cook the berries in the water and when soft add the sugar. Place in a buttered mold with a tight-fitting cover. Sift the flour, baking powder, and salt. Cut in the butter and add the milk to make a soft dough. Drop by spoonfuls on the fruit, cover tightly, and steam over boiling water. The water should come to within one inch of the top of the mold. Steam one hour and serve with Nutmeg Sauce. Serves six to eight.

BLUEBERRY SLUMP

Put a quart of blueberries and half a cup of sugar over the fire until the berries are slightly cooked and covered with a thin syrup. Strain off the berries and put the syrup back on the stove. When it begins to boil, drop squares of thinly rolled biscuit dough into the syrup. Cover closely and cook twenty minutes. Serve hot with blueberries poured over the dumplings and with heavy pan cream. Serves six.

APPLE SLUMP

2 cups peeled sliced apples
2/3 cup sugar
1/2 cup water

1 teaspoon cinnamon
Baking powder biscuits

Combine the apples, sugar, water, and cinnamon. Bring to a boil. Cover with the biscuits, place the cover on tightly, and continue cooking for twenty-five minutes or until the biscuits are done. Remove the biscuits, pour the apples over them, and serve with cream. Serves six.

Blueberries, peaches, cherries, or other fruit may be cooked the same way, adding a teaspoon of lemon juice or a little grated lemon rind if the fruit is very sweet.

SHAKER PEACH DUMPLINGS

Peel small peaches and cut in pieces. Put in a kettle with a little water and sugar to sweeten. Cook slowly until a good syrup is formed. Add nutmeg if desired. Make a batter of the following:

1 cup white flour
1 cup whole wheat flour
2 teaspoons baking powder

1 teaspoon sugar
1/2 teaspoon salt
1 cup milk

Drop by the teaspoonful on top of the boiling fruit, cover closely, and steam ten to fifteen minutes. Serve with the fruit in the center of the dish and the dumplings around the edge. Serves six to eight.

NEW ENGLAND SWEET DUMPLINGS

2 cups water
1/2 cup sugar

2 tablespoons molasses
1 tablespoon butter

Mix the above ingredients and bring to a boil. Make a batter of the following ingredients:

1 cup flour
1 teaspoon baking powder

1/8 teaspoon salt
1/2 cup water

Drop by spoonfuls into the boiling syrup. As the dumplings rise to the surface, turn them with a fork. Let them simmer for fifteen minutes. Serve with hot maple syrup. Serves four to six.

CUP CUSTARD

4 cups milk	1/8 teaspoon salt
4 eggs	1/2 teaspoon vanilla
1/2 cup sugar	Grated nutmeg

Scald the milk. Pour slowly over the eggs beaten until foamy with the sugar and salt. Add the vanilla and pour into the buttered custard cups. Sprinkle grated nutmeg over the top. Set in a pan of hot water and bake in a slow oven, 325 degrees F., until firm, about one hour. Serves six to eight.

GINGER CUSTARD

2 cups milk	1/4 teaspoon salt
2 eggs	2 tablespoons ginger syrup
1/4 cup sugar	1/4 cup preserved ginger

Scald the milk. Pour over the eggs beaten with the sugar and salt. Add the ginger syrup. Butter the custard cups, place a small amount of preserved ginger in the bottom of each, and pour in the custard. Bake until firm in a slow oven, 325 degrees F. Serves four.

BAKED POPCORN CUSTARD

2 cups milk	1 tablespoon cornstarch
2 cups popped corn	1/4 cup sugar
1 egg	1/8 teaspoon salt

Pour the milk over the popcorn and let it stand. Beat the egg, add the other ingredients, drain off the milk, and mix it with the egg mixture. Put the soaked popcorn into a buttered baking dish, pour the custard over it, and bake in a moderate oven, 350 degrees F., until the custard is set, about half an hour. Serve with cream. Serves six.

POPCORN PUDDING

4 cups milk

4 eggs

1/2 cup sugar

1/4 teaspoon salt

1 teaspoon vanilla

1 cup popcorn

1/2 cup sweetened whipped cream

Make a boiled custard of the milk, eggs, sugar, salt, and vanilla. Cool slightly and add the popcorn. Serve with sweetened whipped cream. Serves six to eight.

TIPSY PUDDING

Break or crumble stale spongecake or sunshine cake. Allow one-half cup sherry for three cups cake crumbs. If this does not moisten all the crumbs, add a little more, but do not allow the crumbs to get soggy. Put the crumbs in the bottom of a glass dish, and fill the dish with cold boiled custard to which two tablespoons of rum are added. Sprinkle with chopped toasted almonds. Serves six.

TRIFLE

Cut a spongecake in half, spread with a thick layer of jelly or preserved or candied fruits. Cover with the other half of the cake and soak in sherry. Let stand one hour. Pour a soft custard flavored with one-fourth cup sherry or two tablespoons rum over the cake, and serve with whipped cream. A few toasted chopped almonds may be sprinkled over the top. Serves six to eight.

APPLE FOOL

2 pounds apples

1/2 cup brown sugar

1/2 cup water

Strip lemon peel

2 cloves

1-inch stick cinnamon

1 cup soft custard

Cut the apples into quarters without peeling or coring. Add the sugar, water, and spices. Cook until soft. Strain and mix with the cup of soft custard. Serves six.

APPLEDORE BIRD'S-NEST PUDDING

6 apples   4 eggs
2 cups water   4 tablespoons sugar
1 cup sugar   1/8 teaspoon salt
4 cups milk

Pare and core the apples. Make a syrup of the water and sugar, and simmer the apples in it until they are tender. Be sure they do not fall apart. Put in a buttered baking dish and cover with a custard made of the remaining ingredients, following the directions for baked custard. Bake in a slow oven until the custard is firm. Serves six.

To make a richer dessert, the centers of the apples may be filled with chopped preserved fruits or nuts and the custard flavored with lemon. Serve with Currant Wine Sauce.

APPLE SNOW

6 apples   3 beaten egg whites
Grated rind and juice of 1 lemon 1/8 teaspoon salt
1/2 cup sugar

Pare and slice the apples. Steam them until tender, then run them through a sieve. When cold, add the lemon juice and rind, sugar, egg whites beaten stiff, and salt. Serve in sherbet glasses. Serves six. The glasses may be half filled with soft custard, and the apple mixture heaped on top.

WHIPS

Beat a pint of rich cream, add sugar to taste, and vanilla, sherry, almond, or rum flavoring. Serve very cold by itself in a sherbet glass, over trifles, or with wine jelly. Serves four to six.

LEMON WHIP

1 quart cream   1/2 pint wine
2 cups sugar   Juice of 4 lemons

Beat the cream stiff, add the other ingredients. Serve in tall glasses. Serves four to six.

NEWPORT WHIP

1 pint sweet or sour cream
1/2 cup fruit juice

Juice of 1/2 lemon
1/2 cup powdered sugar

Beat the cream stiff, add the other ingredients. Chill and serve in tall glasses. Serves four to six.

WINE JELLY

2 tablespoons gelatin
1/2 cup cold water
Juice of 2 lemons

3 1/2 cups sherry
Sugar

Soak the gelatin in the cold water. Heat the lemon juice and sherry, dissolve the gelatin in the sherry, add sugar to taste, and chill. Serves eight.

MAST ROAD SNOW PUDDING

2 cups water
1/4 cup cornstarch
1/2 cup sugar

Juice of 1 large lemon
3 egg whites

Heat one and three-fourths cups of the water in a saucepan. Mix the remaining quarter cup with the cornstarch. When the water boils, stir in the cornstarch mixture. Place in the top of a double boiler. Add the sugar and cook until transparent. Remove from the heat and stir in the lemon juice. Fold in the stiffly beaten egg whites. Turn into custard cups and chill. Serves six. When firm, unmold and cover with the following sauce.

Yellow Sauce

2 cups milk
3 egg yolks, beaten
1 teaspoon cornstarch

Pinch of salt
1/3 cup sugar
1 teaspoon vanilla

Heat the milk and turn gradually onto the beaten egg yolks. Mix the cornstarch and salt with the sugar. Stir slowly into the milk and eggs. Cook over hot water until the mixture thickens. Beat well and when cool add the vanilla. Makes about two cups of sauce.

CRANBERRY TAPIOCA

2 cups cranberries	3 tablespoons minute tapioca
1 cup cold water	1 cup boiling water
3/4 cup sugar	1 tablespoon orange juice

Chop the cranberries, add the cold water and sugar. Cook until soft. Put the tapioca and boiling water in the top of a double boiler and cook ten minutes, stirring occasionally. Cool. Stir in the cranberry mixture and the orange juice. Turn into a mold and chill. Serve with cream. Serves six.

IRISH MOSS BLANCMANGE

1/2 cup Irish moss	Juice of 1 lemon
4 cups milk	Pinch of salt
2 tablespoons sugar	

Soak the moss in a little cold water for ten minutes. Clean and pick over. Bring the milk to the boiling point and add the moss. Simmer gently until the consistency of cream. Strain. Add the rest of the ingredients and pour into molds. When cold serve with sugar and cream. Serves six.

BLANCMANGE

2 cups milk	1/4 cup sugar
2 tablespoons cornstarch	1/4 teaspoon salt
1/4 cup cold milk	1 teaspoon vanilla

Heat the milk, add the cornstarch dissolved in the cold milk, sugar, and salt. Cook until the mixture begins to thicken. Remove from the fire and add the vanilla. Serves four to six.

BLUEBERRY FLUMMERY

2 cups blueberries   1/2 cup sugar
1/4 cup water   Juice of 1 lemon
3 teaspoons cornstarch   1/4 teaspoon salt

Cook the blueberries in the water until soft. Strain and mix with the remaining ingredients. Cook until thick. Mold and chill. Serve with heavy cream. Serves four.

Blackberries or raspberries may be used instead of blueberries.

APPLE CRUNCH

8 apples   3/4 teaspoon cinnamon
1/4 cup butter   1/8 teaspoon salt
1/2 cup flour   1/4 cup white wine
3/4 cup sugar

Pare and slice the apples thin. Put them in a buttered casserole. Mix the butter and flour with the sugar, cinnamon, and salt. Sprinkle this over the apples. Pour the white wine over the top. Bake in a moderate oven until the apples are done. Serves six.

ICED CABINET PUDDING

1 cup chopped candied fruit   1/2 cup sugar
Spongecake   1/4 teaspoon salt
1/2 cup wine   1 tablespoon gelatin
3 cups milk   1/2 cup cold water
4 egg yolks

Put the candied fruit and spongecake in a quart mold. Add the wine and let stand. Make a custard of the milk, egg yolks, sugar, and salt. Cook until it begins to thicken. Add the gelatin soaked in the cold water. Stir until dissolved. Pour the custard over the cake; cover and chill. Serve garnished with currant jelly cut in cubes. Serves six to eight.

CRANBERRY GRANITE

1 quart cranberries   2 cups sugar
3 cups water   Juice of 2 lemons

Boil the cranberries in the water until soft. Strain, add the sugar, and stir until dissolved. When cold, add the lemon juice and freeze to a mush. Makes about one quart.

12. DOUGHNUT CROCK AND COOKY JAR

Social life in the royal province of New Hampshire was stately and opulent. The wealthy families who lived along the Piscataqua River entertained lavishly and as formally as did their relatives and friends in England.

Hawthorne, who was continually delving into New England's past for material for his stories, was particularly interested in a party given in Kittery by a member of the Cutts family. He described in detail the elaborate dress of the distinguished guests who gathered in the great reception rooms of the manor house. He also made notes about the refreshments. "Among the eatables," he wrote, "a silver tub, of the capacity of four gallons, holding a pyramid of pancakes, powdered with white sugar."

Pancakes were highly prized by the eighteeth-century Piscataqua gentry, who still clung to the traditions of their ancestors. Shrove Tuesday was Pancake Day to these Church of England people. Some of the older ones remembered, as children in England, the ringing of the pancake bell, the signal for them to go from door to door singing:

"We come a-shroving
For a bit of pancake."

It must have been a gigantic task to make enough pancakes for a large party. Each cake was baked separately and then rolled. The women in the family as well as the servants were requisitioned to help. Pantry supplies were unstinted. Even a recipe designed for the family called for sixteen eggs, one quart of milk, a pound of butter, and the same of sugar and flour. Wine and nutmeg were used for the rich flavoring.

The recipe for party pancakes given in this chapter omits the wine and the nutmeg from the batter, but basically it is the same as the old-time rule. So if you want to try your hand at party pancakes, here they are.

The word pancake, however, does not always mean the rolled delicacy filled with jelly or jam and powdered with sugar. It is also applied to small cakes made by dropping batter from a spoon into deep fat and to hotcakes baked in a skillet or on a griddle. Griddlecakes, known in some sections as slapjacks, flapjacks, or flannel cakes, are great favorites with all New Englanders. There is an art to cooking them properly and turning them at exactly the right time. To flip flapjacks high in the air and then let them fall again on the other side is a featured accomplishment of Maine guides and lumber camp cooks. Our grandmothers baked the cakes on soapstone griddles and piled them high in a covered nappy, with butter spread lavishly on each cake. There are many reliable rules for griddlecakes, but most New England cooks prefer sour milk for mixing them.

It is difficult for any bred-in-the-bone New Englander to picture a time when doughnuts built around holes did not fill a special stone crock on the butt'ry shelf. But the earliest doughnuts were quite unlike these golden rings in shape. The drop cakes, fingers, squares, rounds, and twists of dough were known by a variety of names. In Connecticut, sweet twisted doughnuts were "biled cakes"; in Massachusetts they were fried cakes. In Maine, unsweetened doughnuts were twisters, one of a long list of descriptive terms applied to them in other localities. A jumble in Connecticut did not always mean a cooky. It might be a delicious fried ring of rich sweetened dough; and the simball or cymbal, known both in Massachusetts and Connecticut, was as Oliver Wendell Holmes put it " a kind of genteel doughnut."

One of the great delights of our parents when they were children was visiting grandmother and being allowed to dip into the spicy cooky jar on the pantry shelf. Keeping that jar filled was one of great-grandmother's important responsibilities. Even though cooky making a hundred years ago involved more work than it does now, great-grandmother managed to fit it into her busy day with no apparent effort.

The first cookies were baked in sheets and cut into squares or oblongs when the pan was taken from the oven. Later on, dough rolled half an inch thick was placed in the pan, and a corrugated roller made of wood, ivory, or bone was run over the top. When baked, the cookies were cut along the grooves. Later still, flat cooky disks similar to butter prints with patterns on both sides were used. When done, the cookies were cut along the edge of the pattern.

Fancy-shaped cooky cutters are comparatively recent in date. No excitement compares to that we have all felt at Christmas time when mothers, aunts, and grandmothers made holiday cookies in the shape of birds, hearts, crescents, and stars. Somehow those cookies tasted better than any others we have eaten. The fragrance of spicy evergreens and freshly baked cookies has become to most of us a part of the lost romance of childhood.

No matter how busy grandmother was she always had time to make gingerbread men and monkey faces. We can all remember standing by the kitchen table when we were barely tall enough to see over the edge to watch her trim the gingerbread man's coat. Later came the never-to-be-forgotten day when, with her blue-checked gingham apron tied under our armpits, we were allowed to cut and trim the cookies ourselves.

PARTY PANCAKES

1 cup flour
1/2 teaspoon salt
1 teaspoon sugar
3 eggs, separated

1 cup milk
1 tablespoon salad oil
Jelly

Sift the flour, salt, and sugar. Beat the egg yolks and combine them with the milk. Add a third of the liquid to the dry ingredients and mix thoroughly. Then add the rest of the liquid and the salad oil. Fold in the stiffly beaten egg whites last. Heat a small iron spider; turn in one teaspoon of fat and spread it over the pan. Pour in enough pancake batter to just cover the bottom of the pan. When the pancake is brown, turn it carefully and brown it on the other side. Spread each cake with jelly, roll up, and dust with sugar. Makes eight to ten pancakes.

CRANBERRY PANCAKES

No leavening is used in most pancake batters. But this recipe is a little different: it includes a teaspoon of baking powder.

1 egg
1 1/2 cups milk
1 tablespoon sugar
1 cup flour

1 teaspoon baking powder
1 cup thick cranberry sauce
1 tablespoon melted shortening

Beat the egg and stir it into the milk. Sift the dry ingredients and combine the mixture. Stir in the cranberry sauce and the melted shortening. Drop by spoonfuls on a hot greased griddle. Brown the cakes lightly. Remove from the heat, roll quickly, and dust with powdered sugar. Serve at once with butter. Makes fifteen medium-sized pancakes.

SOUR MILK GRIDDLECAKES

2 1/2 cups flour
1/2 teaspoon salt
1 teaspoon soda

2 cups thick sour milk
2 eggs, well beaten
2 tablespoons melted fat

Sift the flour and salt. Dissolve the soda with a little water and stir into the sour milk. Add the eggs and melted fat, and combine the liquid mixture with the flour. Stir well and drop by spoonfuls on a hot greased griddle. When the tops of the cakes bubble, turn them and bake on the other side until they stop puffing. Serve with butter, maple syrup, or honey. Makes twenty-four medium-sized pancakes.

Corn-meal griddlecakes may be made by substituting two-thirds corn meal for the same amount of white flour.

BLUEBERRY GRIDDLECAKES

Use the recipe for Sour Milk Griddlecakes, making one change. Sift two cups of the flour with the salt, and keep the extra half cup to mix with one and one-half cups of blueberries. Stir the blueberries in last. Makes twenty-four pancakes.

APPLE GRIDDLECAKES

2 cups scalded milk	2 teaspoons baking powder
2 cups fresh bread crumbs	1/2 teaspoon salt
1 tablespoon melted fat	1 tablespoon maple syrup
2 eggs, separated	1 cup chopped apples
1 cup flour	

Turn the hot milk over the bread crumbs, add the melted fat, and let the mixture set until the crumbs are very soft. Rub through a sieve or mash to a paste. Beat the egg yolks until light and add to the crumbs. Sift the dry ingredients and combine with the bread paste. Add the syrup and mix thoroughly. Beat the egg whites and fold in, and quickly stir in the chopped apples. Bake on a hot griddle. Makes twenty-four medium-sized cakes.

NEW ENGLAND BUCKWHEAT CAKES

2 cups buckwheat	Warm water
1 cup graham flour	1/2 yeast cake
1 teaspoon salt	2 tablespoons molasses

Start the batter the night before you plan to serve the cakes for breakfast. Mix the buckwheat, graham flour, and salt with enough warm water to make a thick batter. Dissolve the yeast cake in a little lukewarm water and add with the molasses to the mixure. In the morning, if the batter seems too thick, thin it with warm water. If it smells at all sour, add one-fourth teaspoon soda dissolved in a little warm water. Stir the batter down, and when it rises again pour from the pitcher to form large cakes on a hot griddle. Bake like griddlecakes. Serve with butter or syrup. Makes twenty-four cakes.

BACON WAFFLES

2 cups flour	1 cup milk
2 1/2 teaspoons baking powder	4 tablespoons melted shortening
1/2 teaspoon salt	1/3 cup cooked bacon
2 eggs, separated	

Sift the flour, baking powder, and salt. Add the egg yolks and milk, and beat well. Add the melted shortening and the bacon chopped in small pieces. Beat the egg whites and fold in. Bake in a hot waffle iron. Makes eight waffles.

RYE DROP CAKES

2 1/2 teaspoons baking powder	2 tablespoons molasses
1/2 teaspoon salt	1/2 cup milk
2/3 cup white flour	1 egg, well beaten
2/3 cup rye flour	

Sift the baking powder and salt with the white flour and mix with the rye flour. Add the molasses and milk with the egg, and stir into the dry ingredients. Drop by spoonfuls into hot fat and fry. Serve with butter, maple syrup, or honey. Makes twenty-four cakes.

FRIED PIES

1/2 teaspoon soda	1/2 teaspoon salt
1 cup buttermilk	Flour
1 egg, well beaten	Boiled cider applesauce

Dissolve the soda in a little water and add to the buttermilk. Stir in the egg. Sift the salt with two cups of flour and add more flour to make a dough that will roll. Turn the dough on a molding board and roll to make a thin crust. Cut rounds the size of a small plate. Place a large spoonful of boiled cider applesauce in the center of each round, and roll it over and pinch the edges together like a turnover. Fry in very hot fat. Another method is to fry the rounds one at a time, and pile them alternately with layers of applesauce in a deep dish. Makes ten pies.

MAINE DOUGHGODS

Some people call the small rounds of dough made by the center of the doughnut cutter "doughgods." Others make them as follows:

2 eggs, well beaten	1 teaspoon soda
1 cup rich buttermilk	Flour to mix

Roll out this dough and cut in small squares. Fry like doughnuts. Serve with maple syrup. Makes two dozen.

DUMFUNNIES

1 egg	1 teaspoon soda
2 tablespoons sugar	1 cup sour milk
1/2 teaspoon salt	Flour
1 tablespoon melted butter	

Start these doughnuts at night. Beat the egg with the sugar, and add the salt and butter. Dissolve the soda in the sour milk, stirring it well. Add to the egg mixture. Then stir in enough sifted flour to make a dough stiff enough to knead. After kneading, put the dough in a greased bowl, cover with a clean cloth, and let it stand overnight. In the morning, turn the dough on a floured board, and cut off strips about one and one-half inches wide. Twist them and pinch the ends together. Fry in deep fat. Do not have the lard as hot as for sweetened doughnuts. Let each cake brown on one side before turning it on the other. Dumfunnies are especially good when served with warm maple syrup. Makes three dozen.

FEATHERBEDS

3 teaspoons lard	2 eggs
1/2 teaspoon salt	1 quart light bread sponge
2 cups lukewarm water	Flour

Melt the lard and add with the salt to the lukewarm water. Beat the eggs until light and add to the bread sponge. Combine the mixtures, and add flour until the dough is as stiff as for bread. Let it rise until light. Cut it down, turn on a molding board, and roll out to half an inch thick. Cut in two-inch squares. Let them rise on the board until very light. Fry in deep fat until they are light brown. Featherbeds are delicious when served with warm maple syrup. Makes five to six dozen.

VERMONT OLYCOOKS

2 cups milk	9 cups flour
1 cup sugar	1/2 teaspoon nutmeg
2/3 cup butter	4 eggs, well beaten
1 yeast cake	4 apples, chopped fine
1/4 cup lukewarm water	1/2 pound raisins, chopped fine
1 teaspoon salt	3 tablespoons chopped citron

Scald the milk, add the sugar and one tablespoon of the butter, and cool until bloodwarm. Soften the yeast in the lukewarm water and combine with the first mixture. Sift the salt with three cups of the flour, and add. Let this sponge rise until light. Melt the rest of the butter and stir in the nutmeg and eggs. Add to the sponge with the remaining flour. When the dough is light, stir it down and turn on a board. Knead and roll out. Cut in rounds and let them rise on the board until light. Then put a teaspoon of the mixture of the chopped apples, raisins, and citron in the center of each round. Moisten the edges of the rounds with cold water, and press the edges together like turnovers. Let them rise until very light. Fry in deep hot fat. Roll in powdered sugar. These olycooks, which originated in old Dutch kitchens of the Hudson River Valley, will keep three weeks. Makes six dozen.

SHAKER RAISED DOUGHNUTS

3 medium-sized potatoes	2 tablespoons homemade yeast,
2 cups sifted flour	or 1 yeast cake
1 teaspoon salt	Flour

Boil the potatoes and mash them, saving the water. While still hot, add the two cups of sifted flour. Then add enough of the water in which the potatoes were boiled to make a batter. Stir in the salt. When the batter is lukewarm, add the yeast and flour enough to knead. Let the dough rise overnight. In the morning cut it down, turn on a floured molding board, and roll out half an inch thick. Cut the dough in pieces about three inches long and two inches wide. Let them rise on the board for ten minutes. Fry in deep fat. These doughnuts should be full of large holes when broken open. Serve with maple syrup. Makes four dozen. (If yeast cake is used, dissolve it in one quarter cup lukewarm water.)

DOWN-EAST SOUR MILK DOUGHNUTS

1 tablespoon thick sour cream	1 cup sugar
2/3 cup thick sour milk	Pinch of ginger
1 rounded teaspoon soda	1/3 teaspoon salt
1/3 cup sweet milk	Flour
1 egg, well beaten	

Mix the sour cream and sour milk. Dissolve the soda in the sweet milk and stir quickly into the sour mixture. Add the well-beaten egg and sugar. Sift the ginger and salt with one cup of flour. Then add sifted flour to make a dough that can be handled and will not stick to the board when you roll it. Fry only a few doughnuts at a time, not over four or five. Turn them just as soon as they rise to the top, and keep turning until done. Check the heat of the fat by frying a few small rounds cut from the centers of the doughnuts. Makes four dozen.

MOLASSES DOUGHNUTS

A Connecticut woman who is noted for her molasses doughnuts supplied this recipe. "The frying is very important," she says. "You must not get the lard too hot, or the doughnuts will brown on the outside before they are thoroughly cooked through. If you can get the real old New Orleans molasses, it will give a wonderfully rich light color to the cakes," she adds.

1 egg, well beaten	5 cups flour
1 cup molasses	1 teaspoon salt
1 cup sour milk	1 teaspoon soda
1 teaspoon melted shortening	3/4 teaspoon ginger
1/4 cup sugar	1 teaspoon cinnamon

Mix the egg, molasses, sour milk, and shortening. Sift the sugar with the flour, salt, soda, and spices. Combine the mixtures and stir until smooth. Add enough flour to make a dough that will roll. Turn the dough on a floured board and roll to one-quarter inch thick. Cut out doughnuts and fry in deep fat. Turn them as soon as they come to the top. Watch carefully, for molasses doughnuts burn more easily than those sweetened with white sugar. Roll the doughnuts while warm in sugar. Makes five dozen.

ELDERFLOWER FRITTERS

Cut elderflowers at the height of bloom. Soak in brandy with a stick of cinnamon for one hour. Remove the coarse stems and dip each cluster in a rich egg batter. Drop by spoonfuls into deep hot fat, frying until light brown. Drain on brown paper. Sprinkle with powdered sugar and orange juice, and serve.

OLD-FASHIONED SUGAR COOKIES

1 1/2 cups sugar　　　　　　2 teaspoons cream of tartar
1 1/2 cups butter　　　　　　1 teaspoon soda
2 eggs　　　　　　　　　　　Flour
1/2 cup milk

Cream the sugar and butter, beat in the eggs. Add the milk with the cream of tartar and soda dissolved in it. Add enough flour to roll. The dough should be very soft. Roll one-quarter inch thick, cut, and bake in a hot oven, 400 degrees F., twelve minutes. Makes six dozen.

BROWN SUGAR COOKIES

1 1/2 cups brown sugar　　　1 teaspoon cinnamon or ginger
2/3 cup butter　　　　　　　1/2 teaspoon soda
2 eggs　　　　　　　　　　　4 cups flour
2 tablespoons milk

Cream the sugar and butter. Add the eggs and milk. Sift the spice and soda with the flour. Mix well and roll thin. Bake in a hot oven, 400 degrees F., ten to twelve minutes. Makes five dozen.

JUMBLES

1 cup butter　　　　　　　　4 eggs
2 cups sugar　　　　　　　　6 cups flour
1 cup milk　　　　　　　　　Spices if desired
1/2 teaspoon soda

Cream the butter and sugar. Add the milk with the soda dissolved in it, then the beaten eggs and flour. Roll thin in sugar. Cut with a dough-nut cutter and bake in a moderate oven, 375 degrees F., ten minutes. Makes six to seven dozen.

DAISY WOODWARD'S SOUR CREAM COOKIES

1 cup sugar	1/2 teaspoon salt
1 egg	Flour
1 cup thick sour cream	1 teaspoon vanilla
1 teaspoon soda	

Cream the sugar and egg. Add soda dissolved in sour cream. Sift the salt with the flour and mix well. Add the vanilla. Use just enough flour to roll. This should be soft dough. This is important! Cut and bake in a moderate oven, 375 degrees F., ten to twelve minutes. Makes five dozen.

HARRIET'S OLD-FASHIONED MOLASSES COOKIES

1 cup lard	3 teaspoons soda
4 1/2 cups flour	1/4 cup cold water
2 cups dark molasses	1 teaspoon salt
1/4 cup sugar	1 tablespoon ginger
1 egg	1 tablespoon cinnamon

Cut the lard into the flour. Add the rest of the ingredients, including the soda dissolved in the water. The dough should be quite soft. Roll a little more than one-quarter inch thick. Cut and bake in a hot oven, 400 degrees F., for eight to ten minutes. Makes five dozen.

GINGERBREAD MEN

3/4 cup molasses	1/2 teaspoon salt
1/4 cup brown sugar	1 teaspoon ginger
1/3 cup shortening, melted	1 teaspoon cinnamon
1 egg	3 teaspoons baking powder
3 cups flour	

Mix the molasses, sugar, and melted shortening. Add the egg and beat well. Add the dry ingredients sifted together. Chill the dough. Roll it out and cut. Make faces and trimmings with whole cloves, currants, rice, and raisins. Bake in a moderate oven, 375 degrees F., about twelve minutes. Makes three dozen.

MONKEY FACES

1 egg	1 teaspoon soda
1 cup sugar	2 cups flour
2 tablespoons butter	Raisins
1/2 cup sour milk	

Mix the egg, sugar, and butter. Add the sour milk mixed with the soda. Add flour. Drop by the spoonful on a buttered baking sheet. Press in two raisins for eyes and one for the mouth. Bake in a moderate oven, 375 degrees F., for twelve minutes. Makes three dozen.

GINGER COOKIES

1 cup butter	1 teaspoon soda
1 cup sugar	1 teaspoon ginger
1 cup molasses	2 teaspoons baking powder
1/4 cup hot water	4 cups flour

Cream the butter and sugar. Add to the molasses the hot water and soda. Add this to the butter and sugar mixture, and mix in the ginger, baking powder, and flour sifted together. Let stand half an hour. Roll very thin and bake in a hot oven, 400 degrees F., eight to ten minutes. Makes seven dozen.

HARD GINGERSNAPS

1/2 cup brown sugar	1 cup molasses
1/2 cup shortening	1 teaspoon soda
1 tablespoon ginger	1 tablespoon water
1 teaspoon salt	Flour

Cream the sugar and shortening, adding the ginger and salt. Boil the molasses, pour it over the sugar mixture, and cool. Add the soda dissolved in the water and just enough flour to make a soft dough. Chill. Roll very thin and cut. Bake in a hot oven, 400 degrees F., ten to twelve minutes. Makes three and a half dozen.

CARAWAY SEED COOKIES

1/3 cup butter
1 cup sugar
1 egg
1/4 cup milk
1/3 teaspoon soda

1/2 teaspoon nutmeg
1/2 teaspoon cinnamon
1/2 teaspoon caraway seed
2 cups flour

Cream the butter and sugar, add the egg. Mix the milk and soda, and add it with the spices and flour to the first mixture. Chill and roll thin. Sift sugar over the top, cut, and bake in a moderate oven, 350 degrees F., ten to fifteen minutes. Makes three dozen.

BETSY'S CONNECTICUT SPICE COOKIES

1/2 cup shortening
1/2 cup sugar
1/2 cup molasses
1 egg
1 tablespoon vinegar
2 cups flour
1/4 teaspoon cloves

1/4 teaspoon allspice
1 teaspoon cinnamon
1/2 teaspoon ginger
1/2 teaspoon salt
1 teaspoon soda
1/2 cup chopped dates

Cream the shortening and sugar. Add the molasses, egg, and vinegar. Beat well. Sift the flour with the spices, salt, and soda. Mix well. Add the dates and drop by spoonfuls on a cooky sheet. Bake in a moderate oven, 375 degrees F., twelve to fifteen minutes. Makes three dozen.

MINCEMEAT HERMITS

1 1/2 cups sugar
1/2 cup butter
2 eggs
1 teaspoon salt
1 teaspoon soda
1/2 cup sour milk

3 cups flour
1 teaspoon cinnamon
1/2 teaspoon cloves
1/2 teaspoon nutmeg
1 cup mincemeat

Cream the sugar and butter, add the eggs and salt, and the soda dissolved in the milk. Sift the flour and spices. Mix well, add the mincemeat, and drop by spoonfuls on a greased cooky sheet. Bake in a moderate oven, 350 degrees F., twelve to fifteen minutes. Makes six dozen.

AUNT HAT'S OLD-FASHIONED SOFT HERMITS

1 cup sugar	1 teaspoon cloves
1/2 cup shortening	1 teaspoon cinnamon
1/2 cup sour milk	1/2 teaspoon salt
1/2 cup molasses	1/8 teaspoon nutmeg
1 teaspoon soda	1 cup chopped raisins
1 teaspoon cold water	1 egg, well beaten
1 cup flour	Flour

Cream the sugar and shortening. Mix the sour milk and molasses, add the soda dissolved in the cold water, and mix this with the sugar and shortening. Sift the cup of flour with the spices and mix with the raisins. Add to the first mixture and stir in the well-beaten egg. Add enough flour to make a dough to spread about half an inch thick on a cooky sheet. Bake in a moderate oven, 375 degrees F., fifteen minutes. Cut in squares while hot. Makes six dozen.

HICKORY NUT COOKIES

2 tablespoons butter	1 cup flour
1/2 cup sugar	1 teaspoon baking powder
1 egg	1/4 teaspoon salt
2 tablespoons milk	3/4 cup chopped hickory nuts

Cream the butter and sugar, add the egg and milk. Sift the flour with the baking powder and salt. Add to the first mixtures, fold in the nuts, and drop by the spoonful on a buttered cooky sheet. Garnish with a whole nut. Bake in a moderate oven, 375 degrees F., for five to eight minutes. Makes three dozen.

NEW HAMPSHIRE FILLED COOKIES

4 cups flour	1 cup sour cream
2 teaspoons baking powder	1 cup sugar
1/2 teaspoon salt	1 egg, beaten
1/2 teaspoon soda	1 teaspoon lemon extract

Sift the first four ingredients. Mix the sour cream, sugar, egg, and flavoring. Add to the flour mixture, roll thin, and cut in rounds. Place a teaspoon of filling on half the cookies and cover with the others. Sprinkle with sugar, and bake ten minutes in a hot oven, 400 degrees F. Makes three dozen.

Filling

1 cup chopped raisins	2 tablespoons flour
1/2 cup sugar	Juice of 1/2 lemon
1/8 teaspoon salt	1/4 cup boiling water

Cook until thick and cool before using.

BUTTERNUT FILLED COOKIES

1/2 cup shortening	1 teaspoon baking powder
1/2 cup maple sugar	1/2 teaspoon salt
1/2 cup maple syrup	1 teaspoon cinnamon
1 egg, beaten	1/2 teaspoon cloves
1/4 cup sour milk	1/4 teaspoon nutmeg
1 teaspoon soda	3 cups flour

Cream the shortening and sugar. Add the syrup and beaten egg. Then add the sour milk and soda. Sift the baking powder, salt, and spices with the flour. Add. Chill one hour. Roll thin and cut in rounds. Cover half of the rounds with butternut filling and cover with the other half. Bake twenty minutes in a moderate oven, 375 degrees F. Makes two dozen.

Filling

Mix one-half cup chopped butternuts with one-half cup honey, one teaspoon flour, and a few grains of salt.

CHRISTMAS CAKES

1 cup powdered coriander seed	3 cups sugar
6 cups flour	1 cup milk
1 pound butter	1 teaspoon soda

Mix the coriander seed and flour. Cream the butter and sugar, and mix the milk with the soda. Add the milk and the flour alternately to the butter and sugar mixture. The last of the flour will have to be kneaded in. Put on a floured board and knead until smooth. Roll three-quarters inch thick, and stamp or cut in fancy shapes. Bake twenty minutes in a moderate oven, 375 degrees F. Makes six dozen.

RICH MADELINES

3/4 pound butter	Grated rind of 1 lemon
2 cups sugar	1/2 nutmeg, grated
4 cups flour	1/2 teaspoon baking powder
9 eggs	Jam
1/2 wineglass brandy	

Cream the butter and sugar. Add the remaining ingredients, and bake in a flat pan ten minutes in a moderate oven, 350 degrees F. The dough should be spread very thin. When baked, take from the oven and cut in squares. Makes five dozen. Spread with strawberry, raspberry, apricot, or plum jam, chopped fruits or nuts. From a spoon drop a thick layer of frosting.

Madeline Frosting

2 egg whites, unbeaten	10 drops vanilla extract
2 cups powdered sugar	Juice of 1/2 lemon
6 drops almond extract	

Combine the unbeaten egg whites with the other ingredients. Mix well and beat until creamy. Drop on the cookies. Store in a covered tin. They will keep for a long time.

BROWNIES

2 eggs	2/3 cup flour
1 cup sugar	1/2 teaspoon vanilla
1/2 cup melted butter	1/2 cup chopped walnuts
2 squares chocolate, melted	

Beat the eggs and sugar. Melt the butter and chocolate and add to the sugar. Stir in the flour, add the vanilla and walnuts. Bake in a moderate oven, 350 degrees F., thirty minutes. Makes one and a half dozen.

BUTTERSCOTCH BARS

1/2 cup melted butter	1 teaspoon baking powder
1 cup brown sugar	1/2 teaspoon salt
1 egg	1 teaspoon vanilla
1 cup flour	3/4 cup nut meats

Mix the butter, brown sugar, and egg. Add the flour sifted with the other dry ingredients. Then add the flavoring and nut meats. Bake in a slow oven, 325 degrees F., for thirty minutes. Cut while hot. Makes one and a half dozen.

POPCORN MACAROONS

1 cup freshly popped corn	1 cup powdered sugar
1 cup walnuts or butternuts	Pinch of salt
3 egg whites	

Chop the popcorn and nut meats or put them through a food chopper. Beat the egg whites stiff and combine with the sugar. Mix with the popcorn and nuts, add the salt. Drop by the spoonful on a buttered cooky sheet and bake fifteen minutes in a moderate oven, 350 degrees F. Makes one and a half dozen.

CAMBRIDGE COCONUT CAKES

3 egg whites   1/2 teaspoon salt
1/2 cup sugar   1/2 cup grated coconut
2 tablespoons flour   1/2 teaspoon vanilla

Beat the egg whites stiff. Add the sugar and flour gradually, beating all the time. Add the coconut and vanilla. Drop by the spoonful on a buttered cooky sheet and bake in a hot oven, 400 degrees F., until delicately brown, eight to ten minutes. Makes two dozen.

13. CAKES OF ALL KINDS

Making a cake three hundred years ago was a matter not under- taken lightly. Hours were spent in getting ready the ingredients for the large loaves that were baked in quantities to last for months. There were no accurate recipes, no reliable methods for testing oven heat. "Hurle in a good quantity of Currants and so Worke all together again, and bake your Cake as you see cause in a gentle Warme oven," were part of the hit-or-miss directions given for cakemaking about the time the Pilgrims set sail for America. The only way you could test that "gentle Warme oven" was with your hand. If the heat scorched it you knew the oven was too hot for cake. All the steps in early cakemak- ing were equally haphazard.

An old-time cake which was traditional in England on Mothering Sunday was later made in New England even where nonconformist ways had taken firm hold. The meaning of the day when good children gave cakes to their mothers in return for blessings might be forgotten in Boston, but just for the pleasure of eating, simnels occasionally came from Puritan ovens. The modern version given in this chapter is easily put together and resembles the ancient cake in flavor.

Another old English recipe, nun's cake, has come down to us through the centuries. For many generations mothers told their daughters how to make it, and the directions finally were written down and recorded in early cookbooks. The recipe was brought to America at an early date and became a favorite of the best New England cooks.

Molasses from the West Indies, spices from Dutch merchantmen, fruits from Spain and Italy went into the New England plum cakes and fruitcakes that were wrapped in homespun linen and hidden for months in stone crocks and japanned boxes. Full of rich ingredients, these early nineteenth-century cakes grew more toothsome as they ripened.

Cakes were frequently named for war heroes and the political figures of the times. Harrison cake honored Old Tippecanoe. Nor was the naming limited to the masculine gender. Molly Stark, wife of the hero of Bennington, gave hers to a somewhat heavy cake that was leavened with pearlash; it called for "spices to your pleasure." You would not be satisfied with this cake, so we are not giving the directions. But there are other cakes of the period which are exceedingly delicious and well worth trying. One named for New Hampshire's Josiah Bartlett is not a fruitcake, and it contains no spices. Originally it was made with sour milk and soda, but later the recipe was improved by using sweet milk and cream of tartar and soda.

For many years, the leavening used in cake batter was the same as the raising agencies in bread. Then someone discovered that pearlash (made from potash) when mixed with molasses made doughs and batters rise. But cakes in which this ingredient was used were for the most part coarse-grained and heavy. There was an improvement in lightness and texture when saleratus or soda was combined with sour milk, molasses, and other acid liquids. Then in the middle of the 1850s cream of tartar made its appearance, introducing a new era in home cake baking. Some years later came baking powder, which eliminated chances for wrong measurements when two ingredients were combined.

Many experienced New England cooks still prefer to use cream of tartar and soda, so we have included a number of cake recipes which list these ingredients. This is the case in the recipe for the delicious one-two-three-four cake which our great grandmothers used to "spice with rose petals." We have substituted liquid flavorings for them. And we also have made a change in listing the ingredients. You will note that they are not arranged in the order of use. The name of the cake tells why.

"My mother told me I couldn't have a beau in to spend the evening until I learned to make ribbon cake, and that was more than fifty years ago," said the notable cakemaker who gave us the recipe for ribbon cake. With the exception of using baking powder in the place of cream of tartar and soda, she still makes the ribbon cakes, which she takes to grange fairs, by the directions her mother taught her in the 1880s.

Layer cakes and cakes of variegated light and dark doughs were the masterpieces of cakemaking in the 1880s. Popular indeed was Dolly Varden cake, named for the gay young woman with her broad-rimmed hat trimmed with cherry ribbons, in Dickens' *Barnaby Rudge*. But harlequin cake was even more elaborate. It boasted a tier of layers in three colors instead of two, built up with a rich lemon filling instead of jelly between the layers. Both Dolly Varden and harlequin were special company cakes. Not so marble cake, which could be whipped up at an instant's notice. But do not confuse marble cake and marbled cake. They are not identical. In the first you drop alternate spoonfuls of white and dark mixtures into the pan. In the second you give the dark spots a slight swirl with the mixing spoon as you drop them into the white dough.

In some parts of New England even today an invitation to "take tea with us this evening" is an old-time way of saying, "Won't you come to supper?"

This cozy six o'clock meal is quite likely to end with a fragrant pot of tea, accompanied by some kind of cake, perhaps a frosted devil's food or a golden spongecake. But frequently it is a warm teacake that is served with butter or preserves.

Among these delicious teacakes are the soft spicy gingerbreads that are eaten hot with butter or whipped cream, or are topped with marshmallows. One recipe in this chapter was used for over half a century by the wife of a village doctor. Elvira Moody was noted for her kindliness and her hospitality. Her table was set for every meal with two extra places for guests, and the chairs were never empty.

More in the category of cookies than cakes were the hard gingerbreads that our great-grandmothers made in large quantities. Eggs and butter were used freely as they were in cakemaking. The ancient Gore gingerbread was made with one pound of butter, one and a half cups of molasses, one and a half pounds of sugar, two pounds of flour, five eggs, and two tablespoons of ginger. "If put in an airtight box it will keep good for several months," the old recipe says.

In Salem a century ago children saved their pennies to buy Molly Saunders' gingerbread. The door of Molly's bakeshop on Central Street was half wood and half glass, and any young customer could peek in at the coveted goodies. When the bell tinkled to announce his entrance, he already had made up his mind whether to pay three cents a cake for the upper shelf gingerbread which had butter or two cents for the butterless lower shelf variety. Molly's secret was boiling the butter with sugarhouse molasses. She rolled the gingerbread flat on tin sheets and printed it with corrugated squares especially made for the purpose. A contemporary says the gingerbread appeared and disappeared with the maker.

But the best-known of all New England gingerbreads was the kind sold on Muster Day or General Training Day. When the companies of militia met on that gala occasion, people came from every outlying hamlet and farm. Long before dawn, wagons unloaded men, women, and children at the parade ground. Peddlers set up booths and went through the crowd selling their wares. But most popular of all the things for sale was hard gingerbread. Everybody bought the great squares and munched them as they watched the festivities and the training activities.

SIMNEL

2 cups butter	2 teaspoons baking powder
2 1/3 cups brown sugar	5 1/3 cups flour
6 eggs	1 pound raisins, chopped
3 tablespoons milk	1/2 pound currants
1/2 teaspoon mace	1/8 pound citron, sliced
1/2 teaspoon cinnamon	Almond paste
1/2 teaspoon ginger	

Cream the butter and sugar. Add the eggs, one at a time, beating as added. Stir in the milk. Sift the spices and baking powder with the flour and add to the first mixture. Beat ten minutes. Fold in the fruit. Butter and lightly flour a long cake tin, nine by twelve inches, and turn in half the batter. Spread with a thin layer of almond paste and cover with the rest of the batter. Bake three hours in a slow oven, 325 degrees F. Ice when cool.

NUN'S CAKE

1 cup butter	1/4 teaspoon salt
1 1/2 cups powdered sugar	3/4 cup milk
5 egg yolks	3 teaspoon caraway seeds
2 egg whites	1/2 teaspoon cinnamon
3 cups pastry flour	2 teaspoons rosewater
2 1/2 teaspoons baking powder	

Cream the butter and sugar until very light. Add the egg yolks, beating well. Stir in the unbeaten egg whites and beat one minute. Sift the flour, baking powder, and salt. Add this alternately with the milk to the first mixture. Stir in the caraway seeds, cinnamon, and rosewater. Butter and lightly flour an eight-by-twelve-inch loaf pan. Bake in a moderate oven, 375 degrees F., for forty-five minutes.

BARTLETT CAKE

1 cup butter	2 teaspoons cream of tartar
2 cups sugar	1 teaspoon soda
4 eggs, well beaten	1 cup milk
1 wineglass whisky	1 cup currants
4 cups flour	

Cream the butter and sugar and stir in the eggs. Add the whisky. Sift the dry ingredients and add them alternately with the milk to the butter and sugar mixture. Lightly flour the currants, and add. Turn into two buttered loaf tins, nine by five by three inches, and bake one hour in a moderate oven, 350 degrees F.

HARRISON CAKE

1 1/2 cups butter	2 tablespoons cinnamon
1 1/2 cups sugar	2 tablespoons mace
1 1/2 cups molasses	6 cups flour
3 eggs, well beaten	1 1/4 cups milk
1 wineglass brandy	1 pound raisins
1 teaspoon soda	1 pound currants
1 tablespoon cloves	1/4 pound citron, sliced
1 tablespoon allspice	1 tablespoon lemon juice

Cream the butter and sugar and stir in the molasses. Add the eggs and brandy. Sift the soda and spices with the flour and add alternately with milk to the butter and sugar mixture. Add the fruit and the lemon juice. Mix thoroughly. Turn into three buttered loaf pans, nine by five by three inches. Bake two and one-half hours in a slow oven, 325 degrees F. This cake will keep a year.

COUNTRY SPICECAKE

This is a delicious and inexpensive spicecake, often made by White Mountain cooks.

1/2 cup shortening
1 1/2 cups sugar
1 egg, well beaten
1 teaspoon soda
1 cup sour milk

3 cups flour
1/2 teaspoon salt
1 teaspoon cinnamon
1/2 teaspoon cloves
1 cup raisins, chopped

Cream the shortening and sugar and add the egg. Dissolve the soda in a little cold water and stir into the sour milk. Add to the first mixture. Sift the dry ingredients, and add. Stir well. Flour the raisins and add last. Bake in a large buttered tin, nine by twelve inches, for forty-five minutes in a moderate oven, 375 degrees F. Cover with any desired white frosting or dust with powdered sugar.

DURHAM APPLESAUCE CAKE

1/2 cup shortening
1 cup sugar
1 egg, well beaten
1 1/2 cups applesauce
4 tablespoons hot water
1 cup dates, chopped
1/2 cup nuts, chopped

2 1/2 cups flour
1 teaspoon soda
1/2 teaspoon salt
1/2 teaspoon cloves
1/2 teaspoon nutmeg
1 teaspoon cinnamon

Cream the shortening and sugar and add the egg. Beat well. Stir in the applesauce and the hot water. Add the dates and nuts, then the dry ingredients which have been sifted together. Turn into two small buttered loaf tins, eight by four by three inches, and bake in a moderate oven, 350 degrees F., for one hour.

DAISY WOODWARD'S DATE CAKE

1 cup brown sugar
Butter size of an egg
1 teaspoon soda
1 cup sour milk
1/4 teaspoon salt

1 teaspoon cinnamon
1/2 teaspoon cloves
2 cups flour
1 pound dates

Cream the butter and sugar thoroughly. Dissolve the soda in a little water and stir into the sour milk. Combine the mixtures. Sift the salt, spices, and flour, and stir in. Stone the dates and cut them up; flour them lightly and add to the batter. Pour into an eight-by-twelve-inch buttered loaf pan. Bake one hour in a moderate oven, 350 degrees F. An egg may be added if desired, but the cake is delicious without it.

ONE-TWO-THREE-FOUR CAKE

1 cup shortening	1 teaspoon cream of tartar
2 cups sugar	1/2 teaspoon soda
3 cups flour	1 cup milk
4 eggs, separated	1 1/2 teaspoons rosewater or
1/4 teaspoon salt	1 teaspoon vanilla

Cream the shortening and sugar until fluffy. Add the egg yolks, one at a time, beating thoroughly after each one is added. Sift the dry ingredients three times. Add alternately with the milk and rosewater to the creamed mixture. Beat the egg whites stiff and fold into the batter. Turn into three square layer-cake tins, eight by eight by two inches. Bake thirty minutes in a moderate oven, 350 degrees F. Put the following filling between the layers, and frost the top and sides.

Coconut-Raisin Filling

1 cup raisins, chopped fine	Pinch of salt
1/2 cup chopped nuts	1 egg white, beaten stiff
1/2 cup grated coconut	

Rose Butter Frosting

4 tablespoons butter	1 1/2 teaspoons rosewater
2 cups powdered sugar	Few drops pink cake coloring
Milk	Pinch of salt

Cream the butter, sift the sugar and add it gradually. Stir in enough milk to make a mixture that will spread. Add the rest of the ingredients and stir vigorously until light and fluffy.

RIBBON CAKE

1 cup butter
2 cups sugar
4 egg yolks, well beaten
1 cup milk
3 1/2 cups flour
3 1/2 teaspoons baking powder
1/2 teaspoon salt
4 egg whites, stiffly beaten

1 1/2 teaspoons vanilla
1/2 cup raisins, chopped
1 cup currants
1 pound citron, sliced
2 tablespoons molasses
2 teaspoons brandy
1 teaspoon cinnamon

Cream the butter and sugar and add the well-beaten egg yolks. Stir in the milk. Sift the flour, baking powder, and salt, and add gradually to the first mixture, stirring in a few spoonfuls at a time. Fold in the stiffly beaten egg whites and add the vanilla. Divide the batter into three parts. Butter three nine-inch long oblong tins. Turn this white batter into two tins. Add the fruit, molasses, brandy, and spice to the remaining batter and turn into the third tin. Bake thirty minutes in a moderate oven, 375 degrees F. Remove the cakes from the tins and put one white layer on a large plate. Spread with red jelly. Place the dark layer next, spread with jelly, and cover with the second white layer. Press lightly with the hand when putting the layers together. Trim the edges of the cake evenly and frost.

Vanilla Icing

1/2 tablespoon butter
2 tablespoons hot milk

1 1/2 cups powdered sugar
1 teaspoon vanilla

Melt the butter in the hot milk. Stir in the sugar and add the vanilla.

DOLLY VARDEN CAKE

1/2 cup butter
2 cups sugar
3 eggs, well beaten
3 1/2 cups flour
1 teaspoon cream of tartar
1/2 teaspoon soda
1/2 teaspoon salt

1 cup milk
1 teaspoon lemon extract
1 tablespoon molasses
1 1/2 cups chopped raisins
1 1/2 cups currants
1 teaspoon cinnamon
1 teaspoon cloves

Cream the butter and sugar. Stir in the eggs. Sift the flour, cream of tartar, soda, and salt. Add alternately with the milk to the first mixture. Stir well and add the lemon extract. Divide the batter in two parts. Add the molasses, fruit, and spices to one part. Butter two square tins, nine by nine inches. Turn the white mixture into one, and the dark mixture into the other. Bake in a moderate oven, 375 degrees F., for thirty minutes. Remove from the oven and put the dark layer on a plate. Cover with red jelly. Put the white layer on top and frost.

Lemon Icing

2 egg whites   Grated rind of 1/2 lemon
Juice of 1 lemon   Powdered sugar

Beat the egg whites stiff. Beat in the lemon juice and add the grated lemon rind. Sift the sugar and add until the icing will spread easily. Use a knife with a broad blade or a spatula to spread the icing on the cake.

HARLEQUIN CAKE

1 cup butter   1/2 teaspoon salt
2 cups sugar   1 cup milk
3 eggs, separated   1 teaspoon vanilla
3 cups flour   2 squares chocolate
3 teaspoons baking powder   Pink coloring

Cream the butter and sugar and add the well-beaten egg yolks. Sift the dry ingredients and add alternately with the milk. Beat the egg whites until stiff and fold in. Add the vanilla. Butter four nine-inch layer-cake pans and pour half of the batter into two of them. Divide the remaining batter in two parts. Add the melted chocolate to one, and stir well. Pour into the third pan. Color the fourth part of the batter with pink coloring and pour into the fourth pan. Bake thirty minutes in a moderate oven, 350 degrees F. When done, arrange the layers in the following order: white, chocolate, white, pink. Put this filling between the layers.

Lemon Jelly

1 egg
1 cup water
Grated rind and juice of 1 lemon

1 cup sugar
2 tablespoons flour

Beat the egg, add the water; add the lemon juice and rind. Mix the sugar with the sifted flour and pour the liquid slowly on it, stirring well. Cook in a double boiler until thick and smooth.

Cover the top and sides of the cake with frosting, doubling the ingredients for a cake of this size.

White Mountain Frosting

1 scant cup sugar
1/3 cup water
1 egg white

Pinch of cream of tartar
1 teaspoon vanilla
2 drops glycerine (optional)

Boil together the sugar and water until the syrup hairs when dropped from a spoon. Beat the egg white stiff. Pour the syrup slowly on it, beating constantly. Place in a bowl over top of the teakettle or in a dish of boiling water and leave until the sugar forms a coating on the side of the bowl. Flavor and beat again. Add the vanilla. The glycerine helps to keep the frosting from cracking when cut. If you use it, add just before the last beating.

MARBLE CAKE

1/2 cup butter
1 cup sugar
2 eggs, beaten
1/2 cup milk
1 3/4 cups flour
1 1/2 teaspoons baking powder
1/2 teaspoon salt

1 teaspoon vanilla
1 tablespoon molasses
2 tablespoons melted chocolate
1 teaspoon cinnamon
1/2 teaspoon nutmeg
White icing and sweet chocolate

Cream the butter and sugar; add the beaten eggs and milk. Sift the dry ingredients. Divide the batter and flavor half with the vanilla. Add the molasses, chocolate, and spices to the second half. Drop alternate spoonfuls of light and dark dough into a buttered oblong cake tin, seven by ten inches. Bake in a moderate oven, 375 degrees F., for forty-five minutes. Frost with any desired white icing. Melt sweet chocolate and pour over the icing in rings.

INEZ'S MARBLED CAKE

1/2 cup butter
2 cups sugar
2 eggs, well beaten
3 cups flour
1 teaspoon cream of tartar
ĸ/2 teaspoon soda

1/2 teaspoon salt
1 cup milk
1 teaspoon vanilla
2 tablespoons cocoa
Hot water

Cream the butter and sugar, and add the eggs. Sift the dry ingredients and add alternately with the milk. Add the vanilla and stir well. Remove three mixing spoonfuls of batter to another bowl. Mix the cocoa with hot water until smooth. Stir into the smaller portion of batter. Pour white batter into a large buttered loaf tin, nine by twelve inches, and drop spoonfuls of chocolate mixture into it, swirling them with the back of the spoon to give a marbled effect. Bake forty-five minutes in a moderate oven, 375 degrees F. Cover the top and sides of cake with frosting.

Chocolate Frosting

1 cup water
3/4 cup sugar
2 squares chocolate, grated
2 tablespoons cornstarch

Pinch of salt
1 teaspoon butter
1 teaspoon vanilla

Put the water, sugar, and chocolate in the top of a double boiler. When the chocolate melts, add the cornstarch, moistened with a little cold water, and the salt. Cook until the mixture thickens, stirring to keep it smooth. Add the butter. When cool, add the vanilla.

OLD-FASHIONED BUTTERNUT CAKE

3/4 cup butter
2 cups sugar
4 eggs
2 1/4 cups flour
1 teaspoon soda
2 teaspoons cream of tartar

1/2 teaspoon salt
1/4 teaspoon cinnamon
3/4 cup milk
1/2 teaspoon lemon extract
1 cup butternuts, chopped

Cream the butter and sugar. Add the eggs, one at a time, beating vigorously after each is added. Sift the dry ingredients and add to the first mixture alternately with the milk. Add the lemon extract. Add the chopped butternuts; the black skins should be removed. Turn into a buttered loaf pan, eight by twelve inches, and bake one hour in a moderate oven, 350 degrees F. Cover the top and sides with White Mountain Frosting, or if the cake is to be eaten soon, use the following:

Butternut Sour Cream Frosting

1 egg white
1 cup thick sour cream
1 cup butternuts, chopped

1/3 cup sugar
1/4 teaspoon salt
1 teaspoon vanilla

Add the egg white to the sour cream. Beat, but be careful not to overbeat. Add the butternuts, sugar, salt, and vanilla. Stir in as lightly as possible. This frosting is very rich.

WHITE BUTTERNUT CAKE

1/2 cup butter
1 1/2 cups sugar
2 cups flour
2 teaspoons baking powder
1/2 teaspoon salt

3/4 cup milk
4 egg whites
1 teaspoon vanilla
1 cup butternuts, cut in rather
   large pieces

Cream the butter until light and fluffy. Add the sugar a few spoonfuls at a time and cream well. Sift the flour, baking powder, and salt, and add alternately with the milk. Beat the egg whites until they stand in peaks. Fold into the batter with the vanilla. Add the butternuts. Turn into two buttered nine-inch square tins. Bake thirty minutes in a moderate oven, 350 degrees F. Cool. Put the following frosting between the layers and on top of the cake.

Esther's Nut Frosting

1 cup sour cream	1 square chocolate
1 cup sugar	1/2 cup chopped butternuts

Put all the ingredients in a saucepan. Place over low heat. When the mixture begins to cook, stir just often enough to prevent burning. When it will form a soft ball when dropped in water, remove the mixture from the heat. Set the saucepan in cold water. Do not stir the frosting. It should not grain, but should be slightly runny and smooth. Walnuts may be substituted for the butternuts.

AUNT MARION'S CARAMEL CAKE

1/2 cup butter	1/2 teaspoon salt
2 cups sugar	1 cup milk
4 eggs	1 tablespoon caramelized sugar
3 cups flour	1 cup walnuts, chopped
3 teaspoons baking powder	

Cream the butter with one cup of the sugar. Beat the egg yolks and add the other cup of sugar. Combine the mixtures. Sift the dry ingredients and add alternately with the milk. Fold in beaten egg whites. Add the caramelized sugar. (To caramelize sugar, put one-half cup of sugar in an iron skillet and stir over a hot fire until dark brown. Add boiling hot water and stir. Use the thick liquid for flavoring.) Add the walnuts. Turn the batter into a loaf tin, nine by twelve inches, and bake forty-five minutes in a moderate oven, 375 degrees F. Cover the top and sides with caramel frosting.

Caramel Frosting

1/2 cup brown sugar	1 tablespoon butter
1/2 cup white sugar	1 teaspoon caramelized sugar
1/2 cup cream	

Put the brown and white sugars and cream in a saucepan and bring to a boil. Boil exactly fifteen minutes. Remove from the heat, add the butter and caramelized sugar. Beat with a fork until creamy. Watch carefully to see that it does not get too stiff.

LADY LANGDON'S WHITE CAKE

1/2 cup butter	2 teaspoons baking powder
2 cups powdered sugar	6 egg whites
1 cup milk	1 1/2 teaspoons rosewater, or
3 cups flour	1 teaspoon vanilla

Cream the butter and sugar until very fluffy. Add the milk gradually. Sift the flour and baking powder and fold in. Beat the egg whites stiff and fold in. Add the flavoring. Turn the batter into a buttered loaf pan, eight by twelve inches. Bake seventy minutes in a slow oven, 325 degrees F. Cover with White Mountain Frosting. This recipe makes a good bride's cake.

FLO'S SOUR CREAM CAKE

2 eggs	1/2 teaspoon soda
Sour cream	Pinch of salt
1 cup sugar	1/2 teaspoon vanilla
1 1/3 cups flour	

Break the eggs in a measuring cup and fill with sour cream. Sift the dry ingredients and combine with the liquid. Add the flavoring and beat thoroughly. Turn into a buttered eight-inch square pan. Bake half an hour in a moderate oven, 375 degrees F.

FLO'S FEATHER CAKE

1 1/2 cups flour	1/4 teaspoon salt
1 cup sugar	2 eggs
1 teaspoon cream of tartar	3 tablespoons melted butter
1/2 teaspoon soda	Sweet milk

Sift the dry ingredients three times. Break the eggs in a cup, add the melted butter, and fill the cup with milk. Combine the mixtures and beat hard with an egg beater for five minutes. Turn into a buttered, eight-inch square tin. Bake half an hour in a moderate oven, 350 degrees F.

Flo's Chocolate Cream Icing

Cream	1 egg, well beaten
5 tablespoons grated chocolate	1/2 teaspoon vanilla
1 cup sugar	

Use enough cream to wet the chocolate. Add the sugar and egg. Put in a dish over the teakettle or in a double boiler. Stir until the ingredients are thoroughly mixed.

BERWICK SPONGECAKE

The beating in this cake should be exactly timed by the clock, and it should be baked in a loaf.

3 eggs, separated	2 cups flour
1 1/2 cups sugar	2 teaspoons cream of tartar
1 teaspoon lemon extract	1 teaspoon soda
1/2 cup cold water	1/4 teaspoon salt

Beat the egg yolks two minutes. Add the sugar, lemon, and cold water, and beat two minutes. Sift the dry ingredients and fold into the first mixture. Beat two minutes. Beat the egg whites stiff and add. Beat two minutes. Turn into a lightly buttered loaf tin, seven by ten inches. Bake in a slow oven, 325 degrees F., for forty-five minutes.

CREAM SPONGECAKE

4 eggs, separated	Flour
1 cup sugar	1 1/4 teaspoons baking powder
3 tablespoons cold water	1/4 teaspoon salt
1 1/2 tablespoons cornstarch	1 teaspoon lemon juice

Beat the egg yolks until lemon colored and add the sugar gradually. Add the cold water and beat again. Put the cornstarch in a measuring cup and fill the cup with flour. Sift with the baking powder and salt. Fold into the egg yolk mixture. Beat the egg whites until stiff and fold in. Add the lemon juice. Turn into a lightly buttered pan, seven by ten inches, and bake in a slow oven, 325 degrees F., for half an hour.

JANET'S ANGEL CAKE

1 cup flour	1 teaspoon cream of tartar
11 egg whites	1 1/2 cups sugar
1/4 teaspoon salt	1 teaspoon vanilla

Remove the eggs from the refrigerator several hours before using and have all the ingredients laid out where the cake is to be mixed. Work very quickly but with a light hand in putting the cake together.

Sift the flour once and measure again. Then sift four times. Beat the egg whites until foamy, add the salt, and beat again. Add the cream of tartar and beat with a wire whisk until the whites will hold their shape in peaks. They should be moist and glossy, but not dry. Sift the sugar and fold in. Add the flavoring. Sprinkle a small amount of flour over the mixture and fold in. Continue doing this until the cup of flour is all used. Turn the mixture into an ungreased tube pan, eight and a half inches. Put in a very slow oven, 275 degrees F., for half an hour, then increase to 325 degrees. Bake thirty minutes longer. When the cake is done, invert the pan in such a way that air will pass around it. When the cake is removed from the pan, dust lightly with powdered sugar. If you prefer a frosted cake, try this frosting.

Marvelous Frosting

2 cups sugar	2 egg whites
1/2 cup white corn syrup	1 teaspoon vanilla
1/2 cup water	6 tablespoons marshmallow cream

Combine the sugar, syrup, and water. Heat slowly, stirring until the sugar is dissolved. Boil gently until the mixture will form a firm ball between the fingers when a little is dropped into ice water. Pour at once over the stiffly beaten egg whites, beating continuously until the mixture thickens and will hold its shape when dropped from spoon. Add the flavoring and marshmallow cream. Spread or heap irregularly over the top and sides of the cake.

MAY IDA'S SUNSHINE CAKE

11 egg whites	1 teaspoon cream of tartar
1 1/2 cups sugar	1/2 teaspoon salt
6 egg yolks	1 teaspoon vanilla
1 cup flour	

Beat the egg whites very stiff. Gradually beat in the sugar. Beat the egg yolks until lemon colored and fold into the egg whites. Sift the flour, cream of tartar, and salt four times. Fold into the egg mixture. Turn into a large tube tin. Put in a cool oven, 275 degrees F., and bake for thirty minutes. Then raise to 325 degrees and bake thirty minutes longer. Invert the cake on a rack for one hour before trying to remove it from the pan.

SILVER AND GOLD CAKE

Gold Part

5 egg yolks	1 tablespoon cornstarch
3 tablespoons cold water	1 teaspoon baking powder
1/2 cup sugar	1/4 teaspoon salt
1/2 cup flour	1 teaspoon orange extract

Beat the egg yolks and beat in the cold water. Sift the dry ingredients and stir in. Add the flavoring. Pour into the bottom of an angel-cake tin.

Silver Part

5 egg whites	1/4 teaspoon cream of tartar
1/2 cup sugar	1/2 cup flour
1/4 teaspoon salt	1/2 teaspoon vanilla

Beat the egg whites until dry. Beat in the sugar, salt, and cream of tartar. Sift the flour and fold in. Add the flavoring. Pour the batter on top of the yellow batter in the tin. Bake like Sunshine Cake.

RODDY'S BIRTHDAY CAKE

4 eggs, separated	1 cup flour
1 cup sugar	1 1/2 teaspoons baking powder
1/4 cup orange juice	1/4 teaspoon salt
1 teaspoon grated lemon rind	

Beat the egg yolks until thick and lemon colored. Add three-fourths of the cup of sugar and beat again. Add the orange juice and lemon rind. Sift the flour, baking powder, and salt twice. Fold into the egg yolks. Beat the egg whites and add the remaining one-fourth cup of sugar. Fold into the batter. Turn into two lightly buttered eight-inch layer-cake tins and bake half an hour in a slow oven, 325 degrees F. Remove from the tins and place the following filling between the layers.

Orange Filling

1 egg yolk	1 tablespoon lemon juice
1/4 cup sugar	1/8 teaspoon salt
Grated rind of 1/2 orange	1/2 cup thick cream
2 tablespoons orange juice	

Cook the egg yolk, sugar, orange rind, and orange and lemon juices until thick. When cool, add the salt and the cream which has been whipped until stiff. Cover the top and sides of the cake with frosting.

Orange Frosting

Grated rind of 1/2 orange
1/2 teaspoon grated lemon rind
2 tablespoons orange juice
1 teaspoon lemon juice

1 egg yolk
1 tablespoon butter
Powdered sugar

Mix the fruit rinds with the juices and let stand fifteen minutes. Cream the egg yolk and butter. Strain the fruit mixture over the egg yolk and butter. Stir in enough powdered sugar to spread well. Cut the edges from the cake and cover the top and sides with the frosting.

HARRIET'S JELLY ROLL

3 eggs
Pinch of salt
1 scant cup sugar
1 cup flour
3 tablespoons milk

1 teaspoon soda
2 teaspoons cream of tartar
1 teaspoon vanilla
Jelly
Powdered sugar

Beat the eggs well and add the salt, sugar, and flour sifted together. Put the milk in a measuring cup, and in it dissolve the soda and cream of tartar. Stir well until the milk foams. Add the vanilla and stir the liquid into the first mixture. Butter a dripping pan, fifteen by ten inches, and line the bottom with paper. Butter again. Pour in batter. Bake in a hot oven, 400 degrees F., fifteen minutes. Cut off the crisp edges of the cake. Turn on a cloth covered with powdered sugar. Remove the paper. Spread the cake with jelly and roll it. Wrap in a cloth.

NEVER-FAIL CHOCOLATE CAKE

1/4 cup butter
1 cup sugar
1 egg yolk
1/2 cup cocoa
Hot water

Sweet milk
1 1/2 cups pastry flour
1 teaspoon soda
1/4 teaspoon salt

Cream the butter and sugar, and stir in the egg yolk. Put the cocoa in a measuring cup, and stir in hot water to make a smooth paste. Fill the cup with sweet milk. Add to the first mixture. Sift the dry ingredients and add. Beat well. Turn into a buttered eight-inch square pan and bake thirty minutes in a moderate oven, 350 degrees F.

White Boiled Frosting

1 cup sugar
1/3 cup boiling water
1 egg white

Pinch of salt
1 teaspoon vanilla

Boil the sugar and water until the syrup will hair when dropped from a spoon. Sprinkle the egg white with a pinch of salt and beat until stiff. Turn the syrup slowly over the egg white, beating constantly with a rotary egg beater. Add the flavoring. Finish the beating, using a large spoon, and spread the frosting on the top and sides of the cake.

ADDIE MERRILL'S CHOCOLATE CAKE

1/2 cup butter
1 1/2 cups brown sugar
1 egg, well beaten
1 teaspoon soda
1/2 cup sour milk

1 1/2 cups flour
1/4 teaspoon salt
1 square chocolate
1/2 cup boiling water
1 teaspoon vanilla

Cream the butter and brown sugar, and add the egg. Dissolve the soda thoroughly in the sour milk, and add. Sift the flour and salt, and stir into the mixture. Dissolve the chocolate in the boiling water, and add to the batter. Add the vanilla. Beat well. Turn into a buttered cake tin, seven by ten inches, and bake half an hour in a moderate oven, 350 degrees F. Frost with Caramel Frosting.

MARJORIE'S DEVIL'S FOOD

1 egg, separated	Butter size of an egg
1 cup milk	1 cup flour
1 cup sugar	1 teaspoon soda
2 squares chocolate, grated	1/2 teaspoon salt

Put the egg yolk, half a cup of the milk, half a cup of the sugar, the chocolate and butter in a double boiler to cook. Stir well. Cook until thick and smooth. Turn into a mixing bowl and add the remaining milk and sugar. Sift the dry ingredients and stir in. Beat the egg white until stiff and fold in. Turn into a buttered nine-inch square cake tin and bake in a very slow oven, 325 degrees F., for half an hour. When cool, remove from the tin and frost.

Fudge Frosting

2 cups sugar	2 tablespoons corn syrup
1/2 cup milk	2 tablespoons butter
3 squares chocolate, melted	1 teaspoon vanilla

Boil together the sugar, milk, chocolate, and corn syrup until the mixture forms a soft ball when dropped in cold water. Add the butter and vanilla. When lukewarm, beat until creamy and spread on the cake.

QUICK CUPCAKES

1 1/2 cups flour	1/4 cup shortening
3/4 cup sugar	2 eggs
2 teaspoons baking powder	Sweet milk
1/2 teaspoon salt	1 teaspoon vanilla
1 teaspoon cinnamon	

Sift the dry ingredients. Melt the shortening in a tin measuring cup. When cool, break in the eggs and fill the cup with sweet milk. Add to the dry ingredients. Beat for three minutes. Bake in twelve buttered muffin tins in a moderate oven, 350 degrees F., for twenty minutes.

Maple Icing

1/2 tablespoon butter	1 1/2 cups powdered sugar
2 tablespoons hot milk	1 teaspoon maple syrup

Add the butter to the hot milk. Stir in the sugar to make an icing that will spread. Beat in the maple syrup last. Add more sugar if necessary.

KISSES

4 egg whites	1/8 teaspoon cream of tartar
1/8 teaspoon salt	1/8 teaspoon vinegar
1 cup sugar	

Beat the egg whites until stiff. Add the salt and sugar gradually, beating continuously. Add the cream of tartar and vinegar, and beat until the whites stand in peaks. Drop in a cooking tin covered with oiled paper. Bake in a slow oven, 325 degrees F., for one hour. One egg makes a dozen meringues.

The above recipe may be baked in a nine-inch buttered pie tin for one hour and served with berries and whipped cream. The individual meringues may be hollowed out, filled with berries or fruit mashed and sweetened, and covered with whipped cream.

BLUEBERRY TEACAKE

1/2 cup butter	1/4 teaspoon salt
3/4 cup sugar	1 cup milk
1 egg	1 teaspoon vanilla
2 1/4 cups flour	1 cup blueberries
4 teaspoons baking powder	

Cream the butter and sugar and add the egg. Stir well. Sift the dry ingredients and add alternately with the milk to the first mixture. Add the vanilla. Flour the blueberries and stir in quickly, being careful not to crush the berries. Turn into a buttered pan and bake in a moderate oven, 375 degrees F., for thirty-five minutes. Serve warm with butter or with pan cream.

APPLE TEACAKE

2 cups flour	1 egg
1/2 teaspoon salt	7/8 cup milk
1/2 teaspoon soda	4 sour apples, peeled and cored
1 teaspoon cream of tartar	1/2 cup sugar, mixed with
1/4 cup shortening	1 teaspoon cinnamon

Sift the dry ingredients and rub in the shortening. Beat the egg and combine with the milk. Stir into the first mixture. Beat well and turn into a shallow buttered baking pan. Cut the apples in eighths and arrange in parallel rows on top of the dough. Press the edges of the pieces of apple into the dough. Sprinkle the sugar and cinnamon over the apples. Bake in a hot oven, 400 degrees F., for twenty-five minutes. Serve hot with butter. The cake dough is not sweetened.

PEACH UPSIDE-DOWN CAKE

4 tablespoons butter	Peach halves, fresh or canned
1 cup brown sugar	Cake batter

Melt the butter and sugar in a frying pan. When thick, cover with peeled halves of fresh peaches or with canned peaches. Pour Quick Cupcake batter over them and bake in a moderate oven, 375 degrees F., for about thirty-five minutes. Remove to a large plate, turning upside down so the fruit will be on top. Serve with flavored and sweetened whipped cream.

CRUMB CAKE

2 cups flour	2 teaspoons baking powder
3/4 cup butter	3/4 cup milk
1 1/2 cups sugar	2 eggs
1/4 teaspoon salt	1/2 teaspoon cinnamon

Rub together the flour, butter, sugar, and salt. Remove half a cup of the mixture. Dissolve the baking powder in the milk and combine with the eggs. Turn into the first mixture. Add the flavoring and pour into a buttered cake pan, seven by ten inches. Add the cinnamon to the reserved half cup of dry mixture, and sprinkle the crumbs over the top of the dough. Bake half an hour in a moderate oven, 375 degrees F. Serve hot with butter. This cake is also good when cold.

ELVIRA MOODY'S GINGERBREAD

1/2 cup shortening	1 teaspoon soda
1 cup boiling water	1/2 teaspoon ginger
1 cup molasses	1/2 teaspoon cloves
1/2 cup sugar	2 1/2 cups flour
1/2 teaspoon salt	1 egg, well beaten

Melt the shortening in the boiling water. Add the molasses and sugar. Sift the remaining dry ingredients. Add the egg last. Mix well. Turn into a shallow buttered pan, nine by twelve inches, and bake twenty minutes in a moderate oven, 350 degrees F.

FLO'S HARD MOLASSES GINGERBREAD

1 cup shortening	2 teaspoons ginger
1 cup hot water	2 teaspoons soda
1 cup molasses	Flour
1 cup sugar	Sugar

Melt the shortening in the hot water. Add the molasses and sugar. Sift the ginger and soda with one cup of flour. Then add enough sifted flour to make a stiff dough. Keep in a cool place overnight. The next day, roll the dough to a half inch thick. Put in a large buttered shallow pan, ten by fifteen inches. Sprinkle with sugar. Cut in squares. Bake about twenty-five minutes in a moderate oven, 375 degrees F. This makes a good Muster Day Gingerbread.

CREAM PUFFS

Put one-half cup of lard and one-half cup of hot water in a saucepan over heat. When the ingredients are boiling hard, slowly add one cup of sifted flour, stirring rapidly from the bottom of the pan into a ball. Remove from the heat. When the dough is slightly cool, stir in three eggs one at a time. Drop by spoonfuls on a buttered pan. Bake for forty-five minutes. Have the oven quick at first, 400 degrees F., then reduce to moderate, 375 degrees. In spite of usual directions, look at puffs while they are baking as often as you like. Split when cool and fill. Makes 8 large or 12 medium-sized cream puffs.

Cream Filling

2 cups milk	3/4 cup sugar
2 tablespoons cornstarch	1 teaspoon butter
Cold milk	1/2 teaspoon vanilla
3 eggs	1/4 teaspoon almond extract

Heat the milk to boiling. Mix the cornstarch with cold milk and stir in. Cook ten minutes, stirring to prevent lumps. Beat the eggs, combine with the sugar, and add to the thickened milk. Cook in a double boiler five minutes. Add the butter. When cool, add the flavoring.

14. MAPLE TREES AND BEEHIVES

I T IS always a miracle when spring comes back to New England. Long
before the first bluebird saucily skims by the kitchen window there
are faint hints of the return of spring. You feel it in your bones even
when the stone walls are hidden under deep drifts of snow. If you live in
the sugar country—in Vermont, in New Hampshire, in Maine—early
in February before the freezing nights and thawing days of sugar
weather set in you begin to think of sap dripping in the buckets hung
on the maples, of sweet steam rising from the sugarhouse evaporator,
of new maple molasses on breakfast pancakes.

New Englanders have used maple sugar since pioneer days. They
learned the secrets of making it from the Indians. In fact, methods of
making maple honey and sugar have not changed in their essentials
since the Indian women hung elm bark buckets on the trees to receive
the "sweet water," and threw hot stones into the sap to make it boil.

A century ago, maple, as most people called it, was commonly used on the table to sweeten the breakfast porridge and the evening cup of tea. The treasured cone of white sugar in its blue or brown paper wrapping was scraped only to make the finest cake or to serve guests at special tea drinkings. Later when big barrels of granulated sugar were on sale in all grocery stores, maple still remained a staple pantry item. Children were given pails of maple sugar for their own use, and their mothers were lavish with it in their cooking. A few pennies bought delicious heart-shaped sugar cakes and crinkly edged patties, and cans of maple syrup and pails of sugar were on sale at farmhouse and store.

There are many New England cooks today who will not get along without maple products. In a way, both syrup and sugar are luxury items, but still they are in great demand. Here and there throughout this book you will find recipes which call for maple products. But we have brought the great part of them, especially those for maple desserts, together here.

First we have told how to prepare Sugar on Snow, or leather aprons or frogs, if you prefer the country names. This is always served at the sugaring-off parties held in the sugarhouses. But you can have sugar on snow if you are miles from a maple orchard. All you need are a can of maple syrup and a pan full of clean snow.

Maple syrup and maple sugar give a delicious flavor to both boiled and baked ham. Use them as you would use molasses or brown sugar. We have given a special rule for cooking a slice of ham with maple syrup and sweet potatoes, a dish that was famous in a well-known mountain resort hotel a generation ago.

If you have not tried maple sugar or maple syrup in muffins and rolls, you have a real treat in store, particularly if butternuts are added. Butternuts are a natural combination with anything maple.

A White Mountain tearoom popular in the 1920s was noted for its delicious cinnamon toast. The secret was the use of maple sugar in place of the white sugar usually mixed with cinnamon. French toast also is improved if the toast is buttered while hot and sprinkled with shaved maple sugar.

One of our most prized recipes was given us by a lineal descendant of

Governor Bradford of old Plymouth. Five generations of women have made these delicious thin cakes for the family's Easter dinner dessert. They are called, for a reason nobody can now explain, Hammond's ears.

Accustomed as they were to honey, it must have been a great surprise to the early settlers to find that there were no honeybees in the New World. Within a few years, however, hives were brought over and every family had several. That bees were regarded as a valuable possession we know from the probate records. Hives of bees were listed among such valuable goods as silver and pewter.

When the first escaping bees made their nests in hollow trees the Indians were much amazed at the Englishman's or white-man's fly. But so great was their love of sweets that in spite of stings they robbed the wild-bee trees just as the bears did, often eating the comb also.

The English had always used honey for making metheglin, that drink almost as old as time. But they used it in many other ways also, in place of sugar and molasses in cooking and on bread and hot cakes. In Mother Goose we find even the queen eating bread and honey. Honey butter was made for hot cakes and stored in a cool place for months at a time.

Today we usually buy strained honey, but in the early days the housewife used the beeswax for as many things as she used the honey. Usually the honeycomb was placed in the sun or near a fire with three sieves under it, each finer than the other. As the honey melted, it was gradually strained through the sieves. Then the comb was tied in a bag of linen or wool with several good-sized pebbles to weigh it down and placed in a kettle of cold water. As the water came to a slow boil, the wax melted and rose to the top, and the impurities remained in the bag.

Domestic bees were kept through the winter in warm cellars or in beehouses. A typical beehouse was seven feet square, seven feet high, with a roof running up into a spire. Those who did not have bees of their own went out in the fall to rob the wild bees. Honey made from maple blossoms came first in the spring, then dandelion and fruit-bloom honey. Midseason clover, or honeysuckle as it was called for a long time, was considered the mildest and best flavored, although many old-timers liked the spicy goldenrod honey of the fall.

SUGAR ON SNOW

Fill large pans with closely packed snow. If you cannot get snow, use a flat cake of ice. Boil the maple syrup until it will wax, that is form a "soft" hard ball when dropped in cold water. Drop the syrup by large spoonfuls on the snow. It will form into shapes that may be twisted on forks or wooden skewers and lifted from the pan. Serve with plain doughnuts, pickles, and coffee.

WAUMBEK HAM STEAK

1 slice ham

4 sweet potatoes, boiled and peeled
1 cup maple syrup

Fry the slice of ham until browned. Slice the sweet potatoes and put in the frying pan with the ham. Add the maple syrup and cook until the potatoes are browned and the syrup is almost absorbed. Serves six.

MAPLE BUTTERNUT MUFFINS

2 cups flour
2 1/2 teaspoons baking powder
1/2 teaspoon salt
2 tablespoons maple spread

3 tablespoons melted shortening
1 egg
1 cup milk
1/2 cup butternuts

Sift the dry ingredients. Mix the maple spread with the melted shortening and add the egg. Stir together until smooth. Mix in the milk gradually, and add to the dry ingredients. Remove the black skins from the butternuts. Chop the nuts and add them to the muffin mixture, and stir in quickly. Turn the batter into well-greased muffin tins and bake twenty minutes in a hot oven, 425 degrees F. Makes one dozen muffins.

MAPLE PINWHEEL ROLLS

Use your favorite recipe for yeast rolls or for baking powder biscuits. Turn the dough on the molding board and roll out to about half an inch thick. Brush with melted butter and cover with one-half cup of shaved maple sugar. Sprinkle with chopped butternuts or walnuts. Roll up like jelly roll and slice. Set the slices on end in a well-greased baking pan and spread the tops with butter. Bake in a hot oven, 475 degrees F., for about twenty minutes.

MOTHER'S MAPLE CREAM SHORTCAKE

Make rich biscuit dough and spread the mixture evenly over two greased pie tins. Brush with melted butter and bake in a hot oven, 425 degrees F., for fifteen minutes. Remove from the oven and spread with the following filling between the two layers and on top.

Maple Cream Filling

3/4 cup maple syrup
1 tablespoon butter
2 egg whites

1/2 cup cream
Vanilla

Cook the syrup and butter until it spins a thread when dropped from a spoon. Beat the egg whites until stiff. Gradually pour the syrup and butter mixture over the eggs, beating constantly. When smooth, add the cream beaten until stiff and a few drops of vanilla. Serves six.

CATHERINE'S MAPLE GINGERBREAD SQUARES

1/2 cup sugar
1/2 cup lard
1 egg
1 teaspoon soda
1/4 cup sour milk
1/2 cup maple syrup

1/2 teaspoon salt
1/2 teaspoon cinnamon
1/2 teaspoon ginger
1/4 teaspoon baking powder
Flour

Cream the sugar and lard, and stir in the egg. Dissolve the soda in a little water and stir into the sour milk. Mix with the maple syrup. Combine the mixtures. Sift salt, spices and baking powder with one cup of flour and stir in. Then add enough sifted flour to make a stiff dough.

Roll out, cut in squares, and bake in a moderate oven, 350 degrees F., about twenty-five minutes. Makes twelve squares.

OLD-FASHIONED MAPLE SUGAR CREAM CAKE

1 cup maple sugar	1/4 teaspoon cinnamon
1 egg	Pinch of salt
1 teaspoon soda	2 cups flour
1 cup sour cream	Granulated maple sugar

Mix the maple sugar with the egg and beat thoroughly. Dissolve the soda in a little cold water and stir into the sour cream. Combine the mixtures. Sift the cinnamon and salt with the flour and fold in. Sprinkle the top with granulated maple sugar. Bake in a seven-by-ten-inch pan for half an hour in a moderate oven, 350 degrees F. Serve hot or cold, plain or with whipped cream.

Maple Whipped Cream

1 cup cream	1/3 cup maple spread

Whip the cream until stiff. Add the maple spread and beat slowly until well mixed. Then beat rapidly until firm.

MAPLE BUTTERNUT CAKE

Make a butternut cake. Bake in two nine-inch layers and cover each layer with filling.

Maple Butternut Filling

1 cup maple syrup	1 cup cream, whipped
1 egg white	3/4 cup chopped butternuts
Pinch of salt	

Boil the syrup until it threads when dropped from a spoon. Beat the egg white stiff and add the salt. Pour the syrup slowly over the egg white, beating all the time. Add the whipped cream and continue beating until the mixture will stand alone. After it is spread on top of the cake, sprinkle with finely chopped butternuts.

MAPLE COTTAGE PUDDING

1 cup maple syrup
1 tablespoon shortening
3 tablespoons sugar
1 egg
1/4 cup milk

1 1/2 cups flour
2 teaspoons baking powder
1/4 teaspoon salt
Nuts

Bring the syrup to the boiling point and pour into a baking dish. Cream the shortening and sugar and thoroughly beat in the egg. Add the milk. Sift the dry ingredients and fold into the mixture. Pour the batter into the syrup and bake in a hot oven, 400 degrees F., for twenty-five minutes. Remove the cake from the oven and turn upside down on a serving plate. Sprinkle with chopped nuts. Serve with plain or whipped cream.

MAPLE BUTTERNUT TARTS

Rich pastry
3 eggs
1/2 cup white sugar
3/4 teaspoon salt

1 cup maple syrup
1 cup butternuts or walnuts,
    chopped
1 teaspoon vanilla

Line eight gem pans with pastry. Beat the eggs slightly, add the other ingredients, and stir well. Pour into the pastry shells. Bake in a hot oven, 450 degrees F., for ten minutes, then reduce to 325 degrees and bake thirty minutes longer.

FLO'S MAPLE CUSTARD PIE

3 eggs
1 teaspoon flour
2 teaspoons white sugar
1/2 cup soft maple sugar

Pinch of salt
3 cups milk
Uncooked pie shell

Beat the eggs slightly. Mix the flour with the white sugar and combine with the maple sugar. Stir into the eggs and add the salt. Heat the milk and pour slowly over the mixture. Arrange the pie shell in a deep nine-inch crockery pie plate. Build up the edges and flute them with the thumb and forefinger. Prick the bottom and sides of the pie shell with a fork. Turn in the egg mixture and bake in a hot oven, 400 degrees F., for ten minutes, then reduce to 325 degrees, and bake until the custard is set. The secret of this pie is not to beat the eggs too much, to heat the milk, and to get the pie shell baked during the first ten minutes of baking. If you prefer, prick the pie shell with a fork and bake for a few minutes in a hot oven. Then remove and turn in the filling and continue baking like custard.

HAMMOND'S EARS

2 cups bread flour   1 teaspoon salt
4 eggs

Sift the flour and salt into a mixing bowl. Make a hole in the center of the mound of flour and break in one unbeaten egg. Mix well. Then make another hole, break in another unbeaten egg, and mix thoroughly. Continue until the four eggs are combined with the flour. When the eggs are mixed in, the flour should be of the consistency of pie crust. Add more flour, if necessary. Turn the dough on a molding board and divide into twelve equal parts. Roll each section as thin as paper and to the size of a dinner plate. Pile one "ear" on top of the other with a little flour between them. Fry in deep hot fat, one at a time. As you fry them, put each one in a pan and pour maple syrup over it. Fry another ear, place on top, and cover with maple syrup. Do this until all the ears are fried. Serve hot, with more maple syrup if necessary. Serves six.

MAINE APPLES IN MAPLE SYRUP

8 apples   2 tablespoons butter
1 cup maple syrup   1 1/2 cups hot water

Peel the apples and cut in halves. Place in a deep baking dish and cover with the maple syrup and butter melted in the hot water. Bake

until the liquid is thick. Serve cold with whipped cream. Serves eight.
Peaches or pears may be substituted for the apples.

JANET'S APPLES IN MAPLE CARAMEL

Pare five apples and cut in halves. Boil one cup of maple sugar and
one-half cup of water for three or four minutes. Add the apples and
cook them until fluffy. Remove the apples and heat the syrup again.
In another saucepan put one tablespoon butter, one teaspoon flour, and
one-half cup cream. When hot, add to the syrup. Boil several minutes
and pour over the apples. Cool and serve. Serves five.

BAKED PEARS IN MAPLE SYRUP

6 large cooking pears   3/4 cup maple syrup
1 tablespoon lemon juice

Peel the pears and cut in halves. Put in a baking dish and turn the
lemon juice and maple syrup over them. Cover the dish and bake in a
very slow oven, not over 275 degrees F., for four hours. Serves six.

NEW HAMPSHIRE MAPLE SALAD DRESSING

1/4 cup lemon juice   1/2 teaspoon salt
1 tablespoon flour   Speck of pepper
1/2 cup maple syrup   1 cup cream

Mix the flour with the lemon juice until there are no lumps. When
cold, stir in the syrup. Cook until it thickens, stirring constantly. Add
the seasonings. When the mixture is cool, whip the cream and fold in.
Serve on any fruit salad.

HONEY BUTTER

Mix one cup of honey with half a cup of butter. Stir until smooth.
Serve on pancakes, sandwiches, waffles, and toast. When butter is scarce,
use one-third cup of butter to each cup of honey.

HONEY RICE PUDDING

2 cups cooked rice	3 eggs
3 cups milk	1 cup raisins
3/4 cup honey	

Mix, pour into a buttered baking dish, and bake one hour in a moderate oven, 350 degrees F. Serves six to eight.

OLD HONEY CAKES

3/4 cup butter	1/2 cup cold water
3 1/2 cups flour	1/2 cup honey
1 teaspoon salt	1 tablespoon lemon juice
1/2 teaspoon soda	1 teaspoon butter
6 tablespoons hot water	

Soften the butter, stir in the flour and continue stirring over low heat until slightly brown. Turn onto a lightly floured board. Make a depression in the center, put in salt and soda dissolved in hot water, and mix well with the hands. Press into two nine-inch buttered pie tins, making a deep depression in the center of each. Bake in a moderate oven, 350 degrees F., until light brown, about one hour. Put water and honey in a saucepan and boil three or four minutes. Add lemon juice and butter. Pour over the cakes. Set in a warm oven until the honey soaks in. Serves twelve.

CONNECTICUT HONEY CREAM CAKE

1/4 cup butter	1 teaspoon salt
1 cup honey	1 teaspoon soda
1/2 cup sugar	1/4 teaspoon cinnamon
2 eggs, beaten	1/4 teaspoon nutmeg
1 cup sour cream	2 1/2 cups flour

Cream the butter, honey, and sugar. Add the beaten eggs and cream. Sift the dry ingredients and stir in. Beat well. Bake in a shallow pan, nine by twelve inches, in a moderate oven, 350 degrees F., for forty-five minutes. Cool in the pan and cut in squares.

HONEY LAYER CAKE

1/2 cup shortening	2 cups flour
1/2 cup honey	3 teaspoons baking powder
1/2 cup sugar	1/4 teaspoon salt
2 eggs, beaten	2 teaspoons cream
1/2 cup milk	

Cream the shortening, honey, and sugar. Add the beaten eggs and milk alternately with the sifted dry ingredients. Add the cream and give two or three good stirs but do not beat. Bake in two layers in a moderate oven, 350 degrees F., until brown.

Honey Icing

1 cup honey	2 egg whites

Boil the honey one minute. Beat the egg whites until stiff and add the honey in a thin stream, beating until stiff enough to hold its shape. This is enough for two nine-inch layers. Honey icings absorb moisture and cannot be kept as regular icings are. Eat immediately.

HONEY ICEBOX COOKIES

1 cup butter	3/4 teaspoon baking powder
1/2 cup honey	1 teaspoon lemon juice
1 egg, beaten	Egg white
1/2 teaspoon grated lemon rind	1/2 cup chopped almonds
4 cups flour	

Cream the butter and honey; add the beaten egg and lemon rind. Stir in the flour and baking powder sifted together. Add lemon juice, form into a roll, chill. Slice cookies, brush them with the egg white, and sprinkle with the chopped almonds. Bake in a moderate oven, 350 degrees F., until light brown, about ten minutes. Makes five dozen cookies.

HONEY CREAM PIE

4 tablespoons butter	Pinch of salt
1/2 cup flour	1/2 teaspoon vanilla
1 3/4 cups milk	1/4 cup honey
3 egg yolks	

Melt the butter, blend in the flour. Add the milk very slowly, stirring constantly. Cook in a double boiler over low heat until thick. Add the beaten egg yolks and cook two minutes. Add the salt. When lukewarm, stir in the vanilla and honey. Pour into a nine-inch baked pie shell and top with meringue.

Honey Meringue

3 egg whites	3 tablespoons powdered sugar
2 tablespoons honey	

Beat the egg whites stiff, add the sugar and honey gradually, beating until the meringue stands up in peaks. Spread on the pie and bake in a slow oven, 325 degrees F., ten minutes or until brown. Serve as soon as possible.

15. PRESERVING KETTLE AND PICKLE JAR

Pickling time in New England homes was one of the most important seasons of the year. It was part of the process of getting ready for winter which dominated the thoughts of each member of the family for a number of months.

Conscientious housewives took great pride in their ability to preserve everything, even some things which we do not consider worth preserving today. So it was that each New England girl learned from her feminine relatives how to spice, pickle, and make jelly of both wild and cultivated fruits; she learned to pickle oysters, lobsters, fish, and nuts; she made sweetmeats, chowchow, and ketchup as well as crock after crock of cucumber pickles. It has been said that during her lifetime the New England housewife preserved tons of food, and certainly from what we read in old journals this is no exaggeration.

It was not that New England women were a particularly Spartan

257

breed who liked to stir the big kettles hung in the fireplace or to stand over the hot kitchen stove. But rows of pickle crocks in the cellar, the apple-butter tub in the attic, the full pantry shelves, all these were a necessary insurance against the long hard winter. A few sour pickles with the weekly oyster stew, pungent mustard pickles for the corned beef, chutney to serve with curry, and conserves and sweetmeats for the heavy dark bread baked for so many years in all New England homes, each one played an important part in keeping the family happy. So New England women accepted their responsibilities and became masters of the art of preserving.

A large-sized kettle, a long-handled wooden spoon kept just for this purpose, jelly tumblers and jam pots, tissue paper, several flat pans, and a small bottle of brandy were the tools for jelly and jam making. Early housewives, and later ones too, always heated the sugar before adding it to the boiling juice. Spread in flat pans, it was put in the oven and kept there with an occasional stirring until it was too hot to touch. In the meantime, fruit juice was boiled for just twenty minutes, no longer, the hot sugar thrown in, and the whole stirred vigorously. The sugar would make a great hiss as it went in, but dissolved very quickly. Then the juice was again brought to a boil. Some cooks claimed that the kettle should be removed from the fire as soon as it began to boil again; others said the jelly should be boiled until it met the jelly test. Probably a great deal depended then, as it does now, on the amount of pectin and the amount of water in the fruit.

After the hot jelly was poured into jars and cooled, rounds of tissue paper soaked in brandy were fitted close over the top of the jelly before the cover was put on. In the days before paraffin was used, the brandy helped act as a preservative.

Currant "jell" was indispensable in all New England homes: it was used to tempt the appetite of invalids, served to the family in puddings and gravies, and used as an accompaniment for partridge and other wild game.

Apple jellies often were flavored with sweet herbs. After bringing the apple juice and sugar to a good boil, a tablespoon or two (depending on the amount of jelly since the herb flavor should not be too strong) of apple or orange mint, rose, geranium, lemon verbena, or lemon balm was added. The jelly was boiled two or three minutes, then strained. Sometimes New England cooks poured the jelly into tumblers and floated a piece or two of herb on top. Spiced apple jelly was made frequently, either by cooking the apples with cloves, ginger, and cinnamon, or by adding two drops of oil of cinnamon to each cup of juice. It was served with meats, particularly wild game.

Of chokecherries, William Wood said, "They so furre the mouth that the tongue will cleave to the roofe. . . . they are as wild as ye Indians." Yet New England women learned to make delicious jelly of chokecherries mixed with apple juice.

Our frugal New England forebears never wasted any of the fruit when they made jelly. They covered the fruit pulp with water, brought it to a boil again, and made a second batch of jelly, or strained the juice and pulp through a coarse sieve for jam. From three-quarters to one cup of sugar was allowed for each cup of pulp. This method of jam making was most common for cherry, wild plum, quince, and other large-seeded fruits. For berry jams, it was believed that currant juice added to the flavor, and many old recipes called for one cup of currant juice to each quart of fruit.

October in New England meant gathering apples for storing and making cider. Everywhere patient horses went round and round all day turning the wheels for the cider press. The creaking of the press, the sound of hammers as farmers repaired the cider barrels filled the crisp autumn air.

Wherever there were sweet apple trees the farmer's wife and often the neighbors for miles around gathered to make cider apple "sass." It was stored in barrels in a cold place and chipped off in pieces during the winter. We have given the recipe as it was made in Sandwich, New Hampshire. When boiled cider applesauce was made, countryfolk would gather to make apple butter also. It often took all night and furnished amusement for young and old.

Old-fashioned barberry sauce was made with either sugar or molasses. In the recipe given in this chapter, the syrup is boiled down, but in other recipes the barberries were boiled for three-quarters of an hour, skimmed out, and covered with boiling hot syrup, and the extra syrup was saved for drinks. Often after the barberries were skimmed out of the molasses, sweet apples were cooked in the syrup until tender, then the barberries added, and the whole brought to a boil. When sugar was used in place of molasses, peeled cut-up pears were often cooked in the syrup.

In late summer or early autumn, elder bushes bear loads of juicy deep purple berries that New England women have always made into wine, pie filling, and preserves. Elderberry chutney is delicious when served with guinea hen, quail, or chicken. Chutneys of all sorts were always on hand to serve with curry, one of the most popular dishes brought from the Far East.

Sweet things in the cupboard may have been for the women of the family, but there was no disputing that pickles were made for the menfolk. In big white crocks in the cellar, nestling under grape leaves, were large and small cucumber pickles, ranging from the sour kind which puckered your mouth as you ate them—and incidentally were used to tell when the children had the mumps—to small sweet pickles served on special occasions. Whole cucumber pickles, sliced cucumber pickles, pickles made with oil, dill, or mixed with cauliflower and onions, each variety was planned for serving with a special meat or fish dish. The New England housewife would no more have forgotten the pickle dish when she laid the table than she would have left off the salt and pepper, the vinegar and mixed horseradish.

CURRANT JELLY

Select currants that are ripe, but not too soft. Clean well and wash. Mash in a porcelain preserving kettle and add half a cup of water for each two quarts of fruit. Bring to a boil, stirring to keep from burning. Boil ten minutes. Strain through a jelly bag. Measure the juice, and to each cup of juice add three-quarters cup of sugar. Bring slowly to a boil and test frequently. When two drops hang together, pour into hot clean jars. Allow to cool, then cover with paraffin. A mixture of half currants and half raspberries makes an excellent jelly.

Jelly Test

To test jelly take a small amount in a spoon and allow to cool slightly. Then let it drop from the side of the spoon. If the drops cling together it is done. Some cooks pour a small amount of jelly into a saucer and allow it to cool there. If it hardens around the edges the jelly is done.

APPLE AND CRAB-APPLE JELLY

Do not core or peel the fruit, but wash it carefully and cut out blemishes. Cut into quarters, cover with water, and simmer until soft. Drain through a jelly cloth, allowing four or five hours for the juice to drip through. For each cup of juice allow three-quarters cup sugar. Bring to a good boil, add the sugar, and stir until dissolved. Apple jelly forms very quickly; do not cook too long.

MINT JELLY

Wash and chop mint fine. Add one-quarter cup sugar and one-quarter cup water to each cup of chopped mint, and let stand overnight. Bring to a boil and strain. Follow the directions for apple jelly, adding a few drops of green coloring and one and one-half tablespoons of mint juice for each quart of jelly. Add just before the jelly is poured into the tumblers, mixing well.

GREEN GRAPE JELLY

Follow the general directions for currant jelly, allowing one cup of sugar to each cup of grape juice.

ELDERBERRY AND GRAPE JELLY

Wash and stem the elderberries. Add enough water to cover and cook until soft. Extract the juice from the elderberries, and add an equal amount of grape juice. Follow the directions for currant jelly.

CHOKECHERRY JELLY

Wash and pick over the chokecherries. Cover with water and bring to a slow boil. Simmer until tender. Crab apples or apple cores and parings may be cooked with the chokecherries, adding about half as much apple as chokecherry. If this is not done, use either bottled pectin or two-thirds chokecherry juice and one-third apple juice. Add three-quarters cup sugar to each cup of juice and follow the directions for currant jelly. Chokecherries do not make a clear jelly, so do not be alarmed when it comes out an opaque rose.

QUINCE JELLY

Cut quinces into small pieces, using the core and all. Cover with water and cook until tender. Follow the directions for currant jelly.

BLUEBERRY JELLY

Cut a large orange in very thin slices and let stand overnight in cold water to cover. Add three quarts of blueberries and heat slowly, crushing the fruit. Strain. Bring the juice to a boil, adding one cup of sugar to each cup of juice. Boil ten minutes, skim, and pour into clean hot glasses. Makes about ten to twelve six-ounce glasses.

BEACH PLUM JELLY

Clean the plums. Add half as much water and cook until soft. Strain. Add one cup of sugar to each cup of juice and proceed as for currant jelly.

CIDER JELLY

4 cups sweet apple cider   7 1/2 cups sugar
1 tablespoon lemon or orange rind   1 cup pectin

Combine the cider, rind, and sugar. Heat to the boiling point, stirring constantly. Stir in the pectin, bring to a rolling boil, and boil one minute. Skim and pour into ten to twelve hot six-ounce glasses.

BLACKBERRY, RASPBERRY, OR STRAWBERRY JAM

Wash and pick the berries clean. Measure, allowing three-quarters cup of sugar to each cup of fruit. Add currant juice if desired. Crush the berries and bring to a slow boil, add the sugar, and cook slowly until the mixture thickens.

GOOSEBERRY JAM

Follow the recipe for berry jam, but do not add currants.

SPICED BLUEBERRY JAM

2 pounds ripe blueberries   1/4 teaspoon cloves
Juice of 1 lemon   7 cups sugar
1/2 teaspoon cinnamon   1 cup pectin

Crush the blueberries, add the lemon juice, spices, and sugar. Bring to a full rolling boil, stirring constantly. Boil two minutes, then remove from the heat and add the pectin, stirring constantly. Skim and pour into ten to twelve hot six-ounce glasses.

SANDWICH CIDER APPLESAUCE

Pare and core enough sweet apples to fill a gallon porcelain kettle. Add one-half gallon of boiled cider, cover, and let cook slowly until the apples are dark and tender. Golden sweets were considered the best variety for boiled cider sauce.

GRAPE CONSERVE

1 cup pulped grapes   1/2 small orange
Grape skins   Sugar
6 tablespoons raisins

Pulp the grapes and cook until soft. Put through a sieve and add the grape skins, raisins, and orange cut fine. To every cup of grape mixture add one cup of sugar. Cook until thick. One-quarter cup of nuts may be added to each two cups of mixture.

BAR-LE-DUC

With a needle or embroidery scissors slit and remove the seeds from large perfect gooseberries or currants. Crush imperfect fruit, heat until the juice runs freely, and strain. Allow one and one-half cups of sugar to each cup of juice. Bring to a boil and skim. Add the fruit, boil three minutes, and set aside to let the fruit plump. Pour into jars before it has entirely cooled, or it will jell in the kettle.

A modernized version of the old recipe calls for two cups of cleaned stemmed currants and one and one-half cups of sugar. Bring slowly to a boil, let boil five minutes, and pour into hot clean jars.

APPLE SWEETMEATS

Pare and core the apples. Allow half a pound of sugar to each pound of apples. Make a syrup of the sugar, using two quarts of water to three pounds of sugar. When the syrup is boiling, drop in the apples, and cook until clear. Fill jars half full of apples and fill up with syrup.

BARBERRY SAUCE

Bring equal parts of barberries and molasses to a boil. Skim out the barberries, and let the syrup boil down to half its original volume, making sure that it does not burn. Add the barberries, bring to a rolling boil again, and pour into hot glasses.

APPLE GINGER

3 pounds apples   1/4 pound preserved ginger
Sugar

Pare and core the apples. Cut into small pieces. Cover the parings and cores with water, and boil until soft. Strain and measure. To each one and one-half cups of juice add one cup of sugar, and to the three pounds of apples add two pounds of sugar. Put together, add the ginger, and boil until thick. Makes three to four pints.

PEAR AND QUINCE CHIPS

Pare equal quantities of fruit and slice thin. Add three-quarters cup of sugar and the juice of one-quarter lemon to each cup of fruit. Let stand in a porcelain kettle for ten to twelve hours. Simmer until clear.

SPICED CURRANTS

7 pounds currants	2 tablespoons cloves
5 pounds brown sugar	2 tablespoons cinnamon
2 cups vinegar	

Mix the currants, sugar, and vinegar. Add the spices tied in a bag. Simmer two hours, remove the spices, and bottle. Makes six to eight pints.

SWEET PICKLED GOOSEBERRIES

6 pounds gooseberries	9 pounds sugar
1 pint vinegar	

Remove the blossom end of the gooseberries. Add the vinegar and half the sugar. Cook twenty minutes. Add the rest of the sugar, cook twenty minutes more, and bottle. Makes ten to twelve pints.

SPICED CRAB APPLES

Wash the fruit, but leave the stems on. Add three-quarters pound of sugar to each pound of fruit, one cup of cider vinegar and one cup of water. Tie a dozen cloves, two sticks of cinnamon, and a few blades of mace in a bag. Make a syrup of the sugar, vinegar, water, and spices. Cook the crab apples in the syrup until tender. Bottle. Serve with cold meats, roast pork, or baked ham.

PICKLED CHOKE PEARS

6 pounds choke pears   1 pint cider vinegar
Whole cloves   2 sticks cinnamon
3 pounds maple sugar   1/2 ounce green ginger
1 cup water

Pare the choke pears, but do not core. Leave on the stems, and cut out the blossom ends. Stick a whole clove on each side. Make a syrup of the maple sugar, water, vinegar, and spices. When the syrup is boiling, skim, put in the pears, and cook until tender. Cook only a few at a time so they will keep their shape. Pack in hot jars and cover with boiling syrup. Makes six to eight pints.

White sugar may be used in place of maple sugar and three sticks of cinnamon, one tablespoon of whole cloves, and one tablespoon of allspice in place of cinnamon and ginger.

PICKLED BUTTERNUTS

Gather butternuts soft enough to be pierced with a knitting needle. Let them stand in a strong brine for four or five days, changing the brine twice. Drain, wipe off the fuzz with a coarse cloth. Pierce each nut with a large needle and soak in cold water for six hours. Make a pickle solution of

1 gallon vinegar   3 dozen black peppercorns
1 cup sugar   1 1/2 dozen allspice
3 dozen whole cloves   1 dozen blades mace

Mix the ingredients and boil five minutes. Pack the nuts in jars, and pour vinegar over them. After three days, pour off the vinegar, heat it, and again pour it over the nuts. Repeat in another three or four days, then seal. May be eaten in one month.

ELDERBERRY CHUTNEY

2 pounds elderberries
1 large onion, chopped
1 pint vinegar
1 teaspoon salt

1 teaspoon ground ginger
2 teaspoons sugar
1/4 teaspoon cayenne
1/2 teaspoon mixed spices

Wash the elderberries and remove them from the stems. Put them in a pan and bruise them with a wooden spoon. Add the other ingredients, bring to a boil, and simmer until thick. Put in jars and seal. Makes about three pints.

CHUTNEY

6 ripe or green tomatoes
6 onions
2 cups chopped apples
2 cups chopped raisins
3 cups brown sugar

1/4 cup salt
3 cups vinegar
3 ounces mustard seed
2 ounces preserved ginger
1/4 teaspoon cayenne pepper

Chop the tomatoes and onions; add the apples and raisins. Mix with the other ingredients, and cook slowly for two and one-half hours, stirring occasionally. Makes about eight pints.

CUCUMBER PICKLES

1 gallon cold vinegar
1/4 pound sliced onions
1/4 pound dry mustard
1/4 pound salt
1 ounce white ginger root
1/4 pound whole cloves

1/4 pound stick cinnamon
2 ounces peppercorns
2 tablespoons ground cloves
1 pound brown sugar
Small cucumbers

Mix the first ten ingredients well and turn them into a two-gallon crock. Pick and wash small cucumbers as they grow in the garden and drop them into the pickle mix. When the crock is full, cover with grape leaves.

MUSTARD PICKLES

1 quart small cucumbers	3 green peppers
1 quart small onions	4 quarts water
1 large cauliflower	1 pint salt

Slice the cucumbers and onions; break the cauliflower into bite-sized pieces. Slice the green peppers. Cover with brine made of the water and salt. Let stand overnight. Drain. Bring the brine to a boil, pour over the vegetables, and drain again. Make a dressing as follows:

1 cup flour	2 cups sugar
6 tablespoons mustard	Vinegar
1 tablespoon turmeric	

Mix the dry ingredients well. Add enough vinegar to stir into a smooth paste. When smooth, add enough more vinegar to make two quarts of dressing. Bring to a slow boil, stirring constantly. When smooth and beginning to thicken, add the vegetables. Mix well and bottle. Makes about six pints.

ELIZABETH'S GOLDEN GLOW PICKLES

6 quarts ripe cucumbers	1 1/2 quarts vinegar
1 dozen onions	7 cups sugar
2 green peppers	1/4 cup mustard seed
2 hot red peppers	30 whole cloves
1/2 cup salt	

Cut the cucumbers in cubes and slice the onions. Cut the peppers in inch strips. Cover with the salt and let stand three hours. Drain. Mix with the vinegar, sugar, and spices. Bring to a good boil, bottle, and seal. Makes about twelve pints.

PEPPER RELISH

12 red peppers	3 cups vinegar
12 green peppers	2 cups brown or white sugar
12 onions	3 tablespoons salt

Chop the peppers and onions fine. Cover with boiling water and let stand ten minutes. Drain thoroughly. Add the vinegar, sugar, and salt. Boil twenty minutes and bottle. Makes two to three pints.

SWEET PICKLED ONIONS

4 quarts small white onions	2 cups sugar
1 cup salt	1/4 cup mixed pickling spice
2 quarts vinegar	

Peel the onions, cover with salt water, and let stand overnight. Drain and rinse with cold water. Bring the vinegar, sugar, and spices to a boil and boil five minutes. Add the onions, bring to a boil again, and bottle. Makes about eight pints.

CHILI SAUCE

24 ripe tomatoes	1/4 cup salt
8 onions	1/2 teaspoon cloves
6 red peppers	1/4 teaspoon cinnamon
3 cups vinegar	2 teaspoons allspice
3 cups brown sugar	2 teaspoons black pepper

Peel and chop the tomatoes, and onions. Remove the seeds and chop the peppers. Add the remaining ingredients and cook slowly until thick. Add more salt if necessary. Makes six to eight pints.

CRANBERRY KETCHUP

Cook four pounds of cranberries with one and one-half cups of vinegar until soft. Strain. Rub through a coarse sieve. Add:

4 cups brown sugar	1 teaspoon paprika
1 teaspoon cloves	2 teaspoons cinnamon
1 teaspoon salt	

Simmer slowly until thickened, stirring frequently. Makes six pints.

GRAPE KETCHUP

Wash and stem four pounds of grapes; mash and bring to a boil.
Strain. Cook one pound of tart apples until tender. Strain and combine
with grapes. Add:

4 cups sugar	2 tablespoons cinnamon
1 1/2 cups vinegar	2 teaspoons allspice
1/2 teaspoon salt	2 teaspoons cloves

Boil for twenty minutes, stirring frequently. The spices may be put
directly into the mixture or tied in a bag. If the spices are added directly
to the ketchup mixture, the color will be darker. Makes about six pints.

AUNT HAT'S PICCALILLI

1 peck green tomatoes	5 cups maple sugar
1 cup salt	1 teaspoon cloves
4 onions	1 teaspoon cinnamon
2 green peppers	1 teaspoon allspice
2 red peppers	1/2 teaspoon ginger
5 quarts vinegar	1/2 teaspoon mustard

Chop the tomatoes, add the salt, and let stand overnight. Add the
chopped onions and peppers and the vinegar. Bring to a boil, add the
sugar, and cook fifteen minutes. Add the spices and boil up once. Makes
ten to twelve pints.

WORCESTER CHOWCHOW

2 cups green peppers	1 cup sugar
2 cups red peppers	1/3 cup salt
3 cups chopped cabbage	2 tablespoons mustard seed
2 cups onions	2 quarts vinegar
2 cups green tomatoes	

Chop the peppers, let stand overnight with the salt. Add the other chopped vegetables and seasonings. Boil one hour. Makes about six pints.

BRANDIED PEACHES

4 pounds ripe peaches   2 pounds sugar
Brandy

Scald the peaches and peel them. Stone them if you prefer. Put the sugar and fruit in alternate layers in jars. Fill with brandy and cover tightly.

ROSE BRANDY

Fill a china jar with rose petals. Fill with brandy and cover. The next day, strain and add new rose petals. Do this each day during the rose season, keeping the jar well covered.

Rose brandy was used to flavor custards and cakes.

16. FAMILY BREWING

BELIEVING it to be the root of all human ills, our forefathers avoided drinking water whenever possible. From what we know of sanitation in those days, they were wiser than they realized. It is not surprising therefore that in the early days family brewing was as important as family baking and that every housewife had her favorite recipes.

Until displaced by cider, ales and wines were table drinks in all families. Even children, because of the shortage of milk, were given ale as soon as they could toddle. As a concession to their years, their beer was heated, and it was considered "best . . . not to let them drink their beer till they have first eaten a piece of Brown Bread."

Madeira, claret, and sack, although imported in large quantities in seaport towns, did not always reach the more remote rural areas. All country housewives made their own wines and cordials from cherries, blackberries, currants, and other wild fruits, using them both as beverages and as medicines. When family brewing was so important, every country house had special casks and kegs for wine making. The same sort of kegs may be bought today, or wine may be made in glass jugs. Pour the wine into a cask or jug and attach a rubber hose or a patented bubbler. Seal well with paraffin. When a rubber hose is used, it should be run into a container of water. In this way, gas may escape from the keg, but no air will get into the wine. When all bubbling has stopped, filter the wine either through a flannel cloth or filter paper, and bottle.

When our grandmothers made cherry bounce they usually turned it into a demijohn and shook it every day. Then after two months they strained and bottled it. It was considered better after it had aged six months. Some of the old accounts indicate that cherry bounce was sometimes made with cider and sometimes with rum in the place of whisky.

In addition to fruit wines, metheglin or mead was made in large quantities. A fermented drink dating from the time of Beowulf and probably before, it was first made in this country, from the honey of wild bees. One man said, "Metheglin does stupify more than any other liquor if taken immoderately and keeps a humming in the brain which made one say he loved not metheglin because he was wont to speak too much of the house he came from, meaning the hive."

After a few years, beer and ale were supplanted by cider as a table drink. It has been said that John Adams to the end of his life drank a tankard of hard cider before breakfast. It was served to students in colleges, and no farmer would start the winter without at least a dozen barrels in the cellar. One of the most common winter drinks was spiced cider but when the men of the family tied their drinking napkins under their chins at home or at the tavern they usually drank whisky toddy, apple toddy, grog, or flip. Large covered tankards were kept handy near the fireplace for members of the family and unexpected guests. The iron toddy stick or flip dog was kept hot on the front of the andirons day and night. Many tankards had a hole in the cover through which the heated stick was plunged to keep the drinks at just the right temperature.

Flip, immortalized in Charles Dibdin's sea songs as the favorite beverage of English sailors, can be made in a variety of ways. Compounded of beer and rum sweetened with molasses or dried pumpkin, or of cider and rum with a little lemon and sugar to taste, or perhaps rum or brandy and egg, it was served in tankards and stirred with an iron flip dog. The amount of each ingredient should be a matter of special study. The modernized version in this chapter will serve as a starting point for those who want to experiment. The first essentials in making flips of all sorts, we are told, are to "produce the smoothness by repeated pouring back and forward between two vessels, and beating up the eggs well in the first instance."

Other colonial drinks of note were stonewall, a mixture of cider and rum; bogus or calibogus, rum and beer served cold; and blackstrap, rum and molasses. Every country store had a cask of blackstrap with a salted dried codfish hung slyly alongside—a free lunch to be stripped off and to invite the purchase of another drink.

Posset, spooned from a porringer, was an old English drink very popular in colonial days, particularly at weddings. A recipe attributed to Sir Walter Raleigh and which has a number of variations is given here. Sack, from which it got its name, was a corruption of the Spanish *seco*, meaning dry. It was applied to any dry fortified wine, usually sherry. "Whistle-belly-vengeance," a popular Salem posset, was made of sour beer simmered in a kettle, sweetened with molasses, and poured over brown bread crumbs. This was very thick and had to be eaten with a spoon.

Probably one of the most famous recipes found in culinary literature is the oft-quoted "To make a fine Syllabub from the cow." Appearing in the first cookbook by an American author, *American Cookery, or the Art of dressing viands, fish poultry, and vegetables, and the best mode of making pastes, puffs, pies, tarts, puddings, custards and preserves, and all kinds of cakes, from the imperial plum to plain cake, adapted to this country and all grades of life, by Amelia Simmons, an American orphan, Hartford, 1796,* the recipe reads: "Sweeten a quart of cyder with double refined sugar, grate nutmeg into it, then milk your cow into your liquor, when you have thus added what quantity of milk you think proper, pour half a pint or more, in proportion to the quantity of syllabub you make, of the sweetest cream you can get, all over it."

Until the time of the temperance movement, punch making was an art in New England; every buffet of people of fashion held a punch bowl; every formal dinner began by passing a bowl of punch from hand to hand. It is said that Harrison Gray Otis served ten gallons of punch each afternoon at his Boston home, and that Governor Hancock at a state dinner in 1792 served 136 bowls, each holding about a quart, to eighty diners. In 1757, the following poem was sent to Sir Henry Frankland, probably written by Samuel Mather, son of Cotton Mather:

> *"You know from eastern India came*
> *The skill of making punch, as did the name.*
> *And as the name consists of letters five,*
> *By five ingredients it is kept alive.*
> *To purest water, sugar must be joined,*
> *With these the grateful acid is combined.*
> *Some any sours they get contented use,*
> *But men of taste do that from Tagus choose.*
> *When now these three are mixed with care*
> *Then added be of spirit a small share*
> *And that you may the drink quite perfect see,*
> *Atop the musky nut must grated be."*

Experienced punch makers tell us that for a cold punch the water should always go in first and the spirits last; for a hot toddy, the spirits first and the boiling water last. We who are accustomed to using carbonated water in cold punches add that at the last moment, but put in plain water or tea first.

Most of the punches that were popular in New England were based on English recipes. Fisherman's punch, said by Izaak Walton to be "too good for any but fishermen or very honest men" is one of these. An old recipe for Nonsuch punch advocated mixing the liquors and letting them stand a month before using. The recipe says this is a "delicious and safe drink for a mixed evening party."

Uncle Toby is another English punch widely used in this country. Whether it was named for Tristram Shandy's Uncle Toby, who as you remember "was not a water-drinker . . . except fortuitously upon some advanced posts, where better liquor was not to be had," or whether Uncle Toby was named for the punch we do not know. But we can imagine Uncle Toby and Tristram's father sipping it as they waited for Tristram to be born. In the original recipe, boiling hot stout or porter was added to the other liquors. The recipe given in this chapter has been simplified, but in case stout or porter is available, add one cup just before serving.

Not all New England drinks were alcoholic, however. During the nineteenth century, travelers in New England tell of ginger beer and cookies sold at all country fairs. Edward Everett Hale in *A New England Boyhood* describes election day on Boston Common where "Ginger beer and spruce beer were sold from funny little wheelbarrows, which had attractive pictures of the bottles throwing out their corks by their own improvised action. You might have a glass of spruce beer for two cents, and, to boys as impecunious as most of us were, the dealers would sell half a glass for one cent." As a matter of fact, there was an old New England saying that a clever man was as "full of wit as a ginger-beer bottle is of pop."

ELDERBERRY CORDIAL

Take eight quarts of elderberries with stems removed and boil them with two quarts of water, two teaspoons of whole cloves, two teaspoons of whole allspice, and one stick of cinnamon until the berries are soft. Strain. Add one and a half cups of sugar for each quart of juice, and cook thirty minutes or until it begins to thicken. Strain again, cool, and bottle, adding half a pint of brandy for each quart of juice.

If a very sweet cordial is preferred, the amount of sugar may be increased to two cups for each quart of juice, and the amount of brandy may vary from a wineglass to each bottle to one pint to each quart of juice.

BLACKBERRY BRANDY

Boil crushed blackberries until soft, stirring frequently to keep them from sticking. Strain and add two cups of sugar to each quart of juice.

Boil until the sugar is melted, then cool. Add equal parts of brandy to the juice, and then bottle.

Blackberry brandy may be spiced with cloves and cinnamon, but the spices tend to destroy the delicate berry flavor.

GOOSEBERRY WINE

Pick one gallon of gooseberries when they are half ripe. Crush and add three pounds of sugar. Stir well and let stand three weeks. Strain into a keg and let work two or three months. When it stops fermenting, filter and bottle.

DANDELION WINE

Gather one gallon of dandelion blossoms when the sun is shining so they will be well open. Remove all the stems and pour a gallon of water over the blossoms. Let stand for three days. Put in a large preserving kettle with the rinds of one lemon and three oranges. Boil fifteen minutes and strain. Add the juice and pulp of three lemons and three oranges and three pounds of sugar. When lukewarm, add half a yeast cake dissolved in a little water. Let stand in a warm place one week; strain and put in a cask to work. When it stops working, filter and bottle.

CURRANT WINE

Pick, stem, and mash currants. Strain and to each quart of juice add one and a half cups of sugar and half a cup of water. Stir well, put in a cask, and let ferment about four weeks. Filter and bottle.

RASPBERRY VINEGAR

Place ripe raspberries in a stone crock. Crush slightly and cover with vinegar. Let stand twenty-four hours and strain. Add one and a half cups of sugar for each quart of juice. Scald fifteen minutes, skim, and bottle. A glass of brandy may be added to each quart of juice.

For raspberry shrub, made just like raspberry vinegar, as little as half a cup of sugar for each quart of juice may be used. When ready to serve, take one part raspberry juice to four parts of water, and add a little Jamaica rum or brandy.

GRAPE SHRUB

Cover wild grapes with water and bring to a boil. Strain and add one cup of sugar for each two quarts of juice. Bring to a boil, skim, and bottle.

CHERRY BOUNCE

"To one quart of wild black cherries, add one gallon of good whisky, first bruising the cherries, so as to break the stones. Then shell a handfull of almonds and add them to a half tumbler of white sugar, a quarter of a spoonfull of nutmeg, a quarter of a spoonfull of cloves and a half of a spoonful of cinnamon, all of which should be bruised together in an earthen or metal pot. Let the compound stand a fortnight, and then draw off the liquid. Finally, add a half gallon of best brandy to it and preserve it in airtight bottles, from which it should be served in nip glasses."

GRANDMOTHER'S CHERRY BOUNCE

Crush eight pounds of rum cherries hard enough to crack the stones. Four pounds of sweet cherries and four pounds of sour cherries may be used in place of rum cherries. Put in a deep crock with two and a half pounds of sugar and one gallon of whisky. Stir until thoroughly mixed. Let stand a month, stirring or shaking every day, and another month without touching. Syphon off, strain, and bottle.

MEAD

Add four pounds of honey to one gallon of water—or enough honey to float an egg. Add the rind of one lemon, boil, and skim. Add the juice of one lemon and let stand three days. Skim again and pour into a cask, adding half a yeast cake dissolved in a little water. When it stops working, filter and bottle, or seal in a cask. A pint of brandy or a pint of dry white wine may be added when the liquor is put in the cask.

SPICED CIDER

2 quarts cider
4 whole cloves
1 stick cinnamon

4 whole allspice
1/2 cup light brown sugar
3 or 4 apples

Simmer the cider, spices, and sugar for fifteen minutes. Let stand several hours, strain, and reheat. Bake the apples whole. Serve hot from a large bowl with the apples bobbing on the suface. Two or three pieces of ginger root may be used in place of the spices. Serves eight.

HOT BUTTERED RUM

Put one teaspoon of sugar, a dash of allspice, cloves, and nutmeg in a cup or mug. Add one jigger of rum, one teaspoon of butter, and fill with boiling water.

RUM FLIP

To make a flip, put a quart of ale on the fire to warm. Beat three eggs with half a cup of sugar, one teaspoon of nutmeg, and half a cup of rum. When the ale is nearly boiling, put it in one pitcher and the rum and eggs in another. Pour from one pitcher to the other until smooth as cream.

Put the flip in a tankard near the fire to keep warm. Just before drinking, plunge a heated iron into the drink to make it just the right temperature and to give it the slightly scorched flavor. Serves four to six.

MULLED PORT

Simmer one-quarter cup of sugar, one stick of cinnamon, one slice of lemon, and six cloves in one and a half cups of water. Add one quart of port, bring to a boil, and serve. Serves four to six.

MULLED MADEIRA OR SHERRY WITH EGGS

Add one and a half pints of water to a bottle of Madeira or sherry. Heat. Beat the yolks of six eggs, two cups of sugar, and one teaspoon of nutmeg. Stir well together and add the stiffly beaten egg whites. Pour heated wine slowly on the mixture, stirring constantly to prevent curdling. Pour several times from one dish to another until thoroughly mixed. Serves eight to ten.

RALEIGH'S SACK POSSET

Bring to a boil one cup of dry sherry and one cup of ale. Add one quart of boiling milk or cream. Sweeten with one cup of sugar and flavor with grated nutmeg. Pour into a heated dish and let stand near the fire for several hours. Just before serving, beat in two egg yolks. Serves six.

Another version says to mix the ale and sherry, add beaten eggs and cream, and boil an hour or two. Sweeten to taste and serve with nutmeg. Cool before serving. Still another version omits eggs entirely.

HARVARD MILK PUNCH

Boil one quart of milk, half a cup of sugar, a small stick of cinnamon, and thinly pared lemon rind. Beat the yolks of three eggs and the white of one. Add boiling milk gradually, stirring constantly. Add two wineglasses of rum, and serve with a little grated nutmeg on top. Serves six.

COLD MILK PUNCH

Fill a tumbler with one tablespoon of sugar, two tablespoons of water, and mix well. Add one wineglass of brandy and half a wineglass of rum. Fill one-third full of shaved ice, fill up with milk, and grate nutmeg on top.

TO MAKE THREE GALLONS OF EGGNOG

3 cups powdered sugar
24 egg yolks
2 pints Jamaica rum
3 quarts rye whisky

6 quarts milk
3 quarts cream
24 egg whites
Nutmeg

Mix the powdered sugar with the well-beaten egg yolks. Mix the rum
and whisky and add to the egg yolks, stirring constantly. Mix the cream
and milk, add to the egg and liquor mixture, beating with a rotary
beater. Beat the egg whites stiffly and fold in, stirring until well blended.
Let stand several hours before serving. Sprinkle with nutmeg. Serves
sixty.

OXFORD SYLLABUB

1 cup sherry
1 cup port
1/2 cup brandy

Sugar
Milk and cream

Mix the sherry, port, and brandy. Pour in a punch bowl and fill up
with new milk, adding sugar to taste. Mix well, pour thick cream,
preferably Devonshire cream, over the top, and dust with nutmeg.

Devonshire Cream

Strain sweet milk into a round flat pan. Set aside in a cool room for
twelve to twenty-four hours. Then put the pans on the stove and heat
to about 160 degrees. A thin skin will form over the top, and you will
see small spots that look like melted butter, when it reaches the right
temperature. Do not take from the fire too quickly. Then put the pans
in a cool room and let stand twelve hours. Skim off the cream with an
old-fashioned skimmer with holes in the bottom.

WHITE WINE SYLLABUB

2 cups cream
1 1/2 cups white wine
Juice of 1 lemon

Juice of 1 orange
1/2 cup sugar
Chopped toasted almonds

Beat the cream until frothy; fold in the wine and fruit juices. Serve in glasses with toasted chopped almonds. Serves four to six.

TOM AND JERRY

6 eggs, beaten separately
2 jiggers Jamaica rum
3/4 teaspoon cinnamon
1/4 teaspoon cloves

1/4 teaspoon allspice
4 cups sugar
1 teaspoon cream of tartar

Beat the egg yolks and whites separately, mix, add the rum and spices. Add the sugar until the consistency of thin batter. Stir in the cream of tartar to prevent the sugar from settling to the bottom.

To serve, add one tablespoon of batter to a small glass, one jigger of brandy, fill with boiling water, and sprinkle with nutmeg. Instead of brandy, a mixture of brandy and rum may be prepared ahead of time. Serves four to six.

NONSUCH PUNCH

6 bottles claret
1 bottle brandy
1 bottle sherry
1 pint strong tea

Juice of 3 lemons
Sugar
1/2 pineapple, diced
6 bottles carbonated water

Mix the claret, brandy, sherry, tea, and lemon juice. Let stand twenty-four hours. Just before serving, add sugar to taste and the diced pineapple. Pour over ice, and add carbonated water. Serves forty to fifty.

FISHERMAN'S PUNCH

1 fifth sweet Vermouth
1 fifth sherry
2 fifths whisky
1 pint rum

2 cups lemon juice
1 cup grenadine
2 quarts strong tea
2 quarts carbonated water

Mix all but the carbonated water and let stand twenty-four hours. Pour over a large cake of ice, and add the carbonated water. Serves thirty.

UNCLE TOBY

Rub one cup of sugar on the rinds of two ripe lemons until the sugar is saturated with oil. Put in a bowl with the lemon cut in thin slices and bruise until all the juice is extracted from the lemon and the whole is well blended. Then add a quart of boiling water and stir until the sugar is dissolved. Let the lemon-sugar mixture stand for several hours to blend. Then bring to a boil and add one pint of brandy and one pint of rum. Strain into mugs.

If the punch is too strong, add more water and sugar. The proportions depend largely on the strength of the liquors used. The real secret in making this punch lies in getting all the essence from the lemons when mixing with the sugar. It is excellent to serve after skiing or on a cold winter's evening.

COBBLER

Put two wineglasses, or more if desired, of claret, sherry, or any other wine in a tall tumbler. Add one teaspoon of sugar and fill with crushed ice. Garnish with fresh fruit and serve with a straw or sipper.

CLARET LEMONADE

Add the juice of three lemons and sugar syrup to taste to one bottle of claret. Let stand twenty to thirty minutes to blend. Serve with cracked ice, garnished with orange slices. Serves four to six.

CLARET CUP

1 pint claret

1 pint carbonated water

Juice of 1 lemon

1 glass curaçoa

1 slice cucumber or sprig of borage

1 orange

Grapes

Mint

Mix the claret, carbonated water, lemon, and curaçoa. Let stand for a few minutes with the cucumber slice or the borage. Remove the cucumber slice, pour over ice, and garnish with sliced orange, grapes, and sprigs of mint. Serves four to six.

SWITCHEL

Mix one tablespoon of ginger, one-half cup of sugar, one-quarter cup of vinegar, and four cups of cold water. Boil ten minutes, cool, and chill. Serves four.

FRUIT PUNCH

Juice of 12 oranges
Juice of 12 lemons
2 quarts grape juice

1 1/2 pounds sugar
1 pint water

Mix the fruit juices. Add the sugar boiled with the pint of water. Pour over a large cake of ice, and garnish with pineapple, cherries, and sprigs of mint if desired. Serves twenty-five. Serve with silver and gold cake.

RASPBERRY MINT

1 quart lemonade
6 or 8 mint leaves

1/2 cup crushed raspberries

Chill for two hours, strain, and serve. Serves six.

17. THE TAFFY PULL

THE general store with its rolls of calicoes and serges, its ribbons, buckrams, and laces, its knives, jew's harps, bladders of snuff, its cotton thread and weavers' supplies, its barrels of molasses and apples, and its wooden tubs of hard candies is almost a thing of the past.

When we see a modern candy store window full of rich chocolates and caramels many of us can recall nostalgically the weekly trip to town and how we hung around the candy tubs until the storekeeper or father gave us a small bag to take home. We remember saving pennies to buy old-fashioned chocolate creams shaped like cones, or the hard candies colored on the outside, white on the inside, with fascinating designs of flowers and butterflies running through the center. How we loved the brownies made in the shape of birds and bees and the pink, white, and yellow hearts with "I love you" and other sentimental messages on them. How we treasured the clear lemon and wine drops, sucking them slowly to make them last longer! And the licorice sticks—long black ropes that we nibbled on for days!

With the general store and the hard candy tubs the taffy pull has disappeared too. But when grandmother was young, pulling candy was one of the favorite diversions as the family gathered around the roaring fire on a winter evening. Everyone, old and young joined in the fun, singing songs or listening to the older folk tell tales of the "good old days" as they pulled the creamy sweet-smelling masses of molasses candy and taffy.

Taffy pulling was also a favorite pastime when young people gathered for an evening of fun. Having a partner who knew how much butter to rub on your hands and how to pull and loop the candy was as important at selecting a partner for a dance. And when hands touched briefly or a sly molasses-flavored kiss was exchanged, that was all part of the fun.

No New England Christmas was complete without popcorn balls and colored corn. Sometimes the popcorn was strung and hung on the Christmas tree, at other times the balls were wrapped in colored paper as decorations. But always popping corn and making the sweet syrup for the balls was a part of Christmas preparations.

OLD-FASHIONED MOLASSES CANDY

2 cups molasses	1/8 teaspoon salt
1 cup brown sugar	1 teaspoon butter
1 tablespoon vinegar	1 teaspoon soda

Mix the molasses, sugar, and vinegar. Boil until brittle when dropped in cold water. Add the salt, butter, and soda, stirring in quickly. Pour onto a buttered platter. When cool enough to handle, pull until light.

BUTTERNUT MOLASSES TAFFY

1 cup sugar	1/4 cup water
1 tablespoon vinegar	2 tablespoons butter
1/4 teaspoon salt	1 cup chopped butternuts

Boil the first four ingredients until the syrup forms a hard ball when dropped in cold water. Add the butter. Pour into a shallow buttered pan to cool. When cool enough to handle, sprinkle with nuts and pull until light.

SUGAR CANDY

6 cups sugar
1 cup vinegar
1 cup water

1 tablespoon butter
1 teaspoon soda
Flavoring

Boil the sugar, vinegar, and water until it becomes brittle when dropped in cold water. Add the butter, soda dissolved in hot water, and the flavoring. Pour into a shallow buttered pan. When cool, pull until white.

CREAM CANDY

4 cups sugar
1 cup thick cream
2 cups water

1 tablespoon butter
Pinch of soda
1 teaspoon vanilla

Stir the sugar, cream, and water until the sugar is dissolved. Add the butter and soda, and cook without stirring until a spoonful will crisp when dropped in cold water. Add the flavoring and pour into shallow buttered plates. Cool quickly. When cool enough to handle, pull until the mass is smooth and velvety. Draw into long strips and cut into small pieces.

SALT-WATER TAFFY

2 1/2 cups sugar
2 1/2 cups white corn syrup
2 cups water
1 tablespoon butter

2 teaspoons salt
Flavoring
Coloring

Put the sugar, syrup, and water in a pan and stir until it begins to boil. Boil without stirring until it becomes brittle when dropped in cold water. Add the butter and salt and pour onto a buttered platter. When cool, separate into masses the right size for pulling. Add the flavoring and coloring, pulling it into the mass. Flavor pink with strawberry, green with mint, white with vanilla, yellow with lemon. Pull until creamy. Cut in bite-sized pieces and wrap in waxed paper.

PINE TREE SALT-WATER TAFFY

2 cups sugar	1 tablespoon butter
5 tablespoons water	1/4 teaspoon salt
1/4 teaspoon cream of tartar	1 teaspoon vanilla

Boil the sugar, water, and cream of tartar until it snaps when dropped in cold water. Add the butter, salt, and vanilla. Pour into a shallow buttered pan and cool. Pull until white.

GIBRALTAR ROCK

Hawthorne tells us in his notebooks that he hoped someday to write a children's story about Gibraltars, the confections that were famous in old Salem. They were made by an Englishman named Spencer around 1822 and were sold by his mother who drove a wagon from street to street. Their retail price was a silver penny apiece or four pence, half penny for seven, and Salem children often saved their entire allowance to buy the candies.

2 cups sugar	1 tablespoon vinegar
1 cup water	Vanilla, peppermint, clove flavoring

Boil the sugar, water, and vinegar until it becomes brittle when dropped in cold water. Remove from the fire, cool a little, and flavor. Pour onto a well-buttered plate. When cool enough to handle, pull until white. Cut in three-inch pieces. In several days they will become soft and creamy.

MAPLE FONDANT

1 quart maple syrup	1/2 teaspoon butter

Pour the maple syrup into a saucepan and add the butter. Bring to a boil as quickly as possible. Boil rapidly without stirring until the temperature is between 234 and 238 degrees F. Cover the tines of a fork with cheesecloth and clean off any crystals that have accumulated on the sides of the pan. Skim off any impurities that rise to the surface. Do this as the syrup boils. As soon as the syrup reaches the right temperature, pour into a large dripping pan. Cool gradually to avoid the formation of crystals at the bottom of the pan. Do not move the pan while the mixture is cooling. When the mass has cooled, collect it in the center of the pan with a wooden paddle, being careful not to stir but to use a lifting and beating movement. It will take twenty to forty minutes to work air into the fondant. When no more heat can be felt when the hand is held over the fondant, it may be stirred. Work until the mass is honey-colored and creamy, and continue until it loses its glossy appearance and again becomes hard. Store in tightly covered glass jars.

To use the stored fondant, place in the top of a double boiler and melt over hot water until it becomes like a thin batter. Pour into fancy rubber molds. When completely cooled and firmly set, unmold by bending back the molds.

If you do not want to store the fondant, when it is no longer warm, turn it onto a marble slab and knead until it is creamy and will hold its shape. Mold into desired shapes and garnish with halved nut meats, candied cherries, raisins, or citron. The fondant may be rolled in shredded coconut, chopped nuts, or grated chocolate.

MAPLE FUDGE

For maple fudge use the same ingredients as for maple fondant. Just before turning it into the pan, add chopped butternuts. Stir briskly and turn into molds or a pan. When it has stiffened sufficiently, mark in squares.

The maple syrup and butter may be boiled to the soft ball stage. Then beat until it can be easily handled. Turn onto a slightly floured mixing board and shape into a roll about the size of the wrist. Allow the mixture to cool and cut into slices.

MAPLE FOAM

2 cups shaved maple sugar
1 cup brown sugar
1/2 cup water
1/4 teaspoon cream of tartar

12 marshmallows, cut in bits
2 egg whites
Walnut meats

Combine the maple sugar, brown sugar, and water. Stir in the cream of tartar. Boil to the hard ball stage. Add the marshmallows, cover and let stand five minutes. Beat the egg whites stiff. Pour the sugar mixture over the egg whites and beat until light and the mixture begins to harden. Drop by spoonfuls on waxed paper. Place halved walnut meats on each piece.

MAPLE PANOCHA

1 1/2 cups white sugar
1 cup maple sugar
1 cup milk
1 tablespoon butter

Pinch of salt
1/2 teaspoon almond flavoring
3/4 cup chopped butternuts

Cook the sugar, milk, butter, and salt to the soft ball stage. Set the saucepan in a dish of cold water, being careful not to jar the contents. When it begins to cool, add the flavoring and nuts. Beat until creamy.

NUT CREAM DISKS

2 cups sugar
1/4 teaspoon cream of tartar
1 cup cream

1 cup water
1 cup maple syrup
2 cups walnuts

Mix the first five ingredients. Stir until the sugar is dissolved. Boil without stirring to the soft ball stage. Take from the fire and cool by setting in a pan of cold water. When cool, beat until creamy. Add the walnut meats and drop by the spoonful on waxed paper.

MAPLE WALNUT KISSES

2 cups maple syrup   1 tablespoon orange juice
2 cups corn syrup   1 1/2 cups walnut meats
1/2 teaspoon soda

Boil the maple and corn syrup half an hour. Add the soda and continue cooking until the brittle stage. Remove from the fire and add the orange juice and nuts. Beat.

CHOCOLATE FUDGE

2 cups white sugar   2 squares chocolate
1 cup brown sugar   2 teaspoons vinegar
1 cup milk   2 tablespoons butter

Cook the sugar and milk to the soft ball stage. Add the chocolate, vinegar, and butter. Beat, and add the vanilla.

DIVINITY FUDGE

2 cups sugar   1/3 cup water
2/3 cup corn syrup   2 egg whites
1/2 cup water   1 teaspoon vanilla
2/3 cup sugar   2/3 cup nuts

Put the first three ingredients in a saucepan and boil until the soft ball stage. Ten minutes after starting, put the next two ingredients in a pan and cook to the hard ball stage. Pour the first mixture over the stiffly beaten egg whites, stirring constantly. Then add the second mixture. Add the vanilla, and when creamy the nut meats.

NUT FOAM CHOCOLATE

2 cups sugar   1 teaspoon vanilla
1/4 teaspoon cream of tartar   1 cup nut meats
1/2 cup water   Melted chocolate
2 egg whites

Boil the sugar, cream of tartar, and water until it forms a hard ball. Pour slowly over the stiffly beaten egg whites, beating constantly. Add the vanilla and beat until creamy. Put the nuts in the bottom of a buttered pan and pour the candy over them. Cut into small squares and dip in melted chocolate. Chopped candied cherries may be used in place of the nuts, and candied cherries pressed on top of each piece.

PANOCHA

2 cups brown sugar
2/3 cup milk
1 tablespoon butter

1 teaspoon vanilla
1 cup nuts

Boil the sugar and milk to the soft ball stage. Cool slightly and add the vanilla, butter, and nut meats. Beat until creamy.

TAFFY APPLES

2 cups sugar
1/2 cup water
1/4 teaspoon cream of tartar
1/2 cup butter

1 teaspoon vanilla
1/2 cup cream
6 apples

Cook the first six ingredients until they become brittle when tested in cold water. Clean the apples thoroughly. Leave the stems on or put the apples on lollypop sticks. Dip the apples in the syrup and place on a buttered platter to harden.

FROSTED CURRANTS

Pick fine even bunches of currants. Wash, dry, and dip them in slightly beaten egg white. Drain until nearly dry. Dip in powdered sugar. Dip again in egg white and again in powdered sugar. Dry on waxed paper. Serve by themselves as a confection or use as a garnish for jellies or charlottes.

POPCORN BALLS

1 cup molasses   1/2 teaspoon salt
1/2 cup sugar   3 quarts popcorn
1 tablespoon butter

Boil the molasses and sugar until they become brittle when dropped in cold water. Add the butter. Sprinkle the salt over the freshly popped corn. Pour the hot syrup over the popcorn, stirring to get each piece entirely covered. Dip the hands in cold water and shape the popcorn into balls, being careful not to press them. Wrap in waxed paper.

18. WINTER PICNICS

For approximately five months of the year, Jack Frost is king of New England, especially among the hills and mountains of the northern section where he rules unchallenged. Time was when you set out into the winter wilds with a feeling that you were starting on a hazardous adventure. You may have snuggled among buffalo robes on a sleighing party which ended in an oyster supper at the town hall. Perhaps you chilled the tip of your nose while coasting on Butter Hill. You may have been the gayest of the gay at the moonlight skating frolic. You may have padded away on snowshoes for a fireplace steak fry at a not-too-distant camp. But such a thing as having an honest-to-goodness picnic right out among the snowdrifts never entered your head.

But today—thanks to winter sports—subzero picnics are as popular as those of midsummer. We give all due credit to the small snowshoe clubs, those community affairs that proved you could roast weenies, marshmallows, and apples over an open fire without freezing while you were doing it. But actually it was skiing that coaxed father and mother out into the drifts with the children.

You must make a number of plans ahead for a winter picnic. First you should arrange to hold the meal at midday, for it grows very cold in the mountains when the sun begins to go down. This is even more true at the height of the winter sports season in February than in the shorter days before Christmas. The old adage, "As the days begin to lengthen, the cold begins to strengthen," is not a flight of fancy. But whatever the hour, bring along a warm coat to slip on while you are standing around waiting for the food to be cooked.

The best way to get food and cooking utensils to the picnic spot must also be considered. Sometimes you carry the supplies and equipment in rucksacks, dividing the load among the members of the party. But in the long run it is more satisfactory to choose a spot near a road which is open to winter travel. Then you can bring the supplies in your car or, if you prefer, in a horse-drawn sleigh.

But whatever commissary transportation you choose, see to it that every person is responsible for his own drinking mug, plate, and cutlery. For cooking equipment you will need two long-handled iron skillets, a deep saucepan, a wire corn popper (two if possible), a heavy coffeepot, a can opener, two long-handled mixing spoons, a long-handled fork, and if you have dreams of griddlecakes, a long-handled pancake turner.

Build the fire in a sheltered spot, preferably against a boulder. If possible, bring the fuel from home. Sissy, you say? Perhaps so, but far easier! Time is at a premium on a winter day, and it takes time to hunt fuel. Of course if you are transporting supplies in rucksacks you must get the kindling and wood in the vicinity of the picnic spot. But if you are bringing things in by car, bring the fuel too.

All experienced winter picknickers say that hot soup is one of the best things in the world to take the kinks out of your body and to limber up your disposition after a morning on the trails. Canned soups are invaluable for the rucksack method of transportation. But if the supplies are brought in an automobile, you can include a thermos jug of thick, heavy homemade stew. It is even possible to carry it in a kettle, ready to put over the fire. Wrap the kettle in layers of paper and then in a blanket. It will take only a short time to heat up. Almost any of the stews and thick soups described in Chapter 4 are excellent for the purpose. But the salt pork chowder has proved its worth over and over again.

Baked beans are always delicious on a winter picnic. Bake the beans in an earthen bean pot overnight. Do not remove them from the oven until just before you set out. Wrap the bean pot just as you would wrap the salt pork chowder. If the beans do not seem quite warm enough when dinner is served, quickly reheat in a skillet over the fire.

For picnickers who want to concoct a hot dish right on the spot, we recommend hodgepodge, a favorite with north country people. And steak, of course, is a natural choice for a winter picnic. One of the best ways to cook it is by the old-fashioned method of frying in a skillet. A wire cornpopper is almost indispensable for cooking weenies and bacon. It is also the best utensil for cooking meat cakes over an open fire.

And now about griddlecakes. Make the batter at home and carry it to the picnic spot in cans. Be sure to have a special long-handled saucepan in which to heat the maple syrup. The secret of superfine griddlecakes to be eaten outdoors on a cold day is to have them hot and to literally smother them in hot maple syrup. It is important to have two griddles in operation at the same time, for it is almost impossible for one cook working alone to make the cakes fast enough to satisfy a hungry crowd of skiers. If you can learn to flip the cakes high in the air so they will turn over and land on the griddle again, you will add a lot of color and fun to the party. But frankly the cakes will not taste a bit better than those baked with less fanfare.

No winter picnic can be a real success without coffee. Tea is another beverage that is liked by skiers. It is often served in the warming huts at the end of the day, and makes a fine pickup, the experts say. One ski lodge in the White Mountains specializes in a spiced tea served to guests when they come in from the trails. Hot buttered rum is also a favorite drink served before the great fireplace in a number of New England winter inns.

Inns and hotels in ski areas often arrange picnics for their guests. Such were the affairs inaugurated by Rob Peckett, long-time host of Pecketts-on-Sugar-Hill in the White Mountains and a pioneer in the winter recreational business. He began years ago by taking the guests who came in to the inn for the Christmas holidays or over Washington's birthday to the stone cooking arches he had erected in beautiful wilderness spots. Such feasts were prepared over the great gridirons—broiled chicken, thick steaks, home-cured hams, country sausages, with griddlecakes bathed in hot maple syrup thrown in for good measure! The guests who attended Peckett's picnics in the 1920s when the late Ross Nickerson presided over the feasts will never forget them.

A number of our recipes, including the one for coffee are based on the dishes that were served at these famous meals. We have first described the turnovers that made up the usual dessert, as turnovers make the best ending for an outdoor meal. They are not only delicious and easy to pack, but are perfect to handle when hands are cold.

PECKETT'S APPLE TURNOVERS

Roll rich biscuit dough to half an inch in thickness. Cut in three-inch rounds. Place a spoonful of sweetened cinnamon-flavored applesauce on each piece of dough. Fold the rounds into turnovers. Prick the tops with a fork and brush with milk. Bake twenty minutes in a hot oven at 400 degrees F.

PECKETT'S MINCE TURNOVERS

4 cups cooked chopped meat	2 cups boiled cider
12 cups chopped apples	6 teaspoons cassia
3 cups chopped suet	3 teaspoons cloves
4 cups raisins	1 teaspoon nutmeg
4 cups currants	Juice of 3 lemons
1 1/2 cups molasses	

Mix the ingredients and moisten with the liquor in which the beef was cooked. Simmer until the apples are soft. Make exactly like Apple Turnovers.

GARLIC LOAF

Cut a loaf of French bread lengthwise, but do not let the knife slip straight through. Put in as much butter as you can spare and run a clove of garlic around the sides of the incision. Stuff with cheese. When ready to eat the loaf, heat it thoroughly over the fire. Use a flat rock if you can find one. If not, thrust two sticks through the center of the loaf and hold it over the coals, turning constantly. The rock will give better results, however. When the crust begins to look brown and toasted, and the cheese is melted, the loaf is ready to serve. Slice and eat at once. Serves six.

HODGEPODGE

1 large onion, sliced	1 can kidney beans
1/4 pound suet, chopped	2 large cans tomatoes
1 pound round steak, cubed	4 cups clean snow or water

Fry the onion in the suet until brown. Remove the onion and fry the cubes of steak in the fat until browned on both sides. Return the onion slices. Add the beans, tomatoes, and snow or water. Heat thoroughly. Season with salt and pepper and serve at once. Serves eight to ten.

STEAK IN A SKILLET

Heat the skillet very hot. Throw in the pieces of steak. Shake the skillet vigorously so the meat will not burn. When the pieces are brown on one side, turn and brown on the other side. Put a good-sized piece of butter on each serving and sprinkle with salt and pepper.

COPPERMINE BROOK FRIED POTATOES

2 cups chopped boiled potatoes	2 slices salt pork
1/4 cup diced onions	Salt and pepper

Thoroughly mix potatoes and onions. Put the slices of salt pork in a skillet and try out. Remove the pork when it is crisp and brown. Turn the potatoes and onions into the sizzling hot fat. Sprinkle with salt and pepper. Brown the mixture on one side; then turn and brown on the other side. Serves four.

BRIGAND STEAK

Prepare enough cubes of steak, squares of bread, and sliced onions for the picnic party. Let each person cook his own portion. He puts a square of bread, a cube of steak, an onion ring, and a second square of bread on a sharpened stick and cooks them over the coals until the meat is browned. After removing the materials, they are pressed together and seasoned with salt and pepper to taste.

WRAP-AROUND STEAK

Cut the steak in two-inch squares. Lay a slice of onion on each square and encircle with a slice of bacon. Wrap each portion in waxed paper. When ready to cook, remove the paper and either broil or fry the portion. Season to taste and place between slices of bread.

WINTER PICNIC MEAT CAKES

2 pounds chopped bottom round	1 tablespoon Worcestershire sauce
1/2 teaspoon dry mustard	Salt and pepper
2 tablespoons chopped onion	

Mix the ingredients thoroughly and make into eight flat cakes. Grease a wire corn popper and put in the cakes. Cook over hot coals, turning as necessary.

OVER-THE-COALS CHEESE SANDWICHES

Lay slices of Cheddar-type cheese between thin slices of bread. Fasten the sandwiches to long sticks and toast over the coals until the cheese begins to get runny. Each person toasts his own sandwich.

HOT COFFEE, PICNIC STYLE

Start the coffee at home by mixing a foundation in the proportion of one cup of ground coffee to one cup of water. This will serve six people. Put the mixture in a cheesecloth bag and place in a heavy coffeepot. When ready to serve the coffee, melt clean snow and turn it into the pot. Let it come to a boil and simmer for three minutes. Settle the grounds by adding half a cup of snow. Heat the milk or cream that is used. Crockery mugs will hold the heat better than other kinds.

END-OF-THE-DAY SPICED TEA

1 teaspoon whole cloves
1-inch stick cinnamon
3 quarts water
2 tablespoons black tea

Juice of 3 oranges
Juice of 1 1/2 lemons
1 cup sugar

Tie the spices in a bag and bring to a boil in the water. Add the tea and steep for five minutes. Strain, then add the fruit juices and sugar. Serve very hot. Serves twelve.

19. SPECIAL DAY MENUS

T̲H̲E̲ New Englander was a creature of habit. He liked to know that the baked beans would appear on the Saturday night supper table, that the corned beef would be served on Thursday, that he could count on chicken fricassee for Sunday noon, and that the fresh peas would be ready to serve with the fresh salmon on July 4.

These traditional menus came into popularity over the three hundred years of New England growth. But one special menu was in existence when the Pilgrims landed—the clambake. Associated in most of our minds with the little state of Rhode Island, it was nevertheless the Indian method of cooking clams, and although the menu has been added to over the years, the method remains essentially the same. To quote from an old account:

"Clams, baked in the primitive style of the Indians, furnish one of the most popular dishes on those parts of the coast where they abound, and constitute a main feature in the bill of fare at picnics and other festive gatherings. The method of baking is as follows. A cavity is dug in the earth about eighteen inches deep, which is lined with round stones. On this a fire is made, and, when the stones are sufficiently heated, a bushel or more of soft clams (according to the number of persons who are to partake of the feast) is thrown upon them. On this is put a layer of rockweed gathered from the beach, and over this a second layer of seaweed. Sometimes the clams are simply placed close together on the ground with the hinges uppermost, and over them is made a fire of brush. This is called an Indian bed of clams. Clams baked in this manner are preferred to those cooked in the usual way in the kitchen.

"Parties of ten or twenty persons, or both sexes, are the most common. Often they extend to a hundred when other amusements are added, and on one occasion, that of a grand political mass meeting in favor of General Harrison on the 4th of July, 1840, nearly 10,000 people assembled in Rhode Island, for whom a clambake and chowder were prepared. This was probably the greatest feast of its kind that ever took place in New England."

For the more modern version of the clambake the bed of stones is prepared the same way but other things are added.

CLAMBAKE FOR TWENTY

Prepare the pit and line it with stones. When the stones are hot, rake off the fire, cover with rockweed, add a bushel or more of washed clams, twenty small lobsters, twenty washed potatoes, either Irish or sweet, twenty or more ears of corn, cover with rockweed, tarpaulin, and then sand. Then steam for two hours.

Instead of burying the clams in the unprotected ground, many outdoor cooks heat the stones as above. Then they sink a barrel into the ground and put one-half to one inch of sea water in the bottom. Into this they put half of the hot stones, cover them with seaweed, and then add the clams, lobsters, potatoes, and corn. Add more hot stones more seaweed, cover with a tarpaulin, and steam. By using this method less sand gets into the food.

Properly done, a clambake is a work of art. Many people like to make a sauce for the clams and lobsters, using onion, Worcestershire sauce, ketchup, and other condiments, but plenty of butter and salt and pepper are all that is really necessary.

NEW ENGLAND FISH DINNER

"Cape Cod Turkey" with Egg Sauce

Fried Pork Slices	Boiled Potatoes
Boiled Sliced Buttered Beets	Boiled Onions
Steamed Apple Pudding	Currant Wine Sauce

Tea or Coffee

THURSDAY BOILED DINNER

Vegetables cooked with Corned Beef or Salt Pork
Hot Cream of Tartar Biscuits

Horseradish	Mustard Pickles

Boiled Indian Pudding

SATURDAY NIGHT SUPPER

Baked Beans	Boston Brown Bread
Piccalilli	Mustard Pickles

Coleslaw

Maple Custard Pie	Tea or Coffee

SUNDAY DINNER

Fricasseed Chicken	Dumplings
Tomato Salad	Green Beans

Blueberry Pie

or

Vanilla Ice Cream	Chocolate Cake

SUNDAY BREAKFAST

Fish Cakes   Baked Beans
Scrambled Eggs   Corncakes
Coffee

OYSTER SUPPER

Oyster Stew
Sour Pickles   Hot Rolls
Washington Pie   Apple Pie and Cheese

GRANGE SUPPER

Meat Loaf   Scalloped Potatoes
Pickled Beets   Cabbage Salad
Hot Rolls
All kinds of Pies

FOREFATHERS' DINNER

Plymouth Succotash   Johnnycake
Baked Indian Pudding

THANKSGIVING DINNER

Oyster Stew
Roast Turkey with Stuffing   Cranberry Sauce
Buttered Squash   Buttered Onions
Mince Pie   Apple Pie   Squash Pie
Cracker Plum Pudding

CHRISTMAS DINNER

Roast Goose with Stuffing   Applesauce
Mashed Potatoes   Mashed Turnips
Creamed Onions
Apple Salad
Christmas Plum Pudding   Cold Sauce
Coffee

WHEN NEIGHBORS DROP IN

Corn Popped in the Kettle
Doughnuts and Cheese
Sweet Cider

SUGARING-OFF PARTY

Sugar on Snow   Plain Doughnuts
Sour Pickles
Coffee

MAY BREAKFAST

Sliced Oranges
Fried Brook Trout   Country Fried Potatoes
Popovers
Coffee

FOURTH OF JULY DINNER

Boiled Salmon   New Peas
Buttered Young Carrots   Small Boiled Potatoes
Strawberry Ice Cream

CORN ROAST

Roasted Corn with Butter
Baked Ham   Roasted Potatoes
Coffee

SHORE DINNER

Lobster Stew
Steamed Clams   Fried Clams
Boiled Lobster
French Fried Potatoes   French Fried Onion Rings
Hot Rolls
Apple Pie   Coffee

NORTH COUNTRY COMPANY SUPPER

Cold Sliced Baked Ham   Potato Salad
Parker House Rolls   Grape Jelly
Lemon Tarts   Assorted Cakes
Flummery   Hot Tea

INDEX

Adams, John, 176, 273
Aldrich, Aunt Fanny, ix–x
Alma's pot roast, 92–93
Alma's whole wheat nut bread, 146
Amadama bread, 141
Angel cake, Janet's, 235–236
Apple batter pudding, 189
  vinegar sauce, 189
Apple biscuits, 150
Apple and cabbage salad, 136
Apple crunch, 198
Apple fool, 194
Apple ginger, 264–265
Apple griddlecakes, 204
Apple jelly, 258, 259, 261
Apple pandowdy, xi, 65
  Berry family, 72–73
  with nutmeg sauce, 73
Apple pies, 158–159
  caraway green apple, 161–162
  deep-dish, 158–161
  Marlborough, 162
  Rhode Island greening, 162
Apple salad, 136
Apple slump, 192
Apple snow, 195
Apple sweetmeats, 264
Apple teacake, 242
Apple turnovers, Peckett's, 297
Appledore pudding, 186
  bird's-nest pudding, 195
Apples, Maine, in maple syrup, 252–253
  in maple caramel, Janet's, 253

savory, 123–124
taffy, 292
Applesauce, Sandwich cider, 259, 263
Applesauce cake, Durham, 225
Artichokes, Jerusalem, boiled, 12
  fritters, 12–13
Ashcakes, 7
Asparagus, stewed, 117

Bacon waffles, 205
Baked bean soup, 58
Baking powder biscuit, 155–156
Bar-le-duc, 264
Barberry sauce, 259–260, 264
Barberry tarts, 173
Barlow, Joel, 4
Bartlett cake, 220, 224
Bass, black, baked, ix, 23
  sea, baked, 19
    boiled, 16
    chowder, Rhode Island, 49
Bath buns, 140, 151
Bay State apple johnnycake, 142–143
Bay State brown bread, 139
Bea's date nut bread, 148
Beach plum jelly, 262
Bean porridge, 57
Bean soup, baked, 58
Beans, Boston baked, x, 65–66, 76, 296
  dried lima, 109
  green, and salt pork, 108
  North country, baked soldier, 77
  stewed, 109

Cakes, *continued*
Dolly Varden, 221, 227–228
drop cakes, rye, 205
Durham applesauce cake, 225
Flo's feather cake, 234
Flo's hard molasses gingerbread, 243
Flo's sour cream cake, 233
Harlequin, 221, 228–229
Harriet's jelly roll, 238
Harrison, 224
Inez's marbled cake, 230
Janet's angel cake, 235–236
kisses, 241
Lady Langdon's white cake, 233
marble cake, 229–230
Marjorie's devil's food, 240
Mary Ida's sunshine cake, 236
never-fail chocolate, 238–239
nun's, 220, 223
old honey, 254
one-two-three-four, 226
peach upside-down cake, 242
ribbon, 227
Roddy's birthday cake, 237–238
silver and gold, 236–237
simnel, 220, 223
See also Cookies
Calves' liver and onions, old-fashioned, 98
Cambridge coconut cakes, 218
Candy, 285–293
butternut molasses taffy, 286–287
chocolate fudge, 291
cream candy, 287
divinity fudge, 291
frosted currents, 292
Gibraltar rock, 288
nut foam, chocolate, 291–292
old-fashioned molasses, 286
panocha, 292
pine-tree salt-water taffy, 288

popcorn balls, 293
salt water taffy, 287–288
sugar candy, 287
taffy apples, 292
see also Maple candy
Cape Cod au gratin potatoes, 121
Caramel cake, Aunt Marion's, 232–233
Caraway green apple pie, 161–162
Caraway seed cookies, 213
Carrots, glazed, 112
Casco Bay omelet soufflé, 102
Catherine's maple gingerbread squares, 249–250
Cauliflower, fried, 116–117
Celery, Connecticut baked, 118
with mustard sauce, 118
Cheese muffins, 153
Cheese and rice, baked, 102–103
thick cheese sauce, 103
Cheese sandwiches, over-the-coals, 299
Chef's salad, 127
Cherry bounce, 273, 278
grandmother's, 278
Cherry pie, 164–165
Cherry pudding, steamed, 182–183
Cherrystones (quahogs), 47
Chicken, fried, with cream gravy, New Hampshire, 90
roast, with corn-bread stuffing, 90–91
Shaker fricasseed, 89
Chicken chowder, Pawtucket, 51
Chicken and dumplings, old-fashioned, 89–90
Chicken and oyster pie, 75–76
Chicken pie, small family, 75
Thanksgiving, 73–75
Chicken and pork, Abigail Webster's, 89
Chicken salad, Rhode Island, 135
Chicken soup, 55
Chili sauce, 269

A CATALOG OF SELECTED
DOVER BOOKS
IN ALL FIELDS OF INTEREST

A CATALOG OF SELECTED DOVER
BOOKS IN ALL FIELDS OF INTEREST

CONCERNING THE SPIRITUAL IN ART, Wassily Kandinsky. Pioneering work by father of abstract art. Thoughts on color theory, nature of art. Analysis of earlier masters. 12 illustrations. 80pp. of text. 5⅜ x 8½. 23411-8 Pa. $4.95

ANIMALS: 1,419 Copyright-Free Illustrations of Mammals, Birds, Fish, Insects, etc., Jim Harter (ed.). Clear wood engravings present, in extremely lifelike poses, over 1,000 species of animals. One of the most extensive pictorial sourcebooks of its kind. Captions. Index. 284pp. 9 x 12. 23766-4 Pa. $14.95

CELTIC ART: The Methods of Construction, George Bain. Simple geometric techniques for making Celtic interlacements, spirals, Kells-type initials, animals, humans, etc. Over 500 illustrations. 160pp. 9 x 12. (USO) 22923-8 Pa. $9.95

AN ATLAS OF ANATOMY FOR ARTISTS, Fritz Schider. Most thorough reference work on art anatomy in the world. Hundreds of illustrations, including selections from works by Vesalius, Leonardo, Goya, Ingres, Michelangelo, others. 593 illustrations. 192pp. 7⅛ x 10¼. 20241-0 Pa. $9.95

CELTIC HAND STROKE-BY-STROKE (Irish Half-Uncial from "The Book of Kells"): An Arthur Baker Calligraphy Manual, Arthur Baker. Complete guide to creating each letter of the alphabet in distinctive Celtic manner. Covers hand position, strokes, pens, inks, paper, more. Illustrated. 48pp. 8¼ x 11. 24336-2 Pa. $3.95

EASY ORIGAMI, John Montroll. Charming collection of 32 projects (hat, cup, pelican, piano, swan, many more) specially designed for the novice origami hobbyist. Clearly illustrated easy-to-follow instructions insure that even beginning papercrafters will achieve successful results. 48pp. 8¼ x 11. 27298-2 Pa. $3.50

THE COMPLETE BOOK OF BIRDHOUSE CONSTRUCTION FOR WOODWORKERS, Scott D. Campbell. Detailed instructions, illustrations, tables. Also data on bird habitat and instinct patterns. Bibliography. 3 tables. 63 illustrations in 15 figures. 48pp. 5¼ x 8½. 24407-5 Pa. $2.50

BLOOMINGDALE'S ILLUSTRATED 1886 CATALOG: Fashions, Dry Goods and Housewares, Bloomingdale Brothers. Famed merchants' extremely rare catalog depicting about 1,700 products: clothing, housewares, firearms, dry goods, jewelry, more. Invaluable for dating, identifying vintage items. Also, copyright-free graphics for artists, designers. Co-published with Henry Ford Museum & Greenfield Village. 160pp. 8¼ x 11. 25780-0 Pa. $10.95

HISTORIC COSTUME IN PICTURES, Braun & Schneider. Over 1,450 costumed figures in clearly detailed engravings–from dawn of civilization to end of 19th century. Captions. Many folk costumes. 256pp. 8⅜ x 11¾. 23150-X Pa. $12.95

PIANO TUNING, J. Cree Fischer. Clearest, best book for beginner, amateur. Simple repairs, raising dropped notes, tuning by easy method of flattened fifths. No previous skills needed. 4 illustrations. 201pp. 5⅜ x 8½.　　　23267-0 Pa. $6.95

A SOURCE BOOK IN THEATRICAL HISTORY, A. M. Nagler. Contemporary observers on acting, directing, make-up, costuming, stage props, machinery, scene design, from Ancient Greece to Chekhov. 611pp. 5⅜ x 8½.　　　20515-0 Pa. $12.95

THE COMPLETE NONSENSE OF EDWARD LEAR, Edward Lear. All nonsense limericks, zany alphabets, Owl and Pussycat, songs, nonsense botany, etc., illustrated by Lear. Total of 320pp. 5⅜ x 8½. (USO)　　　20167-8 Pa. $7.95

VICTORIAN PARLOUR POETRY: An Annotated Anthology, Michael R. Turner. 117 gems by Longfellow, Tennyson, Browning, many lesser-known poets. "The Village Blacksmith," "Curfew Must Not Ring Tonight," "Only a Baby Small," dozens more, often difficult to find elsewhere. Index of poets, titles, first lines. xxiii + 325pp. 5⅜ x 8¼.　　　27044-0 Pa. $8.95

DUBLINERS, James Joyce. Fifteen stories offer vivid, tightly focused observations of the lives of Dublin's poorer classes. At least one, "The Dead," is considered a masterpiece. Reprinted complete and unabridged from standard edition. 160pp. 5³⁄₁₆ x 8¼.　　　26870-5 Pa. $1.00

THE HAUNTED MONASTERY and THE CHINESE MAZE MURDERS, Robert van Gulik. Two full novels by van Gulik, set in 7th-century China, continue adventures of Judge Dee and his companions. An evil Taoist monastery, seemingly supernatural events; overgrown topiary maze hides strange crimes. 27 illustrations. 328pp. 5⅜ x 8½.　　　23502-5 Pa. $8.95

THE BOOK OF THE SACRED MAGIC OF ABRAMELIN THE MAGE, translated by S. MacGregor Mathers. Medieval manuscript of ceremonial magic. Basic document in Aleister Crowley, Golden Dawn groups. 268pp. 5⅜ x 8½.　　　23211-5 Pa. $9.95

NEW RUSSIAN-ENGLISH AND ENGLISH-RUSSIAN DICTIONARY, M. A. O'Brien. This is a remarkably handy Russian dictionary, containing a surprising amount of information, including over 70,000 entries. 366pp. 4½ x 6⅛.　　　20208-9 Pa. $10.95

HISTORIC HOMES OF THE AMERICAN PRESIDENTS, Second, Revised Edition, Irvin Haas. A traveler's guide to American Presidential homes, most open to the public, depicting and describing homes occupied by every American President from George Washington to George Bush. With visiting hours, admission charges, travel routes. 175 photographs. Index. 160pp. 8¼ x 11.　　　26751-2 Pa. $11.95

NEW YORK IN THE FORTIES, Andreas Feininger. 162 brilliant photographs by the well-known photographer, formerly with *Life* magazine. Commuters, shoppers, Times Square at night, much else from city at its peak. Captions by John von Hartz. 181pp. 9¼ x 10¾.　　　23585-8 Pa. $13.95

INDIAN SIGN LANGUAGE, William Tomkins. Over 525 signs developed by Sioux and other tribes. Written instructions and diagrams. Also 290 pictographs. 111pp. 6⅛ x 9¼.　　　22029-X Pa. $3.95

CATALOG OF DOVER BOOKS

ANATOMY: A Complete Guide for Artists, Joseph Sheppard. A master of figure drawing shows artists how to render human anatomy convincingly. Over 460 illustrations. 224pp. 8⅜ x 11¼. 27279-6 Pa. $11.95

MEDIEVAL CALLIGRAPHY: Its History and Technique, Marc Drogin. Spirited history, comprehensive instruction manual covers 13 styles (ca. 4th century thru 15th). Excellent photographs; directions for duplicating medieval techniques with modern tools. 224pp. 8⅜ x 11¼. 26142-5 Pa. $12.95

DRIED FLOWERS: How to Prepare Them, Sarah Whitlock and Martha Rankin. Complete instructions on how to use silica gel, meal and borax, perlite aggregate, sand and borax, glycerine and water to create attractive permanent flower arrangements. 12 illustrations. 32pp. 5⅜ x 8½. 21802-3 Pa. $1.00

EASY-TO-MAKE BIRD FEEDERS FOR WOODWORKERS, Scott D. Campbell. Detailed, simple-to-use guide for designing, constructing, caring for and using feeders. Text, illustrations for 12 classic and contemporary designs. 96pp. 5⅜ x 8½. 25847-5 Pa. $3.95

SCOTTISH WONDER TALES FROM MYTH AND LEGEND, Donald A. Mackenzie. 16 lively tales tell of giants rumbling down mountainsides, of a magic wand that turns stone pillars into warriors, of gods and goddesses, evil hags, powerful forces and more. 240pp. 5⅜ x 8½. 29677-6 Pa. $6.95

THE HISTORY OF UNDERCLOTHES, C. Willett Cunnington and Phyllis Cunnington. Fascinating, well-documented survey covering six centuries of English undergarments, enhanced with over 100 illustrations: 12th-century laced-up bodice, footed long drawers (1795), 19th-century bustles, 19th-century corsets for men, Victorian "bust improvers," much more. 272pp. 5⅜ x 8¼. 27124-2 Pa. $9.95

ARTS AND CRAFTS FURNITURE: The Complete Brooks Catalog of 1912, Brooks Manufacturing Co. Photos and detailed descriptions of more than 150 now very collectible furniture designs from the Arts and Crafts movement depict davenports, settees, buffets, desks, tables, chairs, bedsteads, dressers and more, all built of solid, quarter-sawed oak. Invaluable for students and enthusiasts of antiques, Americana and the decorative arts. 80pp. 6½ x 9¼. 27471-3 Pa. $8.95

HOW WE INVENTED THE AIRPLANE: An Illustrated History, Orville Wright. Fascinating firsthand account covers early experiments, construction of planes and motors, first flights, much more. Introduction and commentary by Fred C. Kelly. 76 photographs. 96pp. 8¼ x 11. 25662-6 Pa. $8.95

THE ARTS OF THE SAILOR: Knotting, Splicing and Ropework, Hervey Garrett Smith. Indispensable shipboard reference covers tools, basic knots and useful hitches; handsewing and canvas work, more. Over 100 illustrations. Delightful reading for sea lovers. 256pp. 5⅜ x 8½. 26440-8 Pa. $8.95

FRANK LLOYD WRIGHT'S FALLINGWATER: The House and Its History, Second, Revised Edition, Donald Hoffmann. A total revision—both in text and illustrations—of the standard document on Fallingwater, the boldest, most personal architectural statement of Wright's mature years, updated with valuable new material from the recently opened Frank Lloyd Wright Archives. "Fascinating"–*The New York Times*. 116 illustrations. 128pp. 9¼ x 10¾. 27430-6 Pa. $12.95

PHOTOGRAPHIC SKETCHBOOK OF THE CIVIL WAR, Alexander Gardner. 100 photos taken on field during the Civil War. Famous shots of Manassas Harper's Ferry, Lincoln, Richmond, slave pens, etc. 244pp. 10⅝ x 8¼.   22731-6 Pa. $10.95

FIVE ACRES AND INDEPENDENCE, Maurice G. Kains. Great back-to-the-land classic explains basics of self-sufficient farming. The one book to get. 95 illustrations. 397pp. 5⅜ x 8½.   20974-1 Pa. $7.95

SONGS OF EASTERN BIRDS, Dr. Donald J. Borror. Songs and calls of 60 species most common to eastern U.S.: warblers, woodpeckers, flycatchers, thrushes, larks, many more in high-quality recording.   Cassette and manual 99912-2 $9.95

A MODERN HERBAL, Margaret Grieve. Much the fullest, most exact, most useful compilation of herbal material. Gigantic alphabetical encyclopedia, from aconite to zedoary, gives botanical information, medical properties, folklore, economic uses, much else. Indispensable to serious reader. 161 illustrations. 888pp. 6½ x 9¼. 2-vol. set. (USO)   Vol. I: 22798-7 Pa. $9.95
    Vol. II: 22799-5 Pa. $9.95

HIDDEN TREASURE MAZE BOOK, Dave Phillips. Solve 34 challenging mazes accompanied by heroic tales of adventure. Evil dragons, people-eating plants, blood-thirsty giants, many more dangerous adversaries lurk at every twist and turn. 34 mazes, stories, solutions. 48pp. 8¼ x 11.   24566-7 Pa. $2.95

LETTERS OF W. A. MOZART, Wolfgang A. Mozart. Remarkable letters show bawdy wit, humor, imagination, musical insights, contemporary musical world; includes some letters from Leopold Mozart. 276pp. 5⅜ x 8½.   22859-2 Pa. $7.95

BASIC PRINCIPLES OF CLASSICAL BALLET, Agrippina Vaganova. Great Russian theoretician, teacher explains methods for teaching classical ballet. 118 illustrations. 175pp. 5⅜ x 8½.   22036-2 Pa. $5.95

THE JUMPING FROG, Mark Twain. Revenge edition. The original story of The Celebrated Jumping Frog of Calaveras County, a hapless French translation, and Twain's hilarious "retranslation" from the French. 12 illustrations. 66pp. 5⅜ x 8½.   22686-7 Pa. $3.95

BEST REMEMBERED POEMS, Martin Gardner (ed.). The 126 poems in this superb collection of 19th- and 20th-century British and American verse range from Shelley's "To a Skylark" to the impassioned "Renascence" of Edna St. Vincent Millay and to Edward Lear's whimsical "The Owl and the Pussycat." 224pp. 5⅜ x 8½.   27165-X Pa. $5.95

COMPLETE SONNETS, William Shakespeare. Over 150 exquisite poems deal with love, friendship, the tyranny of time, beauty's evanescence, death and other themes in language of remarkable power, precision and beauty. Glossary of archaic terms. 80pp. 5³⁄₁₆ x 8¼.   26686-9 Pa. $1.00

BODIES IN A BOOKSHOP, R. T. Campbell. Challenging mystery of blackmail and murder with ingenious plot and superbly drawn characters. In the best tradition of British suspense fiction. 192pp. 5⅜ x 8½.   24720-1 Pa. $6.95

THE WIT AND HUMOR OF OSCAR WILDE, Alvin Redman (ed.). More than 1,000 ripostes, paradoxes, wisecracks: Work is the curse of the drinking classes; I can resist everything except temptation; etc. 258pp. 5⅜ x 8½. 20602-5 Pa. $6.95

SHAKESPEARE LEXICON AND QUOTATION DICTIONARY, Alexander Schmidt. Full definitions, locations, shades of meaning in every word in plays and poems. More than 50,000 exact quotations. 1,485pp. 6½ x 9¼. 2-vol. set.
Vol. 1: 22726-X Pa. $17.95
Vol. 2: 22727-8 Pa. $17.95

SELECTED POEMS, Emily Dickinson. Over 100 best-known, best-loved poems by one of America's foremost poets, reprinted from authoritative early editions. No comparable edition at this price. Index of first lines. 64pp. 5$\frac{3}{16}$ x 8¼.
26466-1 Pa. $1.00

CELEBRATED CASES OF JUDGE DEE (DEE GOONG AN), translated by Robert van Gulik. Authentic 18th-century Chinese detective novel; Dee and associates solve three interlocked cases. Led to van Gulik's own stories with same characters. Extensive introduction. 9 illustrations. 237pp. 5⅜ x 8½. 23337-5 Pa. $7.95

THE MALLEUS MALEFICARUM OF KRAMER AND SPRENGER, translated by Montague Summers. Full text of most important witchhunter's "bible," used by both Catholics and Protestants. 278pp. 6⅝ x 10. 22802-9 Pa. $12.95

SPANISH STORIES/CUENTOS ESPAÑOLES: A Dual-Language Book, Angel Flores (ed.). Unique format offers 13 great stories in Spanish by Cervantes, Borges, others. Faithful English translations on facing pages. 352pp. 5⅜ x 8½.
25399-6 Pa. $8.95

THE CHICAGO WORLD'S FAIR OF 1893: A Photographic Record, Stanley Appelbaum (ed.). 128 rare photos show 200 buildings, Beaux-Arts architecture, Midway, original Ferris Wheel, Edison's kinetoscope, more. Architectural emphasis; full text. 116pp. 8¼ x 11. 23990-X Pa. $9.95

OLD QUEENS, N.Y., IN EARLY PHOTOGRAPHS, Vincent F. Seyfried and William Asadorian. Over 160 rare photographs of Maspeth, Jamaica, Jackson Heights, and other areas. Vintage views of DeWitt Clinton mansion, 1939 World's Fair and more. Captions. 192pp. 8⅞ x 11. 26358-4 Pa. $12.95

CAPTURED BY THE INDIANS: 15 Firsthand Accounts, 1750-1870, Frederick Drimmer. Astounding true historical accounts of grisly torture, bloody conflicts, relentless pursuits, miraculous escapes and more, by people who lived to tell the tale. 384pp. 5⅜ x 8½. 24901-8 Pa. $8.95

THE WORLD'S GREAT SPEECHES, Lewis Copeland and Lawrence W. Lamm (eds.). Vast collection of 278 speeches of Greeks to 1970. Powerful and effective models; unique look at history. 842pp. 5⅜ x 8½. 20468-5 Pa. $14.95

THE BOOK OF THE SWORD, Sir Richard F. Burton. Great Victorian scholar/adventurer's eloquent, erudite history of the "queen of weapons"–from prehistory to early Roman Empire. Evolution and development of early swords, variations (sabre, broadsword, cutlass, scimitar, etc.), much more. 336pp. 6⅛ x 9¼.
25434-8 Pa. $9.95

THE INFLUENCE OF SEA POWER UPON HISTORY, 1660–1783, A. T. Mahan. Influential classic of naval history and tactics still used as text in war colleges. First paperback edition. 4 maps. 24 battle plans. 640pp. 5⅜ x 8½. 25509-3 Pa. $14.95

THE STORY OF THE TITANIC AS TOLD BY ITS SURVIVORS, Jack Winocour (ed.). What it was really like. Panic, despair, shocking inefficiency, and a little heroism. More thrilling than any fictional account. 26 illustrations. 320pp. 5⅜ x 8½. 20610-6 Pa. $8.95

FAIRY AND FOLK TALES OF THE IRISH PEASANTRY, William Butler Yeats (ed.). Treasury of 64 tales from the twilight world of Celtic myth and legend: "The Soul Cages," "The Kildare Pooka," "King O'Toole and his Goose," many more. Introduction and Notes by W. B. Yeats. 352pp. 5⅜ x 8½. 26941-8 Pa. $8.95

BUDDHIST MAHAYANA TEXTS, E. B. Cowell and Others (eds.). Superb, accurate translations of basic documents in Mahayana Buddhism, highly important in history of religions. The Buddha-karita of Asvaghosha, Larger Sukhavativyuha, more. 448pp. 5⅜ x 8½. 25552-2 Pa. $12.95

ONE TWO THREE . . . INFINITY: Facts and Speculations of Science, George Gamow. Great physicist's fascinating, readable overview of contemporary science: number theory, relativity, fourth dimension, entropy, genes, atomic structure, much more. 128 illustrations. Index. 352pp. 5⅜ x 8½. 25664-2 Pa. $8.95

ENGINEERING IN HISTORY, Richard Shelton Kirby, et al. Broad, nontechnical survey of history's major technological advances: birth of Greek science, industrial revolution, electricity and applied science, 20th-century automation, much more. 181 illustrations. ". . . excellent . . ."–*Isis*. Bibliography. vii + 530pp. 5⅜ x 8¼. 26412-2 Pa. $14.95

DALÍ ON MODERN ART: The Cuckolds of Antiquated Modern Art, Salvador Dalí. Influential painter skewers modern art and its practitioners. Outrageous evaluations of Picasso, Cézanne, Turner, more. 15 renderings of paintings discussed. 44 calligraphic decorations by Dalí. 96pp. 5⅜ x 8½. (USO) 29220-7 Pa. $4.95

ANTIQUE PLAYING CARDS: A Pictorial History, Henry René D'Allemagne. Over 900 elaborate, decorative images from rare playing cards (14th–20th centuries): Bacchus, death, dancing dogs, hunting scenes, royal coats of arms, players cheating, much more. 96pp. 9¼ x 12¼. 29265-7 Pa. $12.95

MAKING FURNITURE MASTERPIECES: 30 Projects with Measured Drawings, Franklin H. Gottshall. Step-by-step instructions, illustrations for constructing handsome, useful pieces, among them a Sheraton desk, Chippendale chair, Spanish desk, Queen Anne table and a William and Mary dressing mirror. 224pp. 8⅛ x 11¼. 29338-6 Pa. $13.95

THE FOSSIL BOOK: A Record of Prehistoric Life, Patricia V. Rich et al. Profusely illustrated definitive guide covers everything from single-celled organisms and dinosaurs to birds and mammals and the interplay between climate and man. Over 1,500 illustrations. 760pp. 7½ x 10⅛. 29371-8 Pa. $29.95

Prices subject to change without notice.

Available at your book dealer or write for free catalog to Dept. GI, Dover Publications, Inc., 31 East 2nd St., Mineola, N.Y. 11501. Dover publishes more than 500 books each year on science, elementary and advanced mathematics, biology, music, art, literary history, social sciences and other areas.